Politics of Segmentation

When political parties make policy decisions they are influenced by the competition they face from other parties. This book examines how party competition and party systems affect reforms of social protection. Featuring a historical comparison of Italy and Germany post-1945, the book shows how a high number of parties and ideological polarization lead to fragmented and unequal social benefits.

Utilizing a comparative approach, the author brings together two important issues in welfare state research that have been insufficiently investigated. First, the complex influence of party competition on social policy-making, and second, how some social groups enjoy better social protection than others. Moving beyond the two countries of the case study, the book proposes an innovative framework for studying segmentation of social protection and applies this framework to a wider set of 15 advanced welfare states. Overall, this book draws together different strands of research on political parties and on welfare states, and introduces a new argument on how party politics shapes social policy.

An invaluable text on the political economy of the welfare state, *Politics of Segmentation* will be of interest to scholars of political economy, social policy and comparative politics.

Georg Picot is Lecturer in Comparative Social Policy at the University of Oxford, UK.

Routledge/EUI studies in the political economy of welfare
Series editors: Martin Rhodes and Maurizio Ferrera
The European University Institute, Florence, Italy

This series presents leading edge research on the recasting of European welfare states. The series is interdisciplinary, featuring contributions from experts in economics, political science and social policy. The books provide a comparative analysis of topical issues, including:

- reform of the major social programmes – pensions, health, social security
- changing political cleavages in welfare politics
- policy convergence and social policy innovation
- impact of globalization.

Politics of Segmentation

Party competition and social protection
in Europe

Georg Picot

Routledge
Taylor & Francis Group

LONDON AND NEW YORK

First published 2012
by Routledge
2 Park Square, Milton Park, Abingdon, Oxfordshire OX14 4RN

Simultaneously published in the USA and Canada
by Routledge
711 Third Avenue, New York, NY 10017

First issued in paperback 2014

Routledge is an imprint of the Taylor & Francis Group, an informa business

British Library Cataloguing in Publication Data
A catalogue record for this book is available from the British Library

Library of Congress Cataloging-in-Publication Data
A catalogue record has been requested for this book

ISBN 978-0-415-66561-2 (hbk)
ISBN 978-1-138-81246-8 (pbk)
ISBN 978-0-203-13200-5 (ebk)

Typeset in Times New Roman
by Wearset Ltd, Boldon, Tyne and Wear

Contents

Figures

Tables

Acknowledgements

My main support in this book project, which is a substantially revised and extended version of my PhD dissertation, came of course from people. But also music helped me to cope with challenges and occasionally arduous spells. The list of genres, works, and interpreters would be long. But five fine pieces of classical music have recurrently accompanied me on this trip. They ponder on the relation between individual and collective and for this reason may be pertinent to a work on politics and to a young academic in academia: Beethoven's piano concertos.

The first person I would like to thank is Maurizio Ferrera. His advice and guidance in this book project were intellectually stimulating and always helpful. I am very happy to have had him as my mentor and look forward to continue collaborating with him. The Graduate School in Social, Economic and Political Sciences and the Department of Social and Political Studies at the University of Milan gave me the opportunity to come to Italy for what became a professionally and personally invaluable experience. In particular, I would like to thank Paolo Martelli, Francesco Zucchini, and the other faculty members as well as my wonderful PhD companions Basia Szelewa, Francesca Pasquali, and Serida Catalano.

Several other institutions hosted me while working on this book. Thanks to Stefano Sacchi I profited from the supportive and pleasant work environment at the Collegio Carlo Alberto (Research Unit on European Governance) in Turin. A heartfelt 'thanks' goes to my colleagues and friends there – Valeria Sparano, Paolo Crosetto, Patrik Vesan, Krzysztof Nowaczek, and Anna Klabunde – for all the time we shared. Moreover, I spent half a year respectively at the Department of Political Science at the Massachusetts Institute of Technology (MIT) and the Social Science Research Center in Berlin (WZB). In this regard, I am grateful to my respective hosts Suzanne Berger (MIT) and Jens Alber (WZB). The manuscript was completed while working as a lecturer in the very friendly Institute of Political Science, University of Heidelberg, and while collaborating frequently with Philip Manow (now University of Bremen). Apart from the mentioned institutions, I received funding from the Italian Ministry of Education and the MIT-Italy grant of the University of Milan.

I have presented various parts of this research at conferences of the American Political Science Association, the Midwest Political Science Association, the

Council for European Studies, the Italian Political Science Association, and the European Social Policy Analysis Network (ESPAnet). Moreover, I had the chance to discuss my work in the Graduate Workshop of the Center for European Studies at Harvard, the Dissertation Workshop in Comparative Politics and Comparative Political Economy at MIT, the seminar of the WZB Department 'Inequality and Social Integration', the Brown Bag Seminar of the Institute of Political Science Heidelberg, and on workshops organized by ESPAnet and the Network of Excellence on Reconciling Work and Welfare in Europe. Parts of my findings on the German case have been published as an article in *German Politics* (Picot 2009) and have since been further elaborated. I sincerely thank all the discussants, participants, and reviewers on these various occasions for their feedback.

The following people were so kind to read (parts of) the manuscript at different stages and helped improving it by sharing their observations and suggestions: Margarita Estévez-Abe, Agnes Blome, Silja Häusermann, Paul Marx, Dominik Geering, Federico Pancaldi, Ruth Beckmann, and two anonymous reviewers. Apart from the people already mentioned, I have received useful advice during various phases of this work from Philipp Rehm, Claire Dupuy, Bernhard Weßels, Günther Schmid, Sascha Münnich, Werner Jann, Stefano Draghi, Philip Manow, Fabio Franchino, and Antonietta Confalonieri. Furthermore, I would like to thank Henning Katzmann, Elena Bixel, and Sarah Gscheidle for their valuable research assistance. Heidi Bagtazo and Alexander Quayle at Routledge provided professional and friendly editorial guidance. Any shortcomings that may have remained are, of course, my responsibility.

It really is impossible to mention all the friends who made my life so enjoyable while working on this book. By contrast, I have only two parents and I owe a lot to them. Without them I would literally not be here, neither would I be where I am without all the things I learned from them.

Abbreviations

UI	unemployment insurance
UA	unemployment assistance
SA	social assistance
NRR	net replacement rate

Italy

AN	Alleanza Nazionale
CCD	Centro Cristiano Democratico
CGIL	Confederazione Generale Italiana del Lavoro
CIG	Cassa Integrazione Guadagni
CIGS	Cassa Integrazione Guadagni Straordinaria
CISL	Confederazione Italiana Sindacati Lavoratori
DC	Democrazia Cristiana
DP	Democrazia Proletaria
DS	Democratici di Sinistra
FDP	Fronte Democratico Popolare
FI	Forza Italia
IdV	Italia dei Valori
INPS	Istituto Nazionale Previdenza Sociale
IPAB	Istituti Pubblici di Assistenza e Beneficienza
LN	Lega Nord
MSI	Movimento Sociale Italiano
PCI	Partito Comunista Italiano
PD	Partito Democratico
PdCI	Partito dei Comunisti Italiani
PDS	Partito Democratico della Sinistra
PLI	Partito Liberale Italiano
PPI	Partito Popolare Italiano
PR	Partito Radicale
PRC	Partito della Rifondazione Comunista
PRI	Partito Repubblicano Italiano
PSDI	Partito Socialista Democratico Italiano

PSI	Partito Socialista Italiano
PSIUP	Partito Socialista Italiano di Unità Proletaria
RMI	Reddito Minimo di Inserimento
UdC	Unione di Centro
UQ	Uomo Qualunque

Germany

AFG	Arbeitsförderungsgesetz
AVAVG	Gesetz über Arbeitsvermittlung und Arbeitslosenversicherung
BA	Bundesamt [and later: Bundesagentur] für Arbeit
CDU	Christlich Demokratische Union Deutschlands
CSU	Christlich Soziale Union
DP	Deutsche Partei
FDP	Freie Demokratische Partei
GB/BHE	Gesamtdeutscher Block/Bund der Heimatvertriebenen und Entrechteten
PDS	Partei des Demokratischen Sozialismus
SPD	Sozialdemokratische Partei Deutschlands
WZB	Wissenschaftszentrum Berlin für Sozialforschung

Country codes

AT	Austria
AU	Australia
BE	Belgium
CA	Canada
CH	Switzerland
CZ	Czech Republic
DE	Germany
DK	Denmark
ES	Spain
FI	Finland
FR	France
GR	Greece
HU	Hungary
IE	Ireland
IS	Iceland
IT	Italy
JP	Japan
LU	Luxembourg
NL	Netherlands
NO	Norway
NZ	New Zealand
PL	Poland

PT	Portugal
SE	Sweden
SK	Slovak Republic
UK	United Kingdom
US	United States

Part I
Introduction

1 Party competition and social protection

How do party systems and party competition affect the social protection that people get? We know very little about this. We know a good deal about how different political parties (left or right) shape social policy, but research has largely neglected that the actions of these parties depend on the other parties they have to interact with. This book explores the role of party competition in the development of social policy and, more specifically, the fragmentation of social protection, that is, how different groups of people get different levels of protection against social risks.

Party competition is a crucial element of politics in modern democracies. Political parties structure the relationship between citizens and the state. They integrate and represent citizens' interests, and they formulate and adopt policies that have an impact on citizens' lives. While doing so, parties compete with each other for votes, government office, and for the successful implementation of preferred policies. The many aspects of these processes of party politics are not adequately taken into account by scholars trying to explain the development of social policy across time and countries.

The main theory in comparative social policy research regarding political parties distinguishes between families of parties (say, social democratic, secular conservative, or Christian democratic) and assumes that these are linked to specific policies that will be implemented if in government. This theory has contributed a lot to explaining the emergence of different types of welfare states after Second World War. Still today, to know what party is in government often gives us a good idea of what policies to expect. But a social democratic party will act differently if it competes mainly with a secular conservative party than if it competes, say, with a Christian democratic party on the one hand, or a communist party on the other. More generally speaking, what a party does depends on its relative position in the party system. Therefore, the structure of the party system matters.

Among the complexities of party politics, hinted at above, this book will examine the configuration of party systems: how they shape party competition and, in consequence, the policy decisions of parties. Party competition is defined here as the interaction between political parties in a party system. The structure of the party system largely determines the interaction of parties. In this sense, the real independent variable of this study is party systems. But party systems in themselves are static. What has an impact is the interaction that is shaped by them. This is why I often refer to party competition rather than party systems. The mentioned definition of party competition is deliberately broad. It comprises different arenas (electoral, parliamentary, governmental), different objectives (votes, office, policies), and even cooperative as well as strictly competitive behaviour (Bartolini 1999, 2000). However, within this broad definition, we will focus mostly on electoral competition, as will be explained below.

Turning to the dependent variable, social protection, one of its most relevant aspects is how comprehensive or fragmented it is. This aspect is particularly pertinent regarding democratic politics and party competition, being the principal mechanism in conveying social claims to the state. What do different social groups 'get'? Are some groups better and more generously protected against social risks than others? We will consider these questions mainly at the policy level, that is, in terms of the institutional rules as well as the eventual number of beneficiaries. With this focus on the policy 'output' of the state we stay close to the policy decisions of politicians and parties, and we will not delve deeper into the social outcome of policies, which is determined by many other factors that are more remote from political decisions. In addition, studying party competition and differentiation of social rights is interesting because it enables us to examine processes of political inclusion/exclusion that may lead to inclusion/exclusion in public policies and, in the last instance though not covered by this study, to social inclusion/exclusion. For the differentiation of social protection I will use the term 'benefit segmentation', which is explained in more detail in Chapter 3.

In particular, the book will examine policy segmentation in the field of unemployment benefits. This field constitutes an important element of economic security for large parts of the population – not only for the unemployed but also for those who have a job but are concerned about ever becoming unemployed. Unemployment benefits can be defined as public monetary transfers that are paid to the unemployed in order to compensate for their loss of income. Notwithstanding important variations between national labour market regimes, these policies are a crucial part of social protection in all European welfare states.

Moreover, high unemployment levels have put these policies at the centre stage of political debate in most European countries since the 1980s. On the one hand, they are seen as an important protection against the loss of income and as providing the jobless with the necessary resources in order to effectively look for a new job. On the other hand, high levels of unemployment compensation are seen as a burden on public funds and as disincentives to taking up work (Schmid and Reissert 1996). Given the interest in differentiation of social rights, I look deliberately at unemployment benefits in the plural. Unemployment insurance is only the most well-known and usually more generous programme of financial support for the unemployed. Most countries also have needs-based unemployment assistance or social assistance, which are important measures for the unemployed as well.

One of the main objectives of this book is to bring two fields of political science closer together: the literature on political parties and comparative welfare state research. More concretely, the book uses insights from party research in order to learn more about how party politics affects social policy. Therefore, part of the task is to develop a new theoretical argument, which is what most of this chapter is devoted to. This argument is then put to the test in two ways: first and foremost, through a comparative historical analysis of party politics and social protection in Italy and Germany; second, through a cross-sectional analysis of party systems and social protection in advanced welfare states. Italy and Germany are chosen for the case studies because they have widely different party systems but are relatively similar on important other accounts, such as the basic model of welfare state, political institutions, and even party incumbency. In the post-war decades government in both states was headed by Christian democratic parties. Still, the social protection that was put in place in this period differed widely. This was precisely because both Christian democratic parties had to deal with very different contexts of party competition.

What are the findings of this study? First of all, it demonstrates that party competition matters for social protection. Second, it shows how different party systems bring about different patterns of policy segmentation. This can be summarized in three findings: (1) the more parties a party system includes, the more segmented social protection is; (2) ideological polarization of a party system brings about a high degree of policy segmentation; (3) in non-polarized party systems the more specific spatial configuration matters. This point is harder to summarize in one specific finding. In the German case we find that the fundamental 'Hartz reforms' were enabled by the lack of a left-wing competitor to the Social Democrats. In Italy after its party system change in the 1990s we see that bipolar competition between two pre-electoral coalitions has facilitated a reduction of policy segmentation. But ideological differences within each coalition have prevented more structural reforms.

By highlighting the impact of party competition, this study contributes to our understanding of welfare state reform because this aspect has so far been insufficiently recognized. Moreover, the book presents a new way of analysing the differentiation of social rights in the field of unemployment compensation. Using this framework, it takes stock of the segmentation of unemployment benefits across advanced welfare states and it provides a rich comparative account of how unemployment benefits developed in Italy and Germany. Finally, the analysis of party politics in Italy and Germany contains new perspectives on how party systems influenced policy-making. These insights can also be used for research in other policy fields.

Structure of the book

The rest of this and the following chapter develop the theoretical argument and present the research design. After that, the book is divided into two main parts. Part II presents the variation across countries in unemployment benefit segmentation and the development of unemployment benefits in Italy and Germany. Hence, this part sets out the explanandum. Subsequently, Part III shows how party competition (the explanans) influenced policy developments in Italy and Germany as well as variation across advanced welfare states more generally.

The remaining sections of this chapter build the theoretical argument of how party competition affects the segmentation of social protection. The argument involves the number of parties and their positioning in a party system. The more parties there are the narrower the interests they advocate. In terms of positioning, ideologically polarized party systems are likely to produce strong policy segmentation. In non-polarized party systems, the more detailed spatial configuration determines on which voters the attention of parties focuses.

Chapter 2 sets out the methodological approach of the study and explains in more detail why Italy and Germany were selected for the intensive case studies. The party systems of the two states differ strongly. But their differences regarding many other factors (political, institutional, social, and economic) are limited compared to other advanced industrial countries. This set-up makes it possible to distil the effect of different party systems as opposed to other factors. Moreover, the period of investigation comprises the phase of post-war welfare state expansion and the phase of economic austerity since the 1970s. In addition, dynamics of party competition have changed in both states during the 1990s/2000s. These historical changes make it possible to analyse not only the different policy paths between both countries in the phase of welfare expansion, but also to study each country through time, different economic conditions and the effect on policy-making of changes in their respective party system.

The first chapter of Part II (Chapter 3) introduces the conceptual framework for studying the differentiation of social rights in the field of unemployment compensation and applies this framework to today's advanced welfare states. The concept of unemployment benefit segmentation comprises two dimensions: first, how unemployment compensation is divided into various benefit schemes and how inclusive or exclusive these schemes are; second, the differences in generosity between these benefit programmes. The chapter shows the significant differences between advanced welfare states across both dimensions and identifies similar patterns of segmentation.

The following chapter (Chapter 4) describes how unemployment policies in Italy and Germany diverged strongly after Second World War. To this end, the chapter first illustrates how, from the beginning up to 1945, unemployment support evolved very similarly in both countries. Yet, during the post-war welfare expansion Germany established a three-tier system of unemployment benefits with contained differences in generosity and relatively inclusive unemployment insurance (UI). Conversely, Italy developed a system of unemployment compensation with widely different levels of generosity and high fragmentation along occupational lines.

As Chapter 5 shows, reforms of unemployment benefits under austere economic conditions can be distinguished by two sub-phases in both countries.

In Germany between 1975 and the end of the 1990s incremental reforms reduced access to UI and unemployment assistance (UA), and cut back the generosity of social assistance more clearly than for the other two benefit schemes. Between 2002 and 2004 the more radical so-called 'Hartz reforms' abolished the middle tier of the benefit system, thus leading to a dualization of German unemployment compensation. In Italy small reforms of unemployment benefits during the 1980s followed no clear pattern. By contrast, since the end of the 1980s, the wide differences in benefit generosity were incrementally but significantly reduced.

Part III shows how the policy variation presented in the previous part was influenced by party competition. Chapter 6 discusses the explanations of labour market reforms in Italy and Germany by other authors. For the German case institutionalist accounts prevail. This literature predicted policy stability and, accordingly, has difficulties explaining the more fundamental Hartz reforms. In the Italian literature, the relative powers of the working class and institutions have been indicated as important variables. Also the relevance of party competition has been recognized but not yet satisfactorily analysed regarding unemployment benefits.

Chapter 7 points out how the post-war divergence of the Italian and German benefit systems was driven by the two fundamentally different party systems and the competitive dynamics they generated. In Germany the low degree of polarization in the party system and the small number of parties meant that parties competed on programmatic terms and tried to appeal to broad sections of the electorate. At the same time, they focused on the core of the labour force. Only later, under continuing favourable economic conditions, the credit claiming logic of expanding social protection also led to the introduction of social assistance. In Italy, by contrast, ideological polarization prevented programmatic competition and a high number of parties favoured the representation of narrow interests. The strong radical left promoted, first, employment creation and, later, employment protection. As a consequence, unemployment benefits initially were relatively neglected and, subsequently, a few narrow benefit schemes were strongly expanded that formally kept recipients in employment.

Chapters 8 and 9 examine for Germany and Italy respectively the impact that, first, essentially unchanged party systems had under radically different economic conditions and, second, how changing dynamics of party competition affected reform paths. In Germany (Chapter 8), during the phase of incremental retrenchments, centripetal party competition together with public opinion widely in favour of maintaining current welfare levels impeded structural reforms. Given that governments were nevertheless under pressure to act, the resulting reforms imposed losses mainly on marginal and electorally less significant groups. The 'Hartz reforms', by contrast, were adopted after a limited shift in public opinion in favour of reforms. This pushed the Social Democrats to compete harder in the centre of the political spectrum. In doing so, they were not constrained by a relevant left-wing party competitor.

In Italy (Chapter 9) polarization in the 1980s was not as strong as before but still blocked any decisive reforms of unemployment benefits. At the beginning of the 1990s the party system underwent a radical transformation. The new configuration combined centripetal competition between two broad pre-electoral coalitions, and centrifugal competition between parties within each camp. The reduction of generosity differences, but stopping short of a more structural reform, resulted from the compromises found within each camp to deal with these contradictory pressures.

In Chapter 10 I provide evidence that the findings on Italy and Germany can also be applied to other countries. In a first step, I compare party systems and unemployment benefit systems of advanced welfare states at the end of the formative post-war decades. This reveals that countries with a larger number of parties or higher ideological polarization have more segmented social protection. In a second step, I analyse 15 reforms of unemployment benefits in the 2000s and show that reforms in countries with fragmented party systems were more likely to increase the segmentation of unemployment compensation.

Finally, in Chapter 11 I summarize the findings of the book, discuss implications, and indicate future tasks for research. The study demonstrates the relevance of party competition for explaining social policy development. Also the hypothesized relationships between party system characteristics and segmentation of social protection are largely confirmed. Hence, not only is party politics more complex than the story told by the traditional theories of partisan government, but, at least regarding party competition, the neglected aspects of party politics also matter for policy development. The policy implications of other aspects of party politics (such as party organizations) should be investigated more closely in the future.

Theoretical argument

The fundamental starting point for the argument of this study is that party competition has its own dynamics. Political parties mediate between citizens and the state. As such, parties reflect the interests of citizens and their actions are conditioned by the institutions of the state. But they can be reduced to neither of the two sides (Sartori 1990 [1968]). In particular, some theories suggest that parties act in the interests of specific social groups, such as social classes. In fact, the relationship between a party and a certain social group can often be close. However, sometimes organizational ties to the social basis are much weaker and sometimes no specific reference group can be clearly identified at all. Consider, for example, catch-all parties that are not attached to one specific constituency. But consider also, more generally, how party organizations changed historically and, in most advanced industrial states, have become more detached from core constituencies (Kirchheimer 1966; Katz and Mair 1994; von Beyme 2000). If we take political parties as organizations seriously, we cannot simply identify them with a certain social group even if close ties exist. Przeworski and Sprague (1986), in their famous study of electoral socialism, saw the relationship between party and class even driven by the former: 'the relative salience of class as a determinant of individual voting behaviour is a cumulative consequence of the strategies pursued by political parties of the Left' (ibid.: 9).

If parties are to varying degrees autonomous from their electorate they have some freedom in choosing their objectives. The three basic types of objectives that are relevant for parties are maximizing votes, getting into government office, and adopting their preferred policies (Strøm and Müller 1999). For any of these objectives, they are in competition with other parties. This is why, whatever the main objectives, a party's actions are influenced by the context of competition. In particular, we cannot assume that the policy decisions of parties are simply based on the interests of their electoral constituency as traditional theories of partisan government do (e.g. Hibbs 1977; Korpi 1983). This may be the case, but it depends on the existence of a clear core constituency and on the effect of competition with other parties. Therefore, I argue that the context of competition always matters for the actions of a party. This context is structured by the party system.

Green-Pedersen (2001, 2002) has shown how party systems and the logics of coalition formation can affect reforms of social policy. In this book I will focus instead on electoral competition, which, arguably, is of even greater importance to parties. To be sure, parties are not likely to value votes intrinsically and there may be situations when parties face a trade-off between maximizing votes and maximizing one of their other objectives: attaining government office and adopting certain policies. However, votes are instrumentally indispensable for reaching those other goals (Strøm and Müller 1999). They are of fundamental importance because they are institutionally prior to the other objectives. Moreover, some opposition parties may be far from gaining office or having direct policy influence. But they still care about gaining votes and, by competing in the electoral arena, they may influence the strategies of the parties closer to government power. Therefore, for analysing party competition it makes sense to focus, first of all, on electoral competition even if a more complete analysis should take into account the other party objectives and other arenas of party interaction (Bardi and Mair 2008).

How do party systems, through their structuring of electoral competition, affect policy-making and, more particularly, the segmentation of social protection? The most important characteristics of party systems are the number of parties and the positioning of parties relative to each other. I will take in turn how these two aspects matter for the fragmentation of social policy.

Number of parties

The number of parties can be expected to increase the segmentation of social protection. The more political parties there are the narrower the social interests are that they address. This is likely to lead to greater fragmentation of social programmes. A similar point has been made by Ferrera (1993) in his book on the development of different welfare state models. He pointed out that ethnic, linguistic, or religious cleavages, which crosscut party systems, hindered the introduction of universalist policies and favoured more fragmented programmes with occupational principles of coverage.[1] Furthermore the argument that

Estévez-Abe (2008) develops in her book on the Japanese welfare state goes in a similar direction. According to her, electoral systems based on proportional representation create incentives for parties to focus on narrower interests than is the case in electoral systems where only one candidate per district gets elected (see also Cox 1990). Note that the contributions by Ferrera and Estévez-Abe address two of the main reasons that can lead to a high number of parties: many cleavages (Lipset and Rokkan 1967) and a proportional electoral system (Duverger 1959; Nohlen 2009). My argument abstracts from these causes and considers directly the number of parties in the party system.

How the number of parties affects the segmentation of unemployment benefits can be hypothesized more concretely by looking at the institutional characteristics of these policies. Most welfare states have UI as a more generous benefit that can only be claimed by unemployed persons who previously paid sufficient insurance contributions. In addition, most countries have at least one other unemployment benefit that is constructed as a safety net for those jobless people who do not qualify for UI. This can be a dedicated benefit for the unemployed (UA) or it can be a general social safety net (social assistance). These social safety nets provide protection to anyone who passes a means test and, in the case of UA, to anyone who is looking for a job.

The encompassing character of safety nets makes it unlikely that they are actively supported by small political parties. The actual and potential beneficiaries of these programmes are extremely heterogeneous. In addition, due to social marginalization, they are less likely to be politically active (Verba *et al.* 1993; Gallego 2007). These characteristics make it unlikely for a party to focus its attention specifically on this group. However, the size of this group can still be considerable. Consequently, for large parties that have to attract the broadest electoral support possible, it can still be relevant to gain voters among the actual or potential beneficiaries of unemployment or social assistance schemes. Yet on the other hand, these parties may get into conflict with middle class voters who object to generous social protection financed by their taxes and contributions. These parties, therefore, have incentives to provide encompassing but not very generous social protection, which implies little policy segmentation not only in terms of division but also in terms of generosity differences.

Party positions in political space

The spatial structure of the party system generates for each party certain incentives concerning what voters it can and should target in order to raise or maintain its vote shares. These strategic incentives are reflected in the policy choices of parties. They promote policies that appeal to their most important groups of voters. It is important to underline that the most important group of voters in electoral competition can be, but often is not, the long-standing constituency of a political party. Rather, in many competitive situations it is more relevant to attract new voters or to retain voters who are not part of the core constituency and may defect.

It is common to think about parties as situated in a political space. This can be encountered in everyday political discourse when parties are considered to be 'left' or 'right' or 'more left' than another party etc. It has also been the founding idea of a whole branch of party and election research (see the seminal work of Downs 1957; for a general introduction, see Hinich and Munger 1997; on conceptions and operationalizations of political space, see Benoit and Laver 2006: Ch. 1). The most straightforward example of a political space is a general left–right dimension, but political spaces can also be modelled as having more than one dimension and the single dimensions can be based on more specific policy issues (e.g. social policy or immigration policy). The general logic of spatial competition is that parties take the position in political space where they maximize their votes while accounting for the position of the other parties. Individual voters have ideal points in the same political space and choose parties on the basis of which party is closest to them.[2] In spatial analysis, the immediately neighbouring parties of a given party A are its direct competitors (Adams and Somer-Topcu 2009). Hence, if party A moves away from its neighbouring party B (which stays put), party A risks conceding voters to party B. A well-known implication of this way of analysing party competition is that the centre of the distribution of voters in political space is particularly important. When there are only two parties, if voters choose on the basis of proximity, and if voters do not abstain, then the party that occupies the centre will receive all votes on one side of the spectrum plus the centre votes and, therefore, more than half of all votes (this is called the Median Voter Theorem).[3] Spatial analysis had its origins in economic theory and has spawned a huge theoretical and empirical literature, which often employs formal models. However, spatial arguments on party competition can also be understood and applied in a more intuitive way (Sartori 2005 [1976]: 289–92).

When considering the effect of the spatial configuration of a party system on policy-making we have to distinguish first between those party systems that are ideologically polarized and those that are not. The polarization of a party system can be most easily understood as the distance between parties (such as the distance between the two most extreme parties or the mean distance of all parties from the centre weighted by their vote share; Dalton (2008); Rehm and Reilly 2010)). This would be a relative concept of polarization where polarization is a matter of degree. However, we can distinguish party systems where ideological polarization makes a qualitative difference for the logic of party competition compared to other party systems. These are party systems that contain radical opposition parties, also called anti-system parties (Sartori 2005: 117–18). In the following, I will call these party systems ideologically *polarized* or party systems with *ideological polarization* as opposed to non-polarized party systems, and contrary to the more general concept of polarization that may also refer to degrees of polarization.

Following Sartori (2005: 117–18), 'a party can be defined as being anti-system whenever it *undermines the legitimacy* of the *regime* it opposes' (emphasis in the original). This includes ideological as well as more short-lived protest parties. The ideological anti-system parties can be more narrowly defined as those that 'would not change – if [they] could – the government but the very system of government' (ibid.: 118). Sartori stresses that anti-system parties are not necessarily revolutionary parties and do not necessarily operate outside of the established rules of the political system. The main distinguishing criterion is their de-legitimizing impact on the existing political order. The presence of anti-system parties fundamentally changes the logic of party competition. This is why, for our argument, we have to consider polarized and non-polarized party systems separately.

Polarized party systems are characterized by the presence of anti-system parties that are large enough to have an effect on the overall pattern of party competition. However, these parties do not compete in the same way as parties do in a non-polarized system. Their identity and electoral support derives from their radical opposition to the existing order. As a consequence, they are not disposed to compete with moderate parties in terms of policy proposals and they do not conform to the normal incentives of spatial competition. In the logic of spatial competition, anti-system parties would have incentives to move towards centre in order to capture votes from the more moderate parties, while the more extreme voters have no alternative to vote for. However, the electorate of anti-system parties rejects moderate policy programmes that do not challenge 'the system'. Deviations of this kind cause either voter abstention or the emergence of splinter parties that uphold the 'true cause'.[4]

Anti-system parties are usually excluded from government. Nevertheless, in three ways they retain significant influence on the policy process: by outbidding, blocking, and bargaining. First, as they do not carry government responsibility, anti-system parties can attract voters by making far-reaching proposals without being forced to implement them. This outbidding adds to their electoral strength. Thus, even though anti-system parties do not themselves compete on moderate terms, the moderate parties are still forced to react to them. Polarized party systems often have one party or a group of parties in the centre of the political space that are confronted with anti-system opposition from both ends of the (uni-dimensional) political space. In the resulting centrifugal dynamic of competition the moderate parties are torn between both sides and tend to lose votes to the extreme parties (Sartori 2005: 120–1).

Second, in ideologically polarized systems the main conflict concerns the basic structures of state and society and not concrete policy proposals. The 'opposition [of an anti-system party] is not an "opposition of issues" (so little that it can afford to bargain on issues) but an "opposition of principle"' (Sartori 2005: 118). Accordingly, anti-system parties oppose the reforms of moderate parties and try to block them. They can obstruct policy reforms either through veto points in the parliamentary process or by mobilizing mass protest.

Third, the uncompromising conflict between parties is fought on the public stage. But away from public attention party elites can engage in bargaining over legislation. In an otherwise blocked political system, this may often be the only way to introduce some policy change. This change is, however, small-scale and has to bring some benefit to all the parties involved, including policies that target specific electoral constituencies (Cotta 1996; Sartori 1982). Therefore, a polarized party system often brings about particularistic policy-making.[5]

If we consider these characteristics of polarized party systems altogether, we can hypothesize the following effect on social policy. The power of anti-system parties to block policy-making leads to a lack of comprehensive reforms and the resulting elite-level bargaining to particularistically fragmented policies (see also Ferrera 1993). Moreover, the policy preferences of anti-system parties are likely to have a significant impact on policy development through outbidding and bargaining.

In non-polarized party systems – that is, without anti-system parties – all parties are likely to conform to the incentives of spatial competition by trying to capture votes from their main competitors. In these systems it is important to consider the more precise positioning of parties in political space. In this way, we can identify on which voters electoral competition is concentrated. To give an example: in a party system with only two parties, left-wing and right-wing, competition is concentrated on the space between the two parties, that is, on the centre of political space. This is called centripetal competition. If, however, the left-wing party is exposed to competition by a third party further to the left, it cannot concentrate only on gaining voters in the centre as this would mean losing voters to the far-left party. In this way, we can analyse which voters are important for electoral competition. The policy preferences of these voters are more likely to be reflected in policy decisions. Obviously, the voters who are particularly targeted in party competition can change as new parties emerge or established parties change their position (cf. Adams and Somer-Topcu 2009). Because non-polarized party systems are not blocked by ideological conflict, competition is more likely to be based on programmatic proposals rather than particularistic pay-offs to voters.[6] In addition, competition in these systems is generally more sensitive to voter preferences even if not equally sensitive to the preferences of all voters. As explained above, this depends on the specific spatial configuration of the party system.[7]

Precisely because the more specific configuration matters in non-polarized party systems, it is difficult to formulate a general hypothesis on their policy impact. Rather, we have to analyse, regarding specific situations, who are the party competitors of the parties in government. Yet, compared to polarized party systems, we can expect less policy segmentation because the lack of ideological conflict facilitates a programmatic mode of competition. Beyond this the number of parties will matter. Hence, non-polarized party systems with many parties will lead to more fragmented social protection than non-polarized party systems with few parties. And the relative polarization in party systems without anti-system parties is still likely to impede structural reforms. Fundamental reforms need large majorities – but the further away parties are from each other, the less likely is the necessary consensus for these reforms (Tsebelis 2002).[8]

This part of the argument that looks at non-polarized party systems was inspired in part by Kitschelt (2001) who examined which party systems encourage the adoption of restrictive welfare reforms and which systems impede such reforms. One important point in his argument is whether governing parties face an electoral trade-off if they adopt unpopular reforms. This depends essentially on the existence of a left-wing competitor. In addition, Kitschelt highlighted poor credibility of welfare-defending parties, party organizations that favour strategic flexibility, and the salience of the socio-economic policy dimension for party competition as factors that facilitate painful reforms. By contrast, we will concentrate on the spatial configuration of party systems and electoral competition. Thus, we adopt his point on electoral trade-offs, but focus less on the other points, which we will regard rather as potential intervening variables.

The political space this study focuses on is the socio-economic left–right dimension, which concerns economic and social policy in general. Parties that mobilize principally on non-economic (e.g. regional, post-materialist, or religious) issues either do not play a significant role in competition along this dimension or play a different role, as in the case of regionalist or ethno-nationalist parties. These do not mobilize on economic issues but their ideologies have distributive implications.

Party system types

So far we have considered separately the policy implications of the number of parties and their positioning in political space. However, a more synthetic categorization of party systems will be helpful for the analysis. Concerning the more specific spatial configuration of party systems it is hard to come up with general categories. But the number of parties and their ideological polarization is usefully summarized by Sartori's (2005) typology of party systems.

Surprisingly few party system typologies include information on the political positions of parties (for an overview see Wolinetz 2006). The main ingredients of Sartori's (2005) typology, by contrast, are the number of relevant parties and the ideological polarization between them. Relevant parties are either those playing a role in government formation (coalition potential) or those staying out of government but having sufficient blackmail power to change the direction of competition (blackmail potential; ibid.: Ch. 5). Whether a party system is categorized as ideologically polarized depends, as explained above, on the presence of anti-system parties. Sartori calls the number of parties the 'format' of the party system. Polarization, in turn, determines the 'mechanics' of the party system. The mechanics, however, are also reflected in the logics of government formation (such as single-party government, alternative coalitions, shifting coalitions, or minority government).

Sartori identifies four types of competitive party systems: (1) Two-party systems have two relevant parties and low polarization. (2) In predominant party systems there are more than two parties. One of them dominates government, but its dominance does not stifle the competitiveness of the party system. (3) Moderate pluralist systems consist of three to five relevant parties and have no anti-system parties. Either the major parties or alternative coalitions constitute two poles in this type of party system, which leads to a centripetal direction of competition. (4) Polarized pluralist systems have more than five parties.[9]

The presence of anti-system parties at both ends of the ideological spectrum induces a centrifugal dynamic of competition (see also Sartori 1982). Sartori finds that ideological polarization leads to a high number of parties. The only exceptions are those party systems that he calls 'segmented pluralism'. They consist of many parties due to cultural divisions but they are not ideologically polarized. Because of their low polarization the mechanics of these party systems are similar to the moderate pluralist systems. This why Sartori subsumes them in the latter group (Sartori 2005: Ch. 6).

Although Sartori's typology is more than 30 years old it is still widely accepted as the best typology available. Wolinetz (2006) notes that since Sartori's work no significant new typology has emerged. He attributes this to the fact that Sartori's typology successfully 'sorted the available cases, and it did so in a meaningful way' (ibid.: 59; see also Mair 2005). Nevertheless, historical developments have put the usefulness of the typology in question. 'We now have almost no cases of polarized pluralism, save for the now historical instances for which it was developed, and moderate pluralism is increasingly overcrowded,' writes Wolinetz (2006: 59). This suggests that within the group of moderate pluralist systems we should take into account more specific differences in the spatial configurations and dynamics. For example, we can differentiate the directions of competition beyond the general trend of centripetal competition. Even if party competition in moderate pluralism is generally concentrated on the centre there may be shifts of competition to the right or to the left and even centrifugal tendencies in a weak sense. That is to say, electoral competition may shift more to the margins but stops short of becoming fully centrifugal as long as there are no relevant anti-system parties. In this research I will often draw on Sartori's typology but I will supplement it by looking at more detailed dynamics of spatial competition within his broad types.[10]

Situating the argument in the context of welfare state theories

The argument described in this chapter and explored in the rest of this book contributes to explaining social policy development – with a special focus on the segmentation of social protection. The development of social policy is widely studied and research has given rise to a number of well-established theories. Hence, in the following paragraphs I will explain how my argument relates to those established theories. First, I briefly present the most important theories in roughly the order in which they emerged historically. We can broadly distinguish three causal factors that have been highlighted these theories: socioeconomic conditions, class-based political actors, and institutions.

Regarding economic factors, an early influential explanation for the growth of welfare states was the so-called industrialization thesis (Wilensky and Lebeaux 1965; Wilensky 1975). In this view, the social transformations that went along with industrialization (such as urbanization and dependent wage labour) produced new social risks and, consequently, the need for public social protection. At the same time, economic growth provided the resources required for introducing social programmes. The industrialization argument has also been integrated into a larger modernization perspective that, in addition, pays attention to the process of democratization and the extension of political rights (Flora and Alber 1981; see also Marshall 1950). Today economic conditions still play a relevant role in the discussion on welfare state reform. However, after the end of the so-called Golden Age of high economic growth rates and welfare state expansion (1945-70s), the focus has shifted more to socio-economic conditions that constrain or challenge the welfare state. Most famous in this respect is the discussion on globalization (Scharpf 2000). However, the rise of the service sector has posed serious challenges to advanced welfare states (Pierson 2001a; Esping-Andersen 1999; Iversen and Wren 1998; Armingeon and Bonoli 2006). Generally, the positive role of economic growth in facilitating welfare state expansion and the constraining role of austere economic conditions are widely recognized. However, economic factors are not sufficient for explaining actual policy developments, particularly because various states have responded very differently to similar economic conditions.

The mentioned criticism was one of the motivations for scholars to introduce more politics into explanations of welfare state development. At this stage, politics was understood mainly in terms of social class. Most influential in welfare state research was the power resource theory of Walter Korpi (1983; see also Esping-Andersen 1985). According to this approach, social policy development is the result of a struggle between organized social classes. The working class presses for more generous and universal social protection and the success of this battle depends on the strength of trade unions and left-wing political parties. Power resource theory is related to the broader 'partisan politics' approach in comparative political economy (e.g. Hibbs 1977; Castles 1982; M.G. Schmidt 1982). In this approach, parties represent the interests of social classes. The policy objectives of a party correspond to the economic interests of its social constituency, and policy output depends on the partisan composition of government. At first, the focus of this approach was on left parties representing the working class and right parties representing middle and upper classes. Later, it was refined to include Christian democratic parties, which also promoted the growth of the welfare state but emphasizing social insurance and a strong role for the family (van Kersbergen 1995; for an overview see M.G. Schmidt, 2010). Empirically, this approach was powerful in explaining the emergence of different types of welfare state during welfare state expansion (Esping-Andersen 1990; see also Manow 2009).

However, the class-based politics approach was not only applied to the so-called Golden Age of the welfare state but also to the phase of welfare restructuring since the 1970s. Some studies have shown that left parties are less likely to cut back social protection (Korpi and Palme 2003; Allan and Scruggs 2004), while other studies registered a reduced impact of traditional partisan differences (Huber and Stephens 2001). At the same time, some authors, while remaining in a class mobilization framework, have challenged the conventional partisan politics hypotheses. On the one side, Rueda (2005, 2007) maintains that since the 1970s the core constituency of social democratic parties consists of labour market insiders that have a low risk of unemployment and are juxtaposed to an increasing group of precarious labour market outsiders. Consequently, social democratic parties nowadays promote less universal policies because they disregard the needs of marginalized sections of the labour force. On the other side, some studies highlighted that employers have not always opposed greater social protection, as assumed by traditional partisan theory. Rather, in many cases some sections of capital have entered cross-class coalitions that supported the introduction of new social protection (Swenson 2002; Mares 2001).[12]

The main challenge to traditional partisan politics theory came, however, from institutionalist scholars. Pierson's (1996, 2001b) argument that in the era of welfare state reform the political logics have changed decisively because of the extensive welfare state itself, had a huge impact in the field. Existing welfare state structures have created vast groups of voters (in particular, transfer recipients and public employees) with vested interests in maintaining the status quo. Under these conditions, any retrenchment risks severe electoral punishment (see also Flora 1986a; for a cautious assessment of the electoral risk of social policy reforms see Giger 2011). Therefore, reform becomes politically a task of 'blame avoidance' rather than 'claiming credits' for greater social protection as it could be practised previously. The implication of Pierson's argument was that even right-wing parties cannot severely cut back the welfare state. Hence, the traditional partisan differences become blurred.

Other institutionalist scholars have highlighted the role of political institutions in shaping the policy-making process. Thus, research has shown that a high number of 'veto points' impedes the adoption of policy changes. But veto points can influence the kind of policy change by determining which actors can intervene at which stage of the policy process. In this way they can also lead to a more inclusive policy process (Immergut 1992; Birchfield and Crepaz 1998; Swank 2002). Based on institutional arguments, as well, is the 'Varieties of Capitalism' approach. It shows how economic institutions and policies reinforce each other in national economies. This leads to a high stability of specific models of capitalism even in the face of external changes such as globalization (Hall and Soskice 2001). Regarding social policy, it has been maintained that different forms of income protection encourage investment in certain types of skills, which in turn conform to the product strategies of firms (Estevéz-Abe *et al.* 2001).

After institutionalist theories had been challenged for being unable to account adequately for policy change, many studies have discovered that social policy has actually changed more significantly than expected but often as the accumulative result of many incremental shifts (Streeck and Thelen 2005; Hall and Thelen 2009). Nevertheless, a pure focus on institutions can hardly account for what is driving change in the first place. Consequently, these driving forces are usually 'borrowed' by introducing other factors, e.g. socio-economic transformations, political actors, or ideas and discourses (Hall and Taylor 1996: 942).[13]

The welfare state literature has shown convincingly that all three mentioned sets of factors are important for explaining social policy development: socio-economic pressures push governments to act; the partisan composition of government affects the content of new policies; and institutions (policy legacies, political institutions, or economic institutions) condition the direction of reform efforts. Yet, it is striking that party politics, which is arguably at the core of everyday politics in representative democracies, plays such a small role in established welfare state theories. Of course, power resource theory and partisan politics theory have highlighted that parties matter. But in these theories the role of parties is reduced to transmitting interests from a social base to government. As I argue in this book, party politics has a more independent role in policy-making and much of this independent role is shaped by the competition within party systems. This is only one additional aspect in explaining social policy development but accounting for this aspect will yet improve our understanding of what drives policy changes in advanced welfare states.

2 Comparing Italy and Germany

The objective of this study is to show that differences in party systems influence the social protection that states put in place for various groups of citizens. This aim will be pursued, in the first place, by comparing policy developments in two states – Italy and Germany – that have very different party systems but do not differ so strongly on many other important social, economic, and political characteristics. While this historical comparison constitutes the bulk of the analysis, I will conclude by conducting two cross-sectional comparisons of a larger set of advanced welfare states in order to show that my argument applies as well beyond Italy and Germany.

Case selection

Italy and Germany[1] are chosen on the basis of what is called a most similar systems comparative design. To be sure, the two countries differ in many ways. But if we look at them in the wider context of advanced capitalist democracies, they are relatively similar in many aspects that other theories use as independent or intervening variables: the welfare state model, the economic model, post-war economic development, the formal political system, and, not least, the partisan composition of post-war governments. The most remarkable difference between the two states lies arguably in their highly diverse party systems. In fact, some of the unavoidable remaining differences of the other factors have to be seen in the light that we need to choose cases that differ significantly in their configuration of party competition. It is from this point of view that Italy and Germany are remarkably similar in many respects except their party systems. Therefore, this is an almost ideal comparative setting for studying the impact of different party systems.

Most studies in comparative welfare state research assign both Germany and Italy to the group of continental (or conservative or Bismarckian) welfare states. In Esping-Andersen's (1990) important typology they were categorized in this way, which many scholars have adopted since (see e.g. Palier 2010). Indeed, both welfare states are largely built on occupational principles of coverage and rely heavily on status-preserving cash benefits. Moreover, in both countries cash benefits, the structure of the tax system, and the lack of family services encourage a male-breadwinner family model (only since 2004 Germany has introduced some relevant reforms in this respect; Blome *et al.* 2009; Leitner *et al.* 2008; Naldini and Saraceno 2008).

Alternatively, Maurizio Ferrera (1996, 2010) and other scholars have argued that the south European welfare states, including Italy, constitute a distinct type of welfare regime. What distinguishes these welfare states are highly fragmented schemes of income maintenance with wide differences in generosity, a departure from occupationalism by introducing National Health Services, a low degree of state penetration in the provision of welfare, and the frequent abuse of welfare programmes for clientelist purposes.[2] Some of these characteristics have historical roots (such as weak state institutions). But in Italy most have fully emerged only during the phase of welfare state expansion after Second World War. Up to the war, both Italy and Germany were in fact purely occupationalist welfare states (Flora 1986a; Ferrera 1993). In Chapter 4 I will show that unemployment compensation was organized rather similarly in both states up to 1945. Consequently, the marked divergence between Italy and Germany in this policy field after Second World War can hardly be explained by policy legacies or the wider context of welfare institutions. Rather, explaining this divergence constitutes a part of explaining their more general differentiation into two different types of welfare state. After all, fragmented and unbalanced social protection is one of the characteristics that distinguish the south European from the continental welfare state.

In terms of economic models, Italy and Germany are both strongly regulated and coordinated market economies although their modes of economic management differ. Germany is the classic case of a Coordinated Market Economy but Italy shares only some of the features of coordinated capitalism (Hall and Soskice 2001). Consequently, some scholars have considered Italy together with other south European countries as Mixed Market Economies that combine aspects of coordinated and of liberal markets (Molina and Rhodes 2007). Other scholars have seen the Italian case as similar to the French type of state-led capitalism notwithstanding the weakness of Italian state institutions (V. Schmidt 2002b: Ch. 3).

Both the Italian and the German labour market are governed by strict employment protection even if protection specifically against collective dismissals is higher in Italy. Similarly, skill formation in both countries is characterized by a high share of vocational training, but in Germany this is based on the dual apprenticeship system while in Italy it is mainly company-based. Hence, in both labour markets a mixture of industry- and firm-specific skills prevails, but firm-specific skills are yet more widespread in Italy (Estévez-Abe *et al.* 2001). As with differences in the welfare state model, keep in mind that some of the differences in economic coordination and labour market governance have emerged only after Second World War and, therefore, are part of the period under investigation. This applies, in particular, to the regulation of employment security.

Both countries experienced rapid economic growth in the post-war decades. Yet, around the end of Second World War, industrialization was more advanced in Germany than in Italy. In Italy 40 per cent of the labour force was still occupied in the agricultural sector in 1951, while in Germany (in 1950) this proportion was only 23 per cent (Flora *et al.* 1987). However, the strong growth of the economy in the 1950s and 1960s made Italy catch up quickly in terms of industrialization. Consequently, in 1971 only 16 per cent of the Italian labour force was still in agriculture, while 42 per cent was occupied in the industrial sector and 37 per cent in services. In Germany (in 1970) the corresponding shares were 8 per cent in agriculture, 49 per cent in industry, and 44 per cent in services (ibid.). Therefore, differences in economic development had declined significantly.

However, economic development in Italy was continuously characterized by stronger regional disparities than in Germany. The Southern regions (*Mezzogiorno*) have consistently lower per capita income and higher unemployment rates than the Italian North. Unemployment in the South was the main reason why in the 1960s nationwide unemployment rates in Italy did not decline as much as in Germany. On the other hand, since reunification Germany has a notable regional economic divide that runs between the Western and the Eastern *Länder* (Sinn and Westermann 2001). Overall, we do find some structural differences between the Italian and the German economy. Nevertheless, compared to other advanced industrial states both economies have a high degree of coordination in common and both shared very similar paths of post-war economic development, with steep growth in the 1950s and early 1960s, and slow growth combined with high unemployment since the middle of the 1970s.

The parallels in political development are remarkable as well. National unity was established 1861 in Italy and 1871 in Germany. Hence, both countries were 'late-comers' in the process of nationalization (Ziblatt 2006). In the first half of the twentieth century, both states were ruled by fascist regimes: Italy from 1922–43 and Germany from 1933–45. According to Hobsbawm (1994: 112–24), these were in fact the only clear cases of fascism in power, notwithstanding other right-wing authoritarian regimes, and despite the differences between both regimes. After the collapse of fascist rule, both countries consciously adopted constitutions with many checks and balances in order to avoid the concentration of political power. Both states have bicameral parliamentary systems, in which government is normally based on party coalitions and the executive is strongly kept in check by parliament. Still, the way in which parliament exerts its constraining role differs. In Germany the lower house usually does not obstruct government plans due to high coalition and party discipline. Instead, opposition frequently can block legislation in the upper house when the partisan majorities diverge between upper and lower house (but only legislation that concerns *Länder* interests is subject to agreement by the upper house; Lehmbruch 2000; M.G. Schmidt 2002; Scharpf 1985). In Italy, upper and lower houses are symmetric in terms of competence and power. Due to similar electoral rules, even the partisan composition in both chambers broadly corresponded (up to the 1990s). However, in both houses parliamentary groups can exert substantial control over government policies. The political reason for this is the instability of coalitions, which is caused by the divisions in the party system (Sartori 1982: 19–25). Institutionally, the power of parliamentary groups derives from the influential role of parliamentary committees, the involvement of group leaders in agenda setting, and demanding voting rules (Pasquino 2002; Vassallo 2005; Bull and Newell 2005: Ch. 7). Nevertheless, these different workings of parliamentarism have broadly similar constraining effect on the executive in both states.

A more relevant difference in terms of formal political institutions is that Germany, since national unification, was a federal state whereas Italy was founded as a unitary state (Ziblatt 2006). However, starting from the 1970s and continuing today under the pressure of the *Lega Nord* the Italian political system is increasingly decentralizing so that this institutional difference has decreased. At the same time, the policy field that concerns us here, i.e. labour market policy, is one of the few fields in Germany that are centrally administered. Therefore, federalism plays less of a role in this context.

Although Italy and Germany have very different party systems, it is interesting to note the many parallels in the partisan composition of their post-war governments. That is to say, similar parties were in government but they operated in very different environments of party competition. Immediately after the war a consensual approach between the political left and the right prevailed in both countries. However, this collaboration broke up before the first parliamentary elections. Subsequently, during the formative years of post-war reconstruction, from the late 1940s to the beginning of the 1960s, government cabinets were dominated by the Christian democratic party in each of the two states. In subsequent years the left was increasingly included in government. In Italy the Socialist Party participated in government, still led by the Christian Democrats, from the beginning of the 1960s (Tamburrano 1990). At the end of the 1970s even the Communist Party was included in the governing coalition in parliament (but not in the ranks of cabinet). In Germany the Social Democrats entered a 'Grand Coalition' with the Christian Democrats in the middle of the 1960s and became the leading party in a coalition with the Liberals after the end of the 1960s.

In the 1980s, then, both countries registered a shift back to the right. In Italy the Communists ended their support of the executive. The Socialists remained in government but became themselves notably more centrist while the Christian Democrats remained the largest government party. In the same period the German Christian Democrats re-took control of government in coalition with the Liberals. Subsequently, in the middle of the 1990s the composition of government moved again to the left. Centre-left government coalitions came to power 1996 in Italy and 1998 in Germany. In Italy this lasted only up to 2001 when the left lost power to a centre-right coalition again. In Germany the coalition of Social Democrats and Greens stayed in government up to 2005 when another grand coalition (Social and Christian Democrats) was formed.

The parallels of how partisan composition of government evolved over the post-war period are striking. In particular the dominance of Christian democratic parties during the Golden Age of welfare expansion is important (van Kersbergen

1995). According to traditional partisan politics theory, these similarities should have produced similar policy output. At least in the field of unemployment compensation this was not the case. Given, in addition, the many other social, institutional, and economic similarities, this supports our case that the widely different party systems matter. Government actions are shaped by the competitive context in which government parties operate. Even the same partisan composition of the executive can produce different results if the dynamic of party competition that it is exposed to differs.[3]

The differences between the Italian and the German party system will be discussed in more detail in Part III of this book. Suffice it to say that the Italian party system was a clear case of polarized pluralism with a high number of parties, anti-system parties, and centrifugal competition, whereas the German party system was a good example of moderate pluralism with few parties, no relevant anti-system parties, and centripetal competition. This clear difference in logics of party competition motivates the case selection, especially as we regard this against the background of the similarities in partisan composition of government, as well as the similar welfare state models, previous unemployment policy developments, economic models, development paths, and political systems.

Methods

In addition to this basic comparative set-up, the analysis will exploit two broad changes over time: one in economic conditions, and one in party competition itself. This will help us to analyse the impact of party competition under different economic conditions and to conduct additional cross-time comparisons of varying party competition dynamics. In the 1970s the economic context changed from strong, industrially driven growth to low growth rates, high unemployment, the rising importance of the service sector, and increasing international economic integration. As is well known, this economic shift forced governments to abandon welfare expansion and to adopt a restrictive approach to social policy instead (for an overview see Ferrera 2008). However, the basic characteristics of the Italian and the German party systems remained basically unchanged up to the 1990s. Therefore, we can analyse the policy effect of these party systems not only during welfare expansion but also during welfare state restructuring.

Later on in the new economic phase of austerity, the dynamics of party competition changed in both states. At the beginning of the 1990s the Italian party system changed radically. Thereafter, it was characterized by two broad electoral coalitions competing against each other, which introduced a new dynamic of centripetal competition. However, within each coalition, individual parties still tussled between themselves. In Germany changes in party competition were more moderate. The Liberals moved more to the right on socio-economic issues over the course of the 1990s, and in the middle of the 2000s a new party to the left of the Social Democrats emerged. Although German party competition stayed prevailingly centripetal these developments implied some centrifugal tendencies (in a weak sense). These party system changes enable us to study different dynamics of party competition within each country and under essentially similar economic conditions of austerity.

Therefore, we can actually conduct three comparisons. The first compares, cross-sectionally, the policy effects of the different logics of party competition under conditions of economic growth and welfare expansion (1945–70s). The second comparison examines, across time, to what extent the impact of the same party system in each country changed when welfare states entered the phase of economic austerity and welfare restructuring (1970s–90s). Finally, in the third comparison, the economic conditions remain austere but the dynamics of party competition change so that we can compare, again across time for each country, the effects of the reordering of party politics (Germany: 2000s; Italy: 1990s-2000s).

Following the comparative method, we would like to have different values for the independent variable – in our case, party systems – while keeping other variables constant as far as possible (Lijphart 1971; King *et al.* 1994). The first comparison implements this particularly well: apart from some differences in economic structures both countries had similar models of welfare capitalism, experienced similar economic growth, had similar partisan governments, but their party systems were very different. The second comparison is somewhat different because it is not the independent variable but the economic conditions that change. Consequently, this comparison serves less to study the independent impact of party competition. Rather, it is useful in order to examine how the same party systems affect policy-making under different economic conditions in each country. In the third comparison, this design works again very well for the Italian case. Although the early 1990s were generally turbulent years in Italy, the most dramatic change, which triggered many of the subsequent developments, was clearly the breakdown of the old party system. Hence, this is a good occasion to study the effect of a variation in party competition across time. In Germany the changes in party competition were more moderate and accompanied by important other transformations, especially national reunification and its consequences. Therefore, in the German case it will be more difficult to single out the effect of party competition. Fortunately, however, in that period there was a high-profile series of reforms ('Hartz reforms') for which the role of party competition can be examined in more detail.

More generally, the paired comparison (Tarrow 2010) of Italy and Germany does not rely solely on the careful case selection and comparative design but also on tracing the political processes that have led to important reforms. To this end, I draw on party manifestos, newspaper reports, historical literature, and background interviews. This makes it possible to collect more concrete evidence of how party competition has shaped policy development. Moreover, this way can account for more complex processes that a purely comparative design, modelled on the regression method, cannot capture. This regards questions of timing and sequence, interaction between different factors, and possible feedback effect from policy back to party competition (Hall 2003; George and Bennett 2004).

After the historical comparison of Italy and Germany, Chapter 10 will extend the research to a wider set of cases. However, the ambition of this additional step is limited. It is not a full-fledged large-N analysis of the impact of party systems on social protection in its own right. Rather, it provides a first round of evidence that the argument of this book also applies to cases other than Italy and Germany. More precisely, I conduct two cross-sectional comparisons: one for the phase of welfare state expansion and one for the phase of welfare reform. The first comparison confronts, in a cross-tabulation, the party systems that prevailed in the early post-war decades with the segmentation of unemployment benefit systems at the end of that phase. The second comparison analyses, in a multivariate regression, the effect of the number of parties on significant reforms of unemployment benefit levels while controlling for left party government, unemployment, institutional veto points, and path dependence. Both analyses confirm the hypothesized impact of party systems.

Operationalization

How the dependent variable of this study – segmentation of unemployment benefits – is measured, will be discussed in the following chapter. Regarding the independent variable – party systems – the previous chapter has explained that the number of parties matters as well as the positioning of parties. In terms of party positioning, I distinguish between polarized party systems and the more specific spatial configuration in non-polarized party systems.

As is well known among scholars of political parties, to count parties is less obvious than it may seem. Even when we consider only the parties that are represented in parliament, we face the problem that some parties are too small to count them with equal weight as those with double-digit seat or vote shares. Yet, establishing a cut-off point of, say, 5 per cent vote share is arbitrary and can still lead to over- or underestimates. A common solution to the problem is to adopt an indicator that weights parties by their vote shares. The probably most established indicator is the 'effective number of electoral parties'[4] based on the formula by Laakso and Taagepera (1979): the inverted sum of the squared vote shares of all parties. This is a very useful indicator for large-N studies when we lack sufficient knowledge about each of our cases. It does not, however, solve the problem that the size of a party is not a good measure of its political weight. For this reason Sartori (2005: Ch. 5) had proposed rules for counting parties that are based on the political dynamics within a party system. The relevant parties, according to Sartori, are, first of all, those having coalition potential, meaning they play a role in the formation of governments. But some of the parties that never participate in government coalitions can still be relevant if they are strong enough to influence the direction of competition (what Sartori calls 'blackmail potential'). This can be seen from whether they affect the tactics of other parties. For the most part of this study I will rely on Sartori's rules of counting parties: coalition potential and blackmail potential. Only in the cross-sectional comparison of unemployment benefit reforms in advanced welfare states (Chapter 10) will I employ the effective number of electoral parties.

As regards the positions of parties in political space, we first have to keep separate the ideologically polarized party systems. These are the party systems with relevant parties that fundamentally reject the existing political and social order (see previous chapter). Following Sartori (2005) the defining characteristic of these anti-system parties is their de-legitimizing impact on the political system. This can be judged from the party programme as well as other public interventions and standpoints of a party.

For the more specific spatial configuration of party systems, especially in the non-polarized party systems, we need more refined methods for estimating party positions. For this purpose I will draw on the positioning of parties through opinion surveys or expert surveys.[5] Opinion and, especially, election surveys can be used in two ways for measuring party positions: either respondents are asked to locate parties in a certain political space (usually a general left–right axis); or party positions are estimated by the average self-placement of each party's voters (see e.g. Rehm and Reilly 2010). The first method has the advantage that results reflect the perception by the electorate, that is, by the target group of electoral competition itself (Dalton 2008). But the party-placement by respondents is rarer to find in opinion surveys than the self-placement. An additional problem in using opinion surveys is that most of them only use a general left–right dimension for party positions. On this general dimension more specific policy dimensions often get mixed up, such as the different positioning of parties concerning socio-cultural issues (e.g. civil rights and immigration) and socio-economic issues (economic and social policy). As this study is concerned with social policy it has to account for party positions on a socio-economic dimension of competition. For this reason I use the two expert surveys by Laver and Hunt (1992) and Benoit and Laver (2006).[6] These have the additional advantage that experts were asked to estimate the importance of each policy dimension for each party. This helps us to see how important the socio-economic dimension is for the party system overall and whether for some parties this dimension is altogether irrelevant, so that they do not compete on this dimension. For the early decades after Second World War neither survey-based nor expert data on political positions are available. However, the politological and historical literature on party politics in Italy and Germany provides sufficient information on the ideological characteristics of the two-party systems at the time.

Where party competition is programmatic we have to take into account the policy demand of the voters who are in the focus of competition. To this end we can again use public opinion surveys. From these we need to extract items that concern either specifically the preferences for generous unemployment benefits or more generally the preferences for social protection. These policy preferences can then be cross-tabulated with the self-positioning of respondents in political space. In this way, we can, first, infer from the data on party systems where in political space competition is concentrated and, then, identify the policy preferences that prevail in this section of the political space.

Finally, a caveat regarding the ambition of this research is in order: the aim of this study is to highlight the role of party systems in explaining the segmentation of social protection. I control for many other variables in order to show that the remaining variation in policy segmentation is explained by party competition and I show in more detail how party competition affects this variation. To be sure, this does not imply that other factors, such as partisan composition of government, economic conditions, and institutions (see previous chapter) play no role in explaining the development of unemployment benefits in Italy and Germany or the variation in unemployment benefit segmentation across advanced welfare states. After all, the objective of this study is not to explain the development of unemployment benefits as a whole or to fully explain cross-national variation. Rather, I claim that the differences in policy segmentation between Italy and Germany cannot be fully understood without considering the different party systems and, furthermore, that party systems are relevant to explaining policy segmentation also in other welfare states. That economic conditions, partisan government, and institutions matter has been proved often enough. Hence, in this study I focus specifically on party competition without discussing at length the impact of other causal variables.

Part II
Policy segmentation across countries and time

3 Segmentation of unemployment benefits in advanced welfare states today

This book studies the impact of party competition on the differentiation of social rights between different groups of citizens. Before the next chapters track the policy development in Italy and Germany, this chapter discusses how the differentiation of social rights can be analysed in the field of unemployment benefits. Moreover, the chapter provides an overview of how the segmentation of unemployment benefit systems varies across advanced welfare states today.

Differentiation of social rights

T.H. Marshall has powerfully described the egalitarian character of national citizenship and how it expanded from civil rights, to political rights, and social rights. He saw social citizenship as a fundamental challenge to social inequality and class divisions (Marshall 1950). However, as Maurizio Ferrera has pointed out (2005a: 37–52), the construction of national citizenship presupposed, for one thing, the exclusion of non-nationals. But, in addition, the expansion of rights among national citizens often proceeded incrementally and created new distinctions between social groups. In the developed democracies of today, civil and political rights generally extend to all citizens. Yet, many social rights are differentiated and membership boundaries run across the national population.[1] The basic reason for this differentiation lies in the greater costs that social rights involve. While all rights give rise to some 'enablement costs' and 'enforcement costs', social rights involve 'substance costs' in the form of providing social transfers or services. The financing of these costs makes the construction of membership boundaries a complex task that has to take into account material resources and cultural bonds.

Needless to say, Marshall was right in that social rights intervene in the social order that is produced by market and community relations. But how strong their impact is and who will benefit from it is not clear *a priori*.[2] This point was, of course, also made by Esping-Andersen (1990). Welfare states shape social stratification and vary in the kind of effect that they have on the social order. The welfare state 'is, in its own right, a system of stratification. It is an active force in the ordering of social relations' (Esping-Andersen 1990: 23). The precise effect depends on the institutional structures of each welfare state.

Thus, Esping-Andersen (1990) diagnosed that the liberal type of welfare state, as found in English-speaking countries, tends to nurture dualisms as it targets basic social protection on the poor and emphasizes individual responsibility for the rest. By contrast, social democratic welfare states, as in Scandinavia, emphasize broad-based solidarity and therefore tend to contain social differences more effectively. The conservative welfare states of continental Europe tend to reflect traditional social divisions by establishing separate programmes for different social groups, but they also alter the social structure by giving preferable treatment to some groups, such as civil servants. In addition to this three-fold categorization, it has been argued that south European welfare states should be distinguished from their middle European conservative cousins. These welfare states produce yet higher generosity differences and fragmentation in social insurance (Ferrera 1996).

In sum, social rights in modern welfare states are differentiated and citizens are grouped into different membership spaces. So far this perspective has been mainly applied to the macro level. Less research has been conducted on the patterns of differentiation within single policy fields, such as unemployment compensation. However, in two strands of the labour market policy literature, policy boundaries and differentiation do play a role: general comparisons of unemployment benefit systems and research on the rise of non-standard employment.

First, most comparisons between systems of unemployment support consider who has access to this support. Schmid and Reissert (1996) have pointed to the difference between 'insurance-based' and 'welfare-based' systems of unemployment benefits. The former 'establish a close link between previous employment, wages and paid contributions on the one hand and benefits on the other' (ibid.: 243). The latter mainly guarantee a minimum level of income. Accordingly, insurance-based systems are 'biased towards protecting core workers (mostly male and elderly) over marginal workers (mostly young, female and casual), whereas people tend to be more equally treated (with exception of women who are not the main wage-earners) under welfare systems' (ibid.: 248). In a similar vein, Gallie and Paugam (2000) distinguish unemployment benefit systems according to the proportion of unemployed receiving benefits (beneficiary rate), benefit levels and duration, as well as spending on active labour market policies. Their survey of benefit systems is sensitive to the different levels of protection that different groups of unemployed receive. Yet, they do not address clearly the different benefit schemes existing in each unemployment regime, such as UA in addition to UI.[3]

Second, different levels of protection have become an important topic in the literature that studies the rise of non-standard employment (such as part-time, fixed-term, or agency work). The established forms of unemployment compensation are often ill-suited for the needs of this more flexible section of workers. Grimshaw and Rubery (1997) were the first to highlight how eligibility requirements can exclude non-standard workers from receiving benefits in case of unemployment. In many cases this means, more precisely, an exclusion from UI and falling back on assistance schemes (see also Leschke 2008; Clegg 2007;

Berton *et al.* 2009). Clasen and Clegg (2006) have shown that reforms of unemployment benefits in some states have actually exacerbated these divisions, whereas other states have responded by de-differentiating their unemployment compensation. In any case, non-standard workers face problems in other branches of social security as well. Hence, the consistent rise of these new forms of employment in conjunction with the rising importance of service employment and the transformation of household structures has led to a wider debate on processes of dualization and insider–outsider conflicts in European welfare states.[4]

Therefore, the literature demonstrates that differentiation of unemployment protection has become a more pressing issue due to changes in labour markets and that welfare states have reacted in ambiguous ways to the need to adapt their unemployment policies. But so far no study has systematically accounted for how the differentiation of social rights varies cross-nationally in this policy field.

Social rights can be differentiated on two levels: the individual and the group level. On the individual level, they can be differentiated through particularistic administration. For example, if clientelism is pervasive benefits are assigned to individuals in return for their electoral support to specific candidates or parties. On the group level, differentiation consists of different policy programmes for various groups of unemployed. For analysing this group level I use the concept of unemployment benefit segmentation. This is defined as the division of compensation into various schemes and the differences in generosity between them. Hence, the concept has two dimensions. The dimension of division is concerned with the number of benefit programmes and how inclusive or exclusive they are. This dimension is related to the concept of membership spaces and boundaries (Ferrera 2005a). Second, the dimension of generosity differences deals with how much of a difference it makes for an unemployed person to receive one benefit rather than the other.

An overview of cross-national variation

This section takes stock of the variation of unemployment benefit segmentation across 27 OECD countries. For assessing the dimension of division I take account of the various benefit schemes in each state and the shares of unemployed people that profit from them. The dimension of generosity differences will be measured by the replacement rates of the different benefit schemes. In the end, I summarize the variation by identifying groups of countries with similar patterns of segmentation.

Dimension of division

There are three standard types of unemployment benefits. Unemployment insurance is usually financed by employers' and employees' contributions, entitlement is conditional on past employment and contribution records, benefit levels are earnings-related, and durations are limited. Unemployment assistance is financed by the general state budget, entitlement is usually based only on being unemployed and depends on a means test, benefit levels are flat-rate, and duration is unlimited. These first two benefits are sometimes called 'dedicated unemployment benefits'. By contrast, Social assistance (SA) is often relevant for the unemployed but is not a 'dedicated' benefit. SA is often the last resort for unemployed persons, although, of course, it can be claimed by other people with insufficient means to sustain themselves as well. Its characteristics are essentially similar to UA (tax-funded, means-tested, flat-rate, unlimited) but entitlement is just based on being in need and not conditional on being unemployed.

For providing an overview of benefit systems I distinguish three situations that the jobless can find themselves in with regard to unemployment benefits. Most countries have one unemployment benefit that is more generous than others and also more difficult to qualify for. I call this the 'main benefit'. In most cases it is UI. The three benefit statuses of the unemployed can be identified with respect to this more generous benefit. They can be receiving the main benefit, they can have exhausted the maximum duration of the main benefit, or they are not eligible for receiving the main benefit in the first place. In mapping unemployment benefit systems we need to see what kind of benefit a welfare state offers for each qualification status. Drawing on country-specific information on unemployment benefits provided by the OECD (2010a), we can code each benefit system by a sequence of three acronyms that correspond to each qualification status in the mentioned order (main benefit, exhausted main benefit, not eligible; see Table 3.1).

We can see from Table 3.1 that almost all countries have UI as their main unemployment benefit. In most states the unemployed who cannot receive this main benefit have to rely on SA. In 2008, 15 out of 27 countries provided only SA for those not fulfilling the qualifying conditions of UI (including the US, which provides only food stamps). In nine of the other countries the unemployed can fall back on UA, although this is not always unconditional or unlimited. For those unemployed who have exhausted their main benefit the picture is essentially similar, except for the fact that a few countries offer UA specifically for them. Only in Italy no national benefit programme exists for those who cannot claim UI.[5]

For about half of the welfare states considered here, their set of unemployment benefits does not tell us much about segmentation. They provide UI as the main benefit and SA or UA for those who cannot receive the main benefit. Segmentation within these systems depends on how inclusive or exclusive UI is and how much more generous it is compared to the secondary benefit. For the other countries, however, their set of benefit programmes already furnishes us with some indication of segmentation.

Six of these 27 states have as their main benefit either UA or UI with flat-rate benefit levels. Because these benefit levels are the same for all recipients they are usually not very high and, therefore, do not diverge strongly from the subsidiary unemployment benefit. New Zealand and Australia stand out here because both countries have only one benefit (UA) for all unemployed. The other four countries (Ireland, UK, Iceland, Poland) have flat-rate UI as their main benefit.

Table 3.1 Unemployment benefit systems in 27 OECD countries, 2008

Benefit schemes by qualification status			Countries	Remarks
(a)	(b)	(c)		
UI	SA	SA	8 (CA, CZ, DK, JP, LU, NL, NO, SK)	• in Canada SA is regulated by the provinces
UI	SA/UA	SA/UA	4 (PT, ES, HU, SE)	• in Spain SA is regulated by the regions; UA in Sweden refers to the basic insurance scheme
UI	UA	UA	2 (FI, DE)	
UA	UA	UA	2 (AU, NZ)	
UI (flat)	UA	UA	2 (IE, UK)	
UI (flat)	SA	SA	2 (IS, PL) Σ = 6	• in Iceland SA is regulated by the local governments
= flat-rate systems				
UI	(UA)	(UA)	1 (GR)	• UA is conditional and limited
UI	(SA)	(SA)	1 (US)	• not full SA but only food stamps; UI is administered by the states within federal guidelines
UI	–	–	1 (IT) Σ = 3	• benefits other than UI exist, but are restricted to specific occupational groups
= protection gap systems				
UI	UA	SA	3 (AT, FR, CH)	• UA in Austria is earnings-related; UA and SA in Switzerland vary between cantons
UI	UI	SA	1 (BE) Σ = 4	• UI is unlimited, but gets gradually reduced, in some cases down to a flat-rate benefit level
= status-preserving systems				

Source: OECD (2010a: country-specific files).

Notes
Abbreviations in first three columns indicate the benefits for the following sequence of qualification statuses: (a) main benefit, (b) main benefit exhausted, (c) ineligible for main benefit.
SA: social assistance, UA: unemployment assistance, UI: unemployment insurance, UI (flat): UI with flat-rate benefit level.

Note that some UI systems with earnings-related benefit levels can have de facto almost flat-rate benefit levels due to low benefit ceilings (e.g. Denmark). But the question of low ceilings cannot be analysed systematically here.[6]

Three countries in this sample lack financial support for those who cannot receive the main benefit. Greece and Italy do not have minimum income programmes at the national level.[7] So the jobless who cannot claim UI (and neither conditional and limited UA in the case of Greece) have no public income support. In the US the protection of last resort consists only of food stamps and not of a full SA scheme. Consequently, I label the benefits systems in these countries 'protection gap systems'.

Most countries have the same benefit programmes for those jobless who do not qualify for the main benefit and for those who have exhausted the main benefit. In contrast, four countries provide better protection for their long-term unemployed than for the unemployed that cannot get UI in the first place: Austria, Belgium, France, and Switzerland. Therefore, these welfare states make a greater effort to preserve (relatively speaking) the standard of living of unemployed workers even in case of long unemployment spells. In Austria, UA for the long-term unemployed even pays earnings-related benefit levels (as it used to be the case in Germany until 2005), which adds to the status-preserving character of this benefit system. In Belgium UI is paid indefinitely (though the benefit rate decreases after a certain period).

After this overview of the benefit schemes in advanced welfare states we need to know how relevant the different schemes are in terms of the number of unemployed that profit from them. This is a second step to measuring the division of unemployment compensation. The best way to do this is with beneficiary rates, that is, the proportion of the unemployed that receives a benefit. Unfortunately, comparative data for SA is not available because the unemployed recipients are usually not identified among the overall number of recipients. Consequently, I use here administrative data on beneficiaries of dedicated unemployment benefits. The numbers of unemployed are taken from survey data and based on the international definition of unemployment (being out of work, actively looking for work, and available for work). This definition is relatively restrictive and, of course, it comes from a different source than the beneficiary data. For this reason, the beneficiary numbers in some countries exceed the number of unemployed (Figure 3.1). This does not exclude the possibility that at the same time other people in these countries are unemployed according to the international definition but do not receive unemployment benefits (see also Immervoll *et al.* 2004). The beneficiary rates are only available for 22 of the 27 OECD Countries above.

In Figure 3.1 we can discern four groups of countries. To the left of the figure we find some states that provide only UI as a dedicated unemployment benefit, but this benefit is very inclusive: Belgium, Netherlands, Denmark, Norway, and Sweden (in Switzerland UA actually exists as a second dedicated benefit but no beneficiary data is available). The beneficiary rate of Sweden used to be higher but has dropped after a reform implemented in 2007. In the middle range of UI beneficiary rates there are several states that run, in addition, a UA scheme.

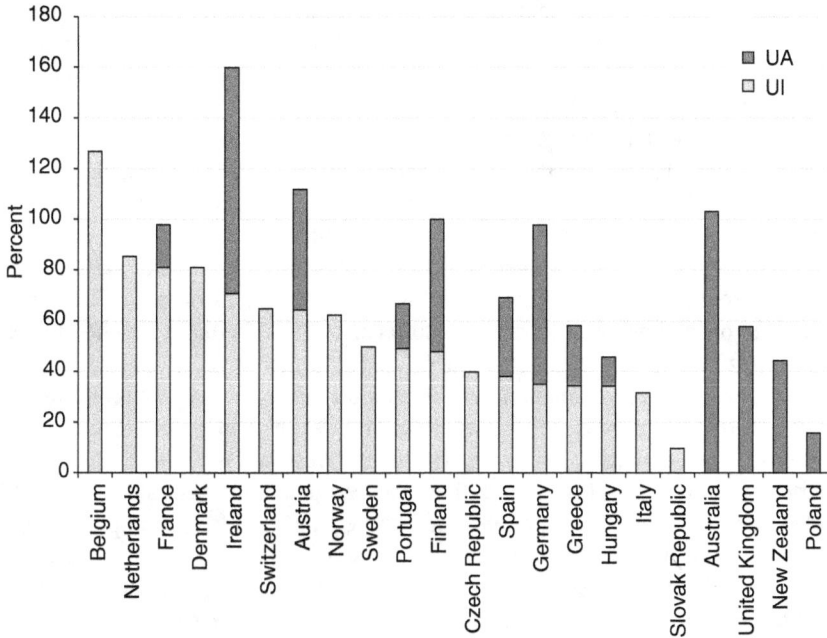

Figure 3.1 Unemployment beneficiary rates in 22 OECD countries, average 2004–8 (source: OECD (2010b), own calculations).

Notes
Number of beneficiaries (administrative data) divided by number of unemployed (survey-based, standardized). Data for UA in Switzerland is missing. In the following cases it is not clear what the data from the source refers to: UI in Sweden refers probably to state-administered basic UI and not to union-administered UI; UA in UK seems to refer to both UI and UA (to contribution-based and to income-based Job-Seekers Allowance); UA in Poland must refer to flat-rate UI as the only other benefit is SA. Data for Greece is based only on 2008, for Poland only on 2005–8.

Among these we have to distinguish the states where all other unemployed are covered by UA: Ireland, Finland, and Germany. In the other countries, for which UI and UA beneficiary rates are shown, UA is limited or conditional so that SA remains relevant for the jobless. Hence, France, Austria, Portugal, Spain, Switzerland, and Hungary have benefit systems with three tiers. To the right of the figure we find states with clearly less inclusive UI. Among these, in the Czech and the Slovak Republic UI is supplemented by SA. But Greece and Italy have no such minimum income benefit. Greece only provides a conditional and limited UA scheme in addition to UI. Therefore, in the latter countries the low inclusiveness of UI has particularly dire consequences. Finally, Australia and New Zealand have UA only. UK and Poland have flat-rate UI, which in the data presumably was registered as UA.

Those unemployed who do not receive dedicated unemployment benefits are likely to claim SA or to have no public financial support. As mentioned, we cannot use SA beneficiary numbers here as they include not only unemployed beneficiaries. Figure 3.1 already gives us some idea of how many unemployed in each country have to get by without receiving a dedicated unemployment benefit: by considering the difference between the cumulative beneficiary rates and the 100 per cent mark. In addition, Immervoll *et al.* (2004) have calculated how many unemployed (following the international definition) respond in labour force surveys that they receive 'unemployment benefits or assistance'. The results are likely to be marred by underreporting and misreporting. Nevertheless, they yield additional information on inclusion/exclusion from dedicated benefits.

Overall, the results by Immervoll *et al.* (2004: 66) confirm the pattern that emerged from the beneficiary rates in Figure 3.1. Italy stands out as in 2001 only 1 per cent of the unemployed declared to receive unemployment benefits. Other countries where, consistent with Figure 3.1, few unemployed (less than 25 per cent) report to receive unemployment support are Greece, Spain, Portugal, Poland, Slovak Republic, and Czech Republic. At the same time, even in the highest-scoring countries (Belgium, Germany, Austria)[8] not more than three-quarters of the unemployed said they receive unemployment benefits. This underlines once more the importance of membership boundaries and policy seg-mentation. The Immervoll *et al.* figures supply us with data on three states, for which we did not have beneficiary rates. The US ranks among the countries with the lowest share of self-reported recipients of unemployment benefits (only 14 per cent). We can speculate that underreporting of receiving benefits is likely to be stronger in the US, given its culture of liberalism. Still, this is the fourth lowest share and below countries such as Slovak Republic, Czech Republic, Spain, and Portugal. Also in Luxembourg relatively few unemployed declare to get unemployment support (21 per cent) and only somewhat more in Iceland (27 per cent).

Dimension of generosity differences

As we have seen, all advanced welfare states apart from Australia and New Zealand have more than one unemployment benefit. Turning to the dimension of segmentation that is concerned with generosity difference, we have to ask: how much of a difference does it make in those countries with more than one unem-ployment benefit, to receive one rather than the other? The most important measure of benefit generosity is the rate of the previous work income that is replaced by benefit income. Here I use net replacement rates that are calculated by the OECD (2010a). These take into account taxes (on previous earned income and on benefit income) as well as additional benefits, such as family and housing benefits. They are calculated by applying the legal benefit regulations to the income situation of hypothetical households. The work income of the hypotheti-cal households is based on the actual average wage in each country. I have com-puted the unweighted averages of four model households (single, single with children, one-earner couple, and one-earner couple with children).

I compare the replacement rate of the main benefit with the replacement rate of those unemployed who have exhausted their main benefit. The OECD calls the former the replacement rate for the initial period of unemployment. This rate is calculated on the assumption of extensive previous contribution and employment records. Hence, in our terms this is the replacement rate of the 'main benefit', which is mostly UI. Unfortunately, the OECD does not calculate replacement rates for those unemployed who do not qualify for the main benefit in the first place. However, in most countries this should be very similar to the replacement rate for the long-term unemployed as they run the same benefit scheme for both groups of unemployed. Only in the countries with status-preserving unemployment benefit systems can this be expected to make a difference. The calculation of the replacement rate of long-term unemployment benefits is based on assumptions that make sure that in any country UI benefits have expired (after five years of unemployment). In order to simplify, I will call the replacement rate for the long-term unemployed 'outsider replacement rate' and the one for the main benefit 'insider replacement rate'.

In Figure 3.2 outsider replacement rates are plotted on the vertical and insider replacement rates on the horizontal axis. It includes a 45 degree line to indicate which countries are close to equal generosity of both benefits. The states with flat-rate benefits as main unemployment benefits are, indeed, closest or even above this line and make up the top left corner of the scatter distribution: Ireland, UK, Australia, and New Zealand. Japan, Belgium, Austria, and Sweden are also close to this angle of the distribution, but remember that Belgium and Austria

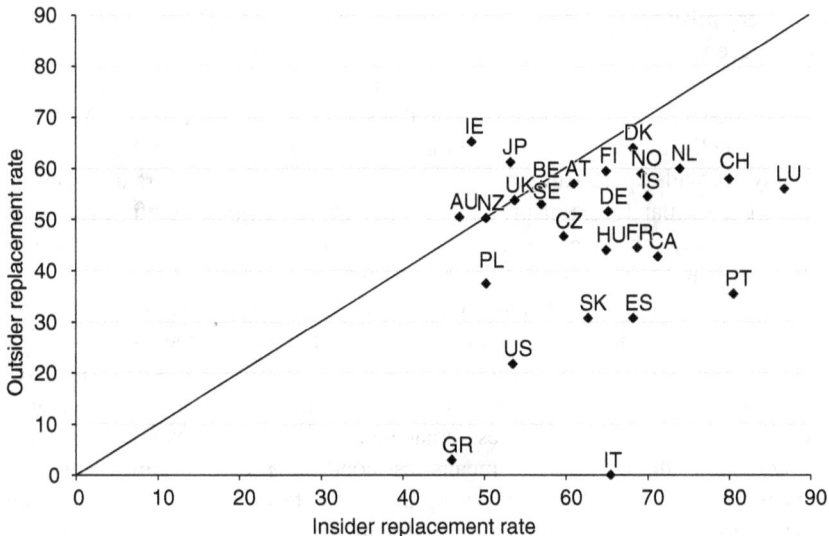

Figure 3.2 Differences in generosity – scatter plot of two unemployment benefit replacement rates in 27 OECD countries, 2008 (source: OECD (2010a), own calculations).

Note
The line is at 45 degrees to indicate equal values on both axes.

pay higher benefits to the long-term unemployed than to those not eligible for UI, which qualifies this apparent equality. Apart from this caveat, the countries in this corner of the distribution make hardly any difference between the long-term unemployed and those on the main benefit, both receiving around 55 per cent of their previous income. In fact, the long-term unemployed in some of these countries are indicated to receive higher benefits. The reason for this is probably that assistance benefits give access to other benefits, such as family or housing.

From this first group of cases we have two directions along which unemployment benefit systems with greater generosity differences are spread. First, those cases to the right that, compared to the flat-rate systems, pay similar benefits to the outsider unemployed but higher benefits to insiders. Here we find the countries from continental and northern Europe. Second, a range of countries spreads downwards. Compared to the flat-rate systems, they pay lower benefits to the outsider unemployed. This difference is particularly strong for the US, Greece, and Italy, which reflects the lack of substantial minimum income schemes in these welfare states. Poland has relatively low benefits for long-term unemployed as well, while other countries, such as the Slovak Republic, Spain, and Portugal, pay not only lower benefits to outsiders, compared to the flat-rate systems, but also higher benefits to the insider unemployed.

Many studies of unemployment benefits rank countries according to 'the' generosity of their unemployment compensation. Usually this measure refers to UI. Figure 3.2 shows that this focus on the generosity of only one benefit scheme can be very misleading. Greece and Ireland or the US and UK have almost identical replacement rates of UI. But in terms of benefit levels for the long-term unemployed they differ widely. And remember that the share of the unemployed that does not receive UI is in most countries substantial (cf. Figure 3.1). Conversely, benefit levels for the insiders in Ireland and Denmark or Australia and Germany are wide apart. But the outsider unemployed in these pairs of countries actually get similar levels of protection. Therefore, we miss significant aspects of variation between unemployment compensation in different welfare states if we look only at the generosity of one benefit scheme.

Using net replacement rates as the measure of generosity has of course some limitations. Other policy features that also determine generosity are the maximum duration, waiting periods, and the strictness of job search requirements.[9] Moreover, all outsider benefits in the states we looked at are means-tested. How the OECD calculates replacement rates of means-tested benefits does not reflect the tightness of means test conditions, e.g. how much of their assets people have to sell before passing the means test or to what extent family members are required to provide financial help. These additional aspects will be taken into account in the case studies on Italy and Germany as well as the more detailed rules of eligibility with regard to the dimension of division. For this survey of advanced welfare states, such detailed analysis was not possible. However, net replacement rates are still a good measure. After all, they address the crucial question: 'How much do I get?'

Patterns of segmentation

Finally, we need to bring together the two dimensions of unemployment benefit segmentation. To this end, I build a cross-table (Table 3.2) that indicates increasing segmentation along both dimensions but distinguishes qualitatively different configurations of benefit systems. On the dimension of division we can summarize the information on kinds of benefit schemes (Table 3.1) and on beneficiary rates (Figure 3.1) by identifying four groups: first, very inclusive benefit systems based on UA or flat-rate insurance; second, countries with inclusive UI; third, benefit systems that are stratified into three tiers; fourth, countries with exclusive UI. Regarding differences in generosity we determined roughly three groups: those countries with equally generous benefits for insiders and outsiders but on a relatively low level; systems that have average benefit levels for the outsider unemployed but pay higher levels to insiders; and countries with only meagre protection for those who are not eligible for UI.

Overall, we find six clusters of countries (see Table 3.2). The Antipodes and the liberal European countries have inclusive assistance-based unemployment benefit systems with almost no differences in generosity, albeit on a low level. This means that these countries have a very low degree of segmentation but with overall only lean protection. Most of the Nordic countries as well as the Netherlands have inclusive insurance-based unemployment support. Their benefit levels for recipients of UI are more generous than for the rest of the jobless. But, as the insurance scheme is relatively inclusive, this difference does not weigh in strongly. Accordingly, segmentation is very moderate as well but on a higher level of generosity than in the assistance-based countries. Belgium and Sweden used to be in this category as well. But, due to recent retrenchments of their insurance benefit levels, their generosity differences have become more similar to the assistance-based systems. Moreover, note that the beneficiary rates of UI in Sweden and Finland are not very high – even though they are still higher than

Table 3.2 Patterns of segmentation in 25 OECD countries, 2008

Division: generosity differences:	Inclusive (assistance-based)	Inclusive (insurance-based)	Stratified (three-tier)	Exclusive (insurance-based)
Equal but low	AU, NZ, IE, UK	BE, (SE)		
Pro-insider		NL, NO, DK, (FI)	AT, FR, CH, PT, (ES)	DE, LU, CZ, (HU), (IS)
Outsider gap				IT, GR, US, (SK), (PL)

Notes

The arrows indicate increasing segmentation, but the two dimensions are not linear. Ambiguous cases are in brackets. Patterns of segmentation are based on: benefit schemes and beneficiary rates for dimension of division, net replacement rates for main and secondary benefit schemes for dimension of generosity differences.

those in the 'exclusive' insurance-based states. Because of this ambiguity Finland and Sweden have been put in parentheses.

Unemployment compensation in most continental countries (France, Austria, Switzerland) is stratified into three tiers. Thus, segmentation here is much clearer, but these welfare states still provide a reasonable safety net for the lowest group through SA. Portugal and Spain also belong to this group of three-tier systems, however the generosity differences in these states are stronger than in the continental states (Spain could almost be considered 'outsider-gap') and their beneficiary rates of UI are lower. Therefore, segmentation is actually somewhat higher.

The other two south European countries (Italy, Greece) are found in the group with strongest segmentation: having exclusive insurance-based systems and lacking adequate protection for labour market outsiders.[10] Interestingly, this group includes the US as well as some central European countries: Slovak Republic and Poland. However, the outsider benefit levels in the latter two countries are not as low as in the rest of this category. Note how, in terms of unemployment benefit segmentation, the US is sharply distinguished from the liberal European welfare states and Antipodes with which it is usually lumped together as liberal welfare states or liberal market economies.

Another heterogeneous group of relatively high segmentation is formed by those countries with exclusive UI and generosity differences in favour of insiders. Here we find Germany after it abolished the three-tier system in 2005 as well as Luxembourg as another continental European state. Moreover, two central European states (Czech Republic and Hungary) as well as Iceland are assigned to this pattern of segmentation, although Hungary and Iceland are again ambiguous cases.

Generally, this chapter has presented the impressive variation in terms of segmentation that we find across advanced welfare states. In some states almost all unemployed are equally protected even if not very generously. In other welfare states some unemployed are protected better than others but the less protected group is rather small. And in yet other countries, some unemployed receive very comfortable protection against income loss while many of the jobless can claim only meagre, or even no benefit at all. The task of this book is not to explain entirely this cross-national variation. In Chapter 10 we will show some evidence that these different patterns were also influenced by the party systems that prevailed during post-war welfare expansion.

Moreover, this overview gives us an idea of the international context within which the German and the Italian cases are situated. Italy belongs to the states with the highest segmentation in unemployment benefits. This emerges from these rather broad indicators even though they are not very well suited to capture the specificities of unemployment compensation in Italy such as the very generous benefits for workers in big industrial firms that are formally only benefits for partial unemployment. Furthermore, the high benefit fragmentation by occupational criteria in Italy is not reflected in the international datasets that I used in this chapter. Germany, on the other hand, has a less segmented benefit system compared to Italy, but, due to its low beneficiary rate of UI and its abolition of the three-tier benefit system, unemployment compensation there is more segmented than in Nordic and European-liberal welfare states and even more than in most other continental states. The next two chapters will analyse more closely how benefit segmentation in Italy and Germany evolved.

4   Italy and Germany

Policy divergence after the Second
World War

Between the end of the Second World War and the 1970s Italy and Germany
established widely different systems of unemployment benefits, although up to
the Second World War these policies had been relatively similar in both states.
In this chapter I will first summarize the policy developments up to 1945, which
reveal many similarities. I will then show how unemployment compensation
diverged from that common starting point.

Similar policy developments up to 1945

Germany

Up to the beginning of the First World War Germany had no national policy of
financial support for the unemployed although there was a political debate about
the introduction of such a policy.[1] Industrialization had brought up unemployment as an evident new social problem and parts of the labour movement
demanded a national response to it. But opposition from employers was uncompromising and government shied away from the issue, citing also practical
difficulties (Faust 1981). Thus, before the First World War financial support for
the unemployed came only from a fragmented range of financially limited funds,
provided by trade unions and municipalities. Apart from these scattered unemployment benefits, the second half of the nineteenth century saw the introduction
of the first labour exchanges on a similarly fragmented basis (run by unions,
municipalities, employers, and commercial services respectively). Some towns
also used public work schemes for alleviating unemployment (*Notstandsarbe-
iten*), but the scope of these measures was very limited (Faust 1981).

The social and labour market disruptions caused by the First World War, as
well as economic planning of war production, prompted the government to intervene more directly in the labour market. Thus, in 1914 the first national scheme
of UA was introduced (*Kriegserwerbslosenfürsorge*). This was a locally administered, means-tested benefit programme, co-financed by national and local funds.
Demobilization after the war called again for government action to dampen the
social impact of unemployment. Indeed the end of the war was accompanied by
fierce workers' revolts in several German cities. The government decided to

extend and to reorganize wartime UA, and in November 1918 the UA (*Erwerb-slosenfürsorge*) was introduced. The scheme was administered by municipalities but financed three-sixths by the national government, two-sixths by the *Länder*, and one-sixth by the municipalities themselves. Transfers were paid after a waiting period of one week and for a maximum of 26 weeks. Eligibility was conditional on a means test. Yet, the scheme was explicitly designed to keep the unemployed out of stigmatized poor relief. *Erwerbslosefürsorge* was meant as a provisional solution until a political agreement was reached on a more comprehensive response to unemployment. However, it took until 1927 to introduce that new policy.

Together with the introduction of the *Erwerbslosenfürsorge* legal provisions were made for a wage supplementation fund for workers on short-time work and for public work schemes (Frerich and Frey 1996: 196). The employment services were reorganized over the following years. In 1920 for the first time a national office for labour market exchange was established (*Reichsamt für Arbeitsvermittlung*). The local branches were run by the municipalities with the equal participation of employers and trade unions. In 1923/4 government reformed UA and put its administration into the hands of the new labour exchange offices. More importantly, the scheme was transformed into a contribution-based benefit. Wage-based contributions had to be paid by all workers (and in equal parts by their employers) that were covered by compulsory health and pension insurance. Consequently, eligibility was reduced to those who had paid at least 13 weeks of contributions during the last 12 months. The means text was maintained nevertheless, which made *Erwerbslosenfürsorge* a hybrid between unemployment insurance and assistance.

With rising unemployment the inadequacy of the existing UA scheme became increasingly blatant. Unemployed who were either ineligible or who had exhausted the benefit fell back on local poor relief. As a consequence, government extended the maximum duration to 52 weeks in 1926. As this proved still insufficient, a supplementary scheme was introduced, the so-called crisis assistance (*Krisenfürsorge*). This second means-tested benefit paid for an indefinite period and was, once more, meant as a provisional measure. Municipalities administered the new programme. Three-quarters of the funding came from national government and one-quarter from municipalities themselves.

The mentioned unemployment crisis of 1925/6 had rendered the structural causes of unemployment yet more evident and, hence, underlined the need for public support of the unemployed (Weisbrod 1981: 190–1). At the same time, employers and trade unions, for different reasons, were unsatisfied with the unemployment benefits already in place (Mares 2001: 60–3; Clasen 1994: 54–5). When unemployment temporarily decreased in 1927 the Act of Labour Exchange and Unemployment Insurance (*Gesetz über Arbeitsvermittlung und Arbeitslosenversicherung*, AVAVG) was adopted, which introduced the first UI in Germany. As with previous contributions to UA, this insurance became compulsory for all workers who were covered by health insurance and, consequently, also covered agricultural workers (Alber 1981). Thus, it was financed through equal contributions from workers and employers, while the national government was supposed to cover deficits (through loans) if necessary. Eligible for receiving benefits were those unemployed who had paid contributions for at least 26 weeks over the last 12 months. Benefit levels were differentiated according to wage groups, to which unemployed were assigned, based on their average wage over the last 13 weeks. On top of this basic benefit came family supplements for each family member (up to a defined maximum). Benefits were paid after a waiting period of seven days and for a maximum period of 26 weeks. If someone was judged to have become unemployed by his own fault, that person could not receive benefits for six weeks. Moreover, nine weeks after the start of payments recipients had to accept job offers from other towns, other occupations and with lower wages compared to their previous job (Frerich and Frey 1996: 199–202).

Unemployment insurance replaced the old assistance scheme (*Erwerbslosenfürsorge*). The crisis assistance (*Krisenfürsorge*), however, was retained for those who exhausted insurance payments and for those who had paid contributions for at least 13 weeks but not for the 26 weeks required for UI. As a last resort there was, as before, locally administered and locally financed welfare assistance (poor relief) for all people in need. Therefore, at this stage Germany had already introduced a three-tier benefit system consisting of UI, crisis assistance, and poor relief.

Apart from introducing UI, the AVAVG restructured national labour market administration. The Imperial Office for Labour Exchange and Unemployment Insurance (*Reichsanstalt für Arbeitsvermittlung und Arbeitslosenversicherung*), as it came to be called, became fully responsible for administering UI. It was now a self-governing public body, jointly run by representatives of employers, workers, and the government. Also the regional and local offices were reorganized along these lines. Apart from employment services and UI, the responsibilities of the *Reichsanstalt* (RA) included career consulting and placement of apprentices.

It soon turned out that the assumptions on future unemployment levels that were underlying the budget of the new RA, and hence the funding of UI, were too optimistic. Already in its first year, and thus still before the Great Depression, the RA ran into financial difficulties and soon had to be supported by loans from the national government. This sparked off a bitter debate about reforming UI. Employers and the national-liberal German People's Party (*Deutsche Volkspartei*, DVP) demanded benefit cuts, whereas trade unions and the Social Democratic Party (*Sozialdemokratische Partei Deutschlands*, SPD) favoured a rise in contributions. The SPD ultimately lost the struggle and in March 1930 deserted the Grand Coalition of Social Democrats, Catholics, Left-liberals, and National-liberals. This caused the downfall of the last parliamentary government of the Weimar Republic (Weisbrod 1981).

The Great Depression meanwhile had sent unemployment soaring, peaking in 1932 at 5.6 million registered unemployed, or 30 per cent of the labour force (Mitchell 1975: 170). The various presidential cabinet governments (1930–3, with their respective heads Heinrich Brüning, Franz von Papen, Kurt von

Schleicher[2]) reacted to this development by strongly cutting benefit rates and eligibility criteria on the one hand and increasing contribution rates on the other. Among other cuts, in June 1932 a means test was introduced after six weeks of receiving UI. One consequence of these retrenchments was that by 1933 only a minority of the unemployed received UI while more and more people were forced into crisis assistance and, especially, local welfare assistance. In September 1932 those receiving local assistance made up 53 per cent of all claimants of unemployment benefits. In fact, the benefit cuts and the rise of contribution rates went so far that, paradoxically, in 1932, when unemployment reached its peak, the RA registered a financial surplus (Frerich and Frey 1996: 203f).

Under National Socialist rule (1933–45) labour market policy was subjected again to the direct control of government and was instrumentalized for war industry. Initially, the system of benefits was by and large retained, although agricultural workers and domestic servants were excluded from UI coverage. However, instead of financial protection for the unemployed, the new regime focused on employment creation and public work schemes. In fact unemployment declined to 2.7 million in 1934 and 430,000 in 1938 (Mitchell 1975: 170). This decrease was largely caused by an expanding war industry and by military conscription, but also by disincentives against the labour market participation of women and by the racist discrimination of foreigners and Jews. In spite of low unemployment and narrow eligibility requirements, contribution rates to UI remained unchanged. The resulting surpluses were redirected, with large sums going towards other purposes such as financing armament. This was also possible because government took direct control of labour market and UI administration (see below).

Given the low unemployment levels, the regime extended the duration of UI indefinitely in 1937 and abolished UA (*Krisenfürsorge*). Two years later UI was transformed into an assistance scheme itself that was closely connected to governmental labour planning and allocation. Henceforth eligibility was no longer based on individual employment records. Rather, everyone available for labour service was eligible, but subject to a means test. Therefore, unemployment benefits became completely secondary to the allocation of labour according the regime's needs.

This focus on allocation was itself made possible by a drastic restructuring of labour market governance. Already in March 1933, almost immediately after Adolf Hitler came to power, self-governance of the RA was abolished. Only a few months later the trade unions were violently suppressed and workers' representation centralized within the new German Labour Front (*Deutsche Arbeitsfront*, DAF) that was controlled by the National Socialists. In 1938 the public employment service was fully integrated into the Ministry of Labour. Its main responsibilities were, by then, the administration of compulsory labour services and labour allocation. After the start of the war, these tasks also included the allocation of prisoners of war and civilian foreigners to forced labour in Germany (Schmid *et al.* 2001: 272–4).

Italy

There was no national policy of financial support for the unemployed in Italy either until the First World War.[3] The 'social question' in general became a central political issue in the last two decades of the nineteenth century. But the upper and middle classes held on to *laissez-faire* principles. The Catholic Church took care of poor relief and objected to interference by the state in this sphere. The labour movement in turn opposed state intervention for ideological reasons (Ferrera 1993: Ch. 6).

The only unemployment benefits before the First World War were supplied by workers' organizations. In fact the first workers' associations emerged with the aim of providing mutual help against social insecurity. The so-called mutual help societies (*società di mutuo soccorso*) organized workers on a local basis and were often associated with centre-left political movements. Many of them later evolved into trade unions (Musso 2002: 112–16). However, in the end they set up mostly social, cultural, and educational activities because systematic financial support for unemployed members was not financially viable within these rather small associations. Even among the emerging trade unions, despite somewhat larger memberships, this was a daunting task. At the national level, only some federations of skilled crafts provided unemployment benefit schemes by the beginning of the twentieth century. Benefit rates of the worker-administered schemes were either flat-rate or differentiated according to previous wage level or professional status. On average they were set at approximately a third of the previous wage. Duration usually depended on the length of previous membership. Many unions verified the unemployment status of claimants by requiring them to report regularly to the union-run office of labour exchange. Overall, the problem of these schemes was that only those workers' associations less in need of unemployment protection were better able to establish a benefit scheme. Consequently, unemployment benefits managed by trade unions generally remained inadequate (Musso 2004: Ch. 6.1).

During the First World War national government set up unemployment benefits for the first time, though these were only patchy and intended as emergency measures. In 1915, when fishing was banned, a benefit was introduced for the fishermen of the Adriatic Sea, and in 1916 the government started to provide lump sum financial support to those associations that offered unemployment compensation. Yet one year later, an unemployment fund was set up for workers in the war production industry, probably in anticipation of the end of the war. In addition, at the beginning of 1918, employers were ordered to pay workers half of their wage if they were kept from working due to energy shortages.

When the ceasefire was announced in November 1918 government faced the worrying prospect of massive unemployment due to the demobilization. Consequently, the government introduced the first comprehensive UA scheme. It was financed from the national budget and was intended as a provisional measure until the end of 1919. The benefit was paid daily for a maximum of 180 days, and its level was differentiated by age, gender, and place of residence;

family supplements were also envisaged. In addition, government introduced a severance payment (*indennità di licenziamento*), according to which laid off employees should receive a one-off payment based on the previous salary and the years of service. Entitlement to this subsidy was limited to white-collar employees with a minimum length of employment within the respective firm (Cherubini and Piva 1998: Ch. 2.2).[4]

In Italy, 1919 was a year of serious social unrest. Trade union membership and labour strikes soared. Due to extensions of suffrage in 1913 and 1919 these social tensions acquired a new political significance (Flora *et al.* 1983: 126). Also unemployment remained a serious problem although between 1901 and 1930 over a million Italians emigrated (Gualmini 1998: 97). Against this background, the government introduced UI in October 1919, replacing the assistance scheme. Covered were all dependent workers including agricultural workers and white-collar employees up to maximum salary level. Excluded were workers below 15 and over 65 years of age as well as home workers, domestic servants, seasonal workers, and public employees. The programme was financed by equal contributions from workers and employers. In addition, for the first three years the state subsidized the scheme with a lump sum, in order to make it immediately viable. The benefit was administered by two different kinds of bodies: regional funds that were administered by provincial governments and occupational funds that were co-governed by workers, employers, and the state. Furthermore, policy administration was supervised by the National Office for Labour Exchange and Unemployment, located at the newly created Labour Ministry.

A worker was eligible to receive benefits from the new insurance fund if he/she had paid at least 36 contributions during the last two years (24 contributions for reduced benefit duration). Once a worker became unemployed he/she had to report to a labour exchange office the next day in order to maintain entitlement. Payments would start on the eighth day of unemployment and last for a maximum of 120 days (90 days, in case of only 24 contributions). If the benefit expired, a recipient could reclaim it only after a break of six months. The benefit level was differentiated according to three wage classes. If an unemployed person refused to take up an adequate job offer or refused to take part in a training measure she could lose his/her benefit entitlement. The same rule also applied if an unemployed was 'devoted to idleness or drunkenness' (Cherubini and Piva 1998: Ch. 2.2).

In 1922 Benito Mussolini and his National Fascist Party (*Partito Nazionale Fascista*, PNF) came into power. Only a year later the fascist regime reformed UI in three main respects. First, on the administrative level the occupational funds were abolished and all policy administration taken over by the National Fund of Social Insurances. Similar to labour market policy in National Socialist Germany, this centralization of policy control provided the fascist state with the necessary discretion to redirect UI funds towards other purposes. In fact, given new restrictions of eligibility (see below), the insurance fund was bound to run annual surpluses, which after 1929 were massively used to raise general state revenue. Second, agricultural workers were excluded from coverage – a significant change given that roughly half of the labour force belonged to this sector. Big landowners had supported the rise of the fascist party and now demanded this step as a pay-off. Additionally, coverage was restricted regarding seasonal workers but extended for white-collar employees. Third, the definition of an 'adequate job offer' was widened and the unemployed were required to report every day to the labour exchange office. As a consequence, those who were unable to show up due to illness, pregnancy, or child birth were barred from receiving payments. Moreover, medical checks and other administrative controls deemed necessary by the insurance fund were allowed for, with the aim of verifying the effective availability for work. Therefore, UI was turned into a powerful tool of social control (Cherubini 1977: 310ff; Ferrera *et al.* forthcoming: Ch. 2).

After fascist social policy had originally been overwhelmingly restrictive, in 1927, a second, more expansive and corporatist phase began. This was characterized by cross-class collaboration, the pervasive state control, and differentiation of policies along occupational lines. However, while other new social programmes were introduced, UI was not expanded. In 1933 the National Fund of Social Insurances was renamed to the National Fascist Institute of Social Protection (*Istituto Nazionale Fascista della Previdenza Sociale*, INFPS) and in 1935 contributions and benefit levels of UI were switched from fortnightly to weekly instalments. This brought them in line with the other social insurances, but did not alter effective levels. Furthermore, the rules concerning so-called voluntary unemployment were tightened.

Generally, a restrictive approach to UI prevailed and benefit levels were rarely updated. This way, the programme became clearly inadequate for the persisting problem of unemployment, particularly in the wake of the Great Depression. Similar to Germany, the regime focused on policies other than unemployment compensation. First, it responded to the crisis by massively expanding the state's role in the economy. The foundation of public enterprises and investments in infrastructure were intended to create work opportunities for the unemployed (Gualmini 1998: 98). Second, in 1934 the regime reduced the weekly working hours from 48 to 40 in order to redistribute employment to the unemployed. The employed workers were not compensated for the resulting reduction in income. Third, the fascist party in 1931 founded public works organizations (*Enti Opere Assistenziali*, EOA) that functioned at the provincial level as a substitute for UA. The EOA offered work for the unemployed in exchange for a cash subsidy or payments in kind. Often these works included the construction of buildings for the fascist movement. According to official statistics 2,880,000 persons took part in this scheme in the winter of 1934/5 (Ferrera *et al.* forthcoming: Ch. 2) – a huge number considering that the amount of registered unemployed was only a third (964,000, Mitchell 1975: 170).[5] Yet, the regime's efforts did not eliminate unemployment. In 1938 there were still 810,000 registered unemployed (Mitchell 1975: 170).

Only relatively late during fascist rule the government expanded UI. In 1937 family supplements were introduced only to be reduced again a few years later.

In 1939 benefit levels generally were raised. However, the rise in benefit levels hardly made up for their loss in real terms due to inflation over the years. Moreover, benefit levels were now distinguished by class. White-collar workers could receive higher benefits than blue-collar workers (Cherubini 1977: 312f.; Ferrera *et al.* forthcoming: Ch. 2). When Italy entered the Second World War in 1941 the government expanded benefits once more by prolonging the maximum duration from 120 to 180 days. In addition, the difficulties of wartime production (energy shortages and supply problems) led to the introduction of wage supplementation for workers on short-time by collective contract (a pre-form of the later *Cassa Integrazione Guadagni*, see below). However, at that time the role of wage supplementation was still limited (Gualmini 1998: 99f.).

Italy and Germany compared

The similarities between the policy development of unemployment benefits in Italy and Germany prior to 1945 are remarkable. In both countries there was no nationwide unemployment benefit before the First World War, only small and dispersed funds – in Germany run by trade unions and municipalities, in Italy only run by trade unions. Both states introduced their first national measures in this field during the First World War even if they were more fragmented in Italy. Directly after the war both countries put national comprehensive UA schemes in place, as a new measure in Italy and as a renewed version of a wartime policy in Germany. The democratic phase between the First World War and fascism saw the introduction of UI in both states, although this happened much earlier in Italy (1919) and relatively late in Germany (1927). These two programmes were somewhat similar in their characteristics such as the graduation of benefit levels by wage classes. In both countries UI did not fare well under fascism. The fascist regimes took direct control of policy administration, redirected unemployment funds towards other purposes, and excluded agricultural workers from coverage. Clearly, both regimes favoured employment creation, public works, and assistance schemes rather than rights-based UI. However, in Italy UI was by and large retained, while in National Socialist Germany it was transformed into UA.

To be sure, the mentioned similarities mainly concern UI. The two benefit systems as a whole did have some relevant differences. In Italy, for most of the time there was no secondary benefit (such as UA or SA) to help those not supported by the primary benefit. Only in 1931 did the fascist regime introduce its public works programme that served in practice as a kind of UA but was not granted on the basis of legal entitlements. At the same time, welfare assistance was largely in the hands of private and church-affiliated institutions and regulated only very loosely by the state. By contrast, in Germany local government had traditionally been responsible for poor relief and in 1924 national legislation established a basic right to local welfare assistance. Moreover, a secondary unemployment benefit was introduced in 1926 (first as a secondary scheme to main UA then secondary to UI). However, this three-tiered benefit system was overturned under National Socialist rule.

The fact that Italy lacked protection for those unemployed who could not receive UI is one aspect that still today distinguishes the Italian from the German system of unemployment benefits. But, it is only one aspect. The ways in which the rest of the benefit system changed after 1945 were not foreshadowed by the previous policy development. Arguably the main peculiarity of unemployment compensation in Italy after the war is not so much that there is no UA to back up UI, but that unemployment insurance degenerated into a very low-paying benefit, while new very generous but narrow benefit schemes were introduced. In the German case the similarity between the post-war and inter-war benefit systems is clearer, but we have to keep in mind that the benefit system inherited from the Nazi regime at the end of the war was totally uprooted and not at all similar to the inter-war situation.

Therefore, two points have to be underlined with respect to the development of unemployment benefits before 1945. First, in comparative perspective, the similarity of the two policy trajectories confronts us with the puzzle why the two benefit systems diverged so clearly after the Second World War. If anything, differences may have been expected to decrease as Italy caught up in economic development and as both states were ruled by Christian democratic parties. Second, even considering each country separately, the policy constellations at the end of the war did not anticipate the future policy development.

The post-war divergence

In the post-war phase of welfare state expansion the Italian and the German systems of unemployment compensation diverged significantly. In those decades both countries experienced rapid economic growth – in both cases coined an 'economic miracle'. The rising living standards changed patterns of consumption and class structures. Unemployment declined throughout the 1950s and reached its historic low in both countries at the beginning of the 1960s. This led to full employment and labour shortages in Germany, while in Italy unemployment persisted, especially in the South. Many Italian workers actually emigrated to Germany, thus reducing the labour surplus in Italy and easing labour shortages in Germany. Regional economic differences were stronger in Italy where the North boomed but the South remained economically backward. Nevertheless, economic expansion was the dominating trend in both countries. Rising tax and contribution revenues enabled both states to expand their welfare state programmes. But how governments used these favourable conditions differed. In the field of unemployment compensation, expansion took fundamentally different paths.

In Germany in this period a full-fledged unemployment benefit system was re-introduced soon after the war: first only provisionally, but in the middle of the 1950s major reforms established the post-war benefit system that afterwards was more or less only linearly expanded. This system of unemployment compensation consisted of three tiers (similar to the pre-war system): relatively generous and inclusive UI; less generous but still earnings-related UA for those with shorter contribution records or those who exhausted their insurance benefit; and, finally, SA for those unemployed (and other people in need) who could not receive any other benefits.

In Italy, by contrast, after some provisional post-war measures, no comprehensive unemployment benefit system was introduced. Unemployment insurance was extended to agricultural workers, but, at the same time, was changed into a flat-rate benefit, not indexed to inflation. Over the 1950s financial support to the unemployed played a minor role in the government's approach to the unemployment problem. Only starting from the early 1960s, the wage supplementation fund for workers on short-time was successively expanded, and ended up becoming a very generous compensation scheme for workers in big industrial firms that were effectively redundant. By this process a very fragmented benefit system was created with huge differences in generosity: core sections of the labour force were highly protected, others could only receive very low UI, but those unemployed who were ineligible for any of the other benefits had no minimum income scheme to fall back on.

Establishing a three-tier benefit system in Germany

The development of unemployment compensation in (West) Germany during the post-war period of social policy expansion and up to the 1970s can be distinguished into three phases: provisional reconstruction and expansion (1945–mid 1950s), establishment of the post-war benefit system (mid 1950s–1961), and linear expansion (1960s–1974).[6]

Provisional reconstruction and expansion

Right after the Second World War, basically the old unemployment benefit system of the Weimar Republic was re-introduced by the Western occupation authorities. As we have seen, under National Socialist rule wartime production and labour allocation had marginalized unemployment benefits and their institutional framework had been uprooted. In the social and economic crisis of the immediate post-war years the lack of labour demand soon became a major problem. The occupation authorities reacted with a wage freeze and labour planning; but soon they reinstalled the 1927 Act of Labour Exchange and Unemployment Insurance (*Gesetz über Arbeitsvermittlung und Arbeitslosenversicherung*). This re-establishing of UI accompanied the gradual re-introduction of market mechanisms into the process of labour allocation. In the American and British zones UA was also set up. As a last resort, local poor relief based on 1924 legislation continued. Coverage of UI was soon extended and benefit levels raised to account for the basic needs of the jobless. As before the war, UI benefit levels depended on the previous wage class, but the earnings-relation was degressive so that according to Schmid *et al.* (2001: 292) the result was almost a flat-rate benefit.

Soon after the foundation of the Federal Republic of Germany (1949) and at the beginning of a long spell of Christian democratic led governments, UI and

UA benefit levels were standardized and increased across the country. UA benefits were now related to previous earnings as well. Minor expansions of coverage and benefit duration followed in the next few years. The first significant intervention in the field of poor relief came only in 1953. This reform, however, clearly improved the assistance to the poor. It clarified that benefits should cover the cost of living. Along these lines the levels of protection were aligned across the local governments, which were responsible for policy administration. A 20 per cent benefit supplement was introduced for specific groups, such as the unemployed. Moreover, the private means were specified that had to be exempted from the means test. In this first phase of provisional reconstruction, therefore, UI and UA were the first to be re-established and adjusted to socio-economic needs. Only with a time lag, was assistance to the poor also improved.

Establishing the post-war benefit system

The reforms of the first years were adopted to take care of the immediate needs that had to be dealt with. At the same time, it was widely agreed that at a later stage a deliberate choice of the post-war policy framework was to be made. This institutionalization of the post-war regime of labour market policy started in 1952 when the Federal Office for Labour Exchange and Unemployment Insurance (*Bundesanstalt für Arbeitsvermittlung und Arbeitslosenversicherung*, BA) was established. This reform, however, had no direct effect on unemployment benefits. The major revision of UI and UA came in 1956, and brought them into the form in which they would characterize the Federal Republic up to 2005: UI was fully standardized at the national level, and benefit levels were increased. They were still based on a table of gradually degressive replacement rates, but were now more closely related to previous earnings. According to Schmid *et al.* (2005: 292), the previous income of average earners was replaced by about 44 per cent. Maximum benefit duration was, as previously, graduated according to contribution records, but the longest possible duration was extended to one year and the contributory requirements for this longest possible duration were relaxed down to three years of insurance-covered employment. There was some discussion whether the upper income limit for compulsory insurance should be abolished so that high-earners would have to pay contributions although typically they faced a lower risk of unemployment. In the end, the income limit was kept and moderately raised.

Regarding UA it was decided that it could be claimed by all those unemployed who have exhausted UI and, in addition, by those who are not eligible for UI but have acquired a lower minimum contribution record. Unemployment assistance benefits remained earnings-related and subject to a means test, but, similar to UI, the benefit was made more generous through higher benefit levels, lower benefit regression relative to income, and a wider scope of means test exempted earnings. The duration of UA was unlimited. All claimants had to do was to reapply after three years. That UA was earnings-related was a peculiarity of the German system. As mentioned in Chapter 3, UA schemes are usually flat-rate (and means-tested), while earnings-related benefit levels are typical of

UI (without a mean-test). Hence, compared to standard UA programmes, the German scheme was closer to the social insurance idea of maintaining social status. 'The guiding idea [of UA] was, in contrast to social assistance, an insurance of the standard of living, even if on a lower level than unemployment insurance' (Schmid *et al.* 2005: 291). Therefore, although at this point proper SA was not yet established, with UI and UA the basic structure of stratification into three tiers was already in place.

A full SA scheme was adopted only five years later. In fact, this reform can be seen as belonging to a different sub-phase of social policy development. M.G. Schmidt (2005: 76) interprets the years 1949–56 as reconstructing social policy and as addressing the most important policy tasks. By contrast, the years 1957–66 were characterized by improving social protection regarding less central needs. Indeed, introduction of SA had a different social and political relevance than the dedicated unemployment benefits. Yet, from our perspective on the system of unemployment benefits as a whole, the SA reform introduced the third and essential element of the post-war benefit system.

After the introduction of UI and UA, unemployment had continued to decline (see Figure 4.1) and some minor expansions of UI coverage were introduced. In 1961, when full employment had already been reached, parliament passed the Federal Social Assistance Act (*Bundessozialhilfegesetz*) that replaced the 1924 poor relief legislation. The law defined a socio-cultural minimum as the standard for benefit levels. This minimum was meant to enable recipients a dignified life and, thus, went beyond merely securing the subsistence of the poor. The reform also strengthened the legal entitlement of needy individuals and extended the scope of the benefits and services that should be provided. The SA was designed

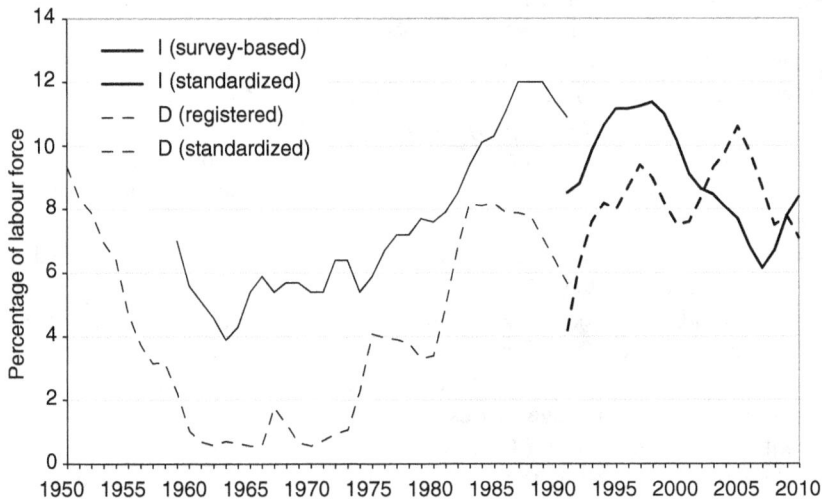

Figure 4.1 Unemployment rates in Italy and Germany, 1950–2010 (sources: OECD (2010b), *Bundesministerium für Arbeit und Soziales* (2007), own calculations).

as a safety net available for all persons without sufficient means to sustain themselves and, therefore, was always relevant for those unemployed who received neither UI nor UA. Furthermore, recipients of UI and UA could apply for a top-up from SA if their benefit transfers fell below the socio-cultural minimum (due to low pervious earnings). However, while we lack precise data, in the years of full employment and given the relatively soft eligibility criteria of UI and UA, it is unlikely that SA had a lot of unemployed claimants. This changed only in the years of mass unemployment after 1975 when eligibility for UI and UA was increasingly restricted.

Linear expansion

In the 1960s and beginning of the 1970s generally favourable economic conditions and full employment continued. From 1966 to 1969 a grand coalition of Christian Democrats and Social Democrats ruled the country that was succeeded by a coalition of Social Democrats and Liberals. Once the main structure of the benefit system was in place, these years were generally characterized by extensions of coverage and increases in generosity that did not affect the structure of the benefit system and were, in this sense, linear. The most significant labour market reform in this period was the Employment Promotion Act of 1969 (*Arbeitsförderungsgesetz*, AFG). It introduced, for the first time in Germany, a comprehensive range of active labour market policies. Re-training and qualification measures were intended to confront problems arising from labour shortages and from the beginning post-industrialization of the labour market. The AFG brought about only minor modifications of unemployment benefits (see below).

Before the AFG, a significant change for UI was that, in line with pension insurance, the upper income limit for compulsory insurance was abolished in 1967. Moreover, the AFG in 1969 extended coverage to additional worker categories that had previously been excluded (miners, some groups of agricultural workers, and apprentices). As a consequence, the proportion of the labour force that was covered by UI rose rapidly from 59 per cent in 1967 to 76 per cent in 1971 (Flora *et al.* 1983). The only significant parts of the work force remaining outside the membership space were civil servants and the self-employed (cf. Alber 1989: 133–9).

Benefits also became more generous. The levels of UI and UA were raised in 1967. Two years later, the AFG tied benefits closer to previous earnings, cancelled the waiting period, and eased the conditions of receipt by obliging the jobless only to accept offers of 'suitable work', while criteria for suitability were not specified. In 1974, UI and UA benefits were again increased and their calculation was changed from wage classes to a defined nominal replacement rate (68 per cent for UI, 58 per cent for UA). A benefit ceiling resulted from the fact that this rate was only applied up to the same income limit that was applied to insurance contributions. However, this income limit was set at a high level so that maximum benefits were high as well.[7] This conformed to the typical status-preserving character of German social insurance.

Regarding SA, the government of Christian Democrats and Liberals (in 1965) had already increased the benefit supplement for special groups (including the unemployed) from 20 to 30 per cent of the basic amount. In 1969 and 1974, contemporaneously with expansions of UI and UA, other improvements of SA were adopted, including higher supplements for family members and a loosening of the means test.

Overall, the phase of linear expansion did not significantly change the three-tier structure that had been previously established. Generosity was augmented across the board so that differences in generosity remained by and large stable even though SA, by virtue of being a minimum income scheme, expanded somewhat less. More importantly, UI and UA became more inclusive through widened boundaries of coverage. The fact that the more generous scheme, UI, was made more accessible diluted the significance of generosity differences.

Therefore, at the end of welfare state expansion, unemployment compensation in Germany was clearly stratified into three tiers (UI, UA, and SA) but inclusiveness of the top tier (UI) was high and generosity differences were limited. In 1974 the net replacement rate of UI was 69 per cent for a worker who previously received the average production worker's wage. Unfortunately this type of data is unavailable for UA. For SA we can only calculate the replacement rate for the standard cash amount that recipients get, which excludes the payments for housing and heating to which recipients are entitled and, therefore, is considerably lower than what beneficiaries actually get. This rate was 37 per cent in 1974.[8] So, the widest generosity difference in the German benefit system at the end of expansion was between at least 37 per cent replacement rate at the low end and 69 per cent at the high end.[9] (For a summary of the most important reforms of unemployment benefits in Germany during this phase, see Table 4.1.)

Fragmentation and generosity differences in Italy

Unemployment benefits in Italy took a very different path from the one chosen in Germany. In the post-war era of welfare state expansion, we can distinguish two broad phases: first, a phase of only provisional reconstruction and, otherwise, neglect of unemployment benefits (1945–63), second, a phase in which only some benefits were selectively upgraded and expanded (1963–mid 1970s).[10]

Provisional reconstruction and policy neglect

The Italian government reconstructed unemployment benefits in the immediate post-war years but during the 1950s did nothing to complement or update the existing benefits. Overall, unemployment compensation played a minor role in government policy during this phase. The benefit system that became characteristic for post-war Italy only emerged subsequently, during the 1960s. After the liberation of Northern Italy from German occupation, provisional governments of national unity ruled the country. Right after the end of fighting, a ban on dismissals was called in order to keep the labour market consequences of the

Table 4.1 Important reforms of unemployment benefits in Germany, 1945–74

Provisional reconstruction and expansion

1947 • unemployment insurance (UI) re-introduced on the basis of 1927 legislation
     • unemployment assistance (UA) re-introduced in British and American occupation zones (Länderrat, 9 September 1947)
1951 • UI and UA benefits raised and standardized nationally (29 March 1951)
1953 • minimum income benefit improved, based on 1924 legislation: defined to cover cost of living, 20% benefit supplement for special groups, minimum exemptions specified for means test (20 August 1953)

Establishing the post-war benefit system

1956 • major reform of UI: benefits raised, benefit degression reduced, eligibility improved, coverage extended (23 December 1956)
     • major reform of UA: eligible are those who have exhausted UI or who fulfil only lower contribution requirements, benefits are earnings-related but means-tested, duration unlimited (26 April 1956)
1961 • major reform introducing social assistance (SA): defined to secure socio-cultural minimum of those in need, individual entitlement strengthened, extended scope of benefits and services (30 June 1961)

Linear expansion

1967 • UI and UA benefit levels raised (10 March 1967)
     • upper income limit of UI coverage abolished (21 December 1967)
1969 • coverage of UI extended, benefit degression of UI and UA reduced, conditions of receiving UI eased, and waiting period abolished ('AFG', 25 June 1969)
     • SA expanded (concerning family supplements, means test, certain additional payments; 14 August 1969)
1974 • benefit levels of UI and UA raised and changed to single defined replacement rate (UI: 68%; UA: 58%; 21 December 1974)
     • SA expanded (again concerning family supplements, means test, certain additional payments; 25 March 1974)

Note
Laws are denoted by the date they were issued by the President of the Federal Republic.

shattered economy in check. This was accompanied by the legal institutionaliza-tion of the wage supplementation fund (*Cassa Integrazione Guadagni*, CIG) for workers with temporarily reduced working hours. The scheme had first been introduced by collective contract in 1941. It only applied to the industrial sector and was initially restricted to Northern Italy, but in 1947[11] CIG was extended to the whole national territory. The nominal replacement rate of hourly wages was set at two-thirds. The benefit could be paid for a maximum of 16 hours per week and 90 days in a year.

Unemployment insurance (*indennità ordinaria di disoccupazione*, continued to exist through the Second World War. In 1946, when the ban on firing was partly lifted and unemployment soared, an additional unemployment benefit (*sussidio straordinario di disoccupazione*) was introduced for workers who did not qualify for UI, but this benefit was restricted to specific contexts of economic crisis. Its implementation was highly discretionary and in the hands of the Min-istry of Labour. One year later the ban on dismissals was lifted for good (Gins-borg 1990: Ch. 3).

In 1947 the coalition of national unity broke up and a longer spell of governments led by the *Democrazia Cristiana* (DC) in coalition with smaller moderate
parties began (this phase is commonly called *Centrismo*). The Constitution of
the Italian Republic came into force in 1948.[12] Unemployment at the time was
high and, especially in the rural areas, the bleak social situation gave rise to wide
mobilizations and violent protests. Nevertheless, unemployment compensation
ranked low in terms of reform efforts, with the only significant reform being
adopted in 1949. The main cause of debate in this reform was actually the establishing of Public Employment Services that previously had been controlled by
the trade unions. With respect to UI the most important change was the extension of coverage to agricultural workers, which was, however, only implemented
several years later. To appreciate the relevance of this step, keep in mind that in
those years the agricultural sector still made up 40 per cent of the Italian labour
force (Flora *et al.* 1987: 551).

A separate scheme was set up for extending UI coverage to agriculture. Given
that frequent periods out of work, seasonal work and underemployment were
normal features of agricultural employment it was clear from the beginning that
an unemployment benefit was difficult to implement. In the end, UI in the agricultural sector took the form of additional income support to agricultural
workers. Those who had paid a minimum number of daily insurance contributions during the previous year were eligible to a certain maximum number of
daily benefits in the subsequent year. In order to receive these payments it was
important to be registered in local records of the agricultural labour force, but
the unemployment status was not effectively controlled.

For both the general and the agricultural UI scheme, the 1949 reform changed
benefit calculation from graduation by wage classes to a flat-rate benefit, set at
200 lira per day, which corresponded roughly to 17 per cent of the average gross
industrial wage at the time. No mechanism of indexation was adopted. Accordingly, the benefit constantly lost real value over the years. The government only
occasionally (in 1957, 1960, 1966, 1974) raised the benefit level in order to
contain the constant devaluation. Despite the modest level of UI payments, they
were still a welcome supplement to household income, especially in the more
depressed areas of the rural South. Moreover, receiving UI also granted access to
family benefits and health care coverage. (At the time health care was still
insurance-based, as the National Health Service was not introduced until 1978).
Due to the high demand for these assets and the weakness of bureaucratic structures, especially in the *Mezzogiorno*, UI soon became an object of clientelist
exchanges (Ferrera 1984: 207–10). As mentioned, the extension of UI to the
agricultural sector was not implemented straight away; the necessary decree was
not adopted until six years after the reform. This, however, helped to increase
the proportion of insured persons in the labour force significantly, rising from 15
per cent at the beginning of the 1950s to 40 per cent at the beginning of the
1960s (Flora *et al.* 1983).

The 1949 reform also established a public works programme that was made
the basis for receiving payments of the *sussidio straordinario* and that was

administered in a highly discretionary way. In fact, the government focused on public works in order to combat unemployment rather than paying mere unemployment compensation. In quantitative terms this was reflected by the fact that in the beginning of the 1950s as much was spent on public works as for UI (see Ferrera *et al.* forthcoming: Ch. 2). Another important measure, the reform of agrarian land distribution, was meant to address the plight of the rural poor (Ginsborg 1990: Ch. 4), as was the introduction of a fund for public investments in the South (*Cassa per il Mezzogiorno*). No relevant changes were adopted within the SA arena. Poor relief continued to be delivered by a plethora of private and church-affiliated institutions (*Istituti Pubblici di Assistenza e Beneficienza*, IPAB) and by the public *Enti Communali di Assistenza*. The sector was only loosely regulated on the basis of a law from 1890 and no national minimum standards existed.

Overall, the extension of coverage to agriculture was a significant step in this period but unemployment benefits played a subordinate role in the government's approach to the post-war crisis and unemployment. With the introduction of the wage supplementation fund (CIG) the seed was planted for some of the following expansions that created new and generous unemployment benefits. However, at that time, CIG did not function as an unemployment benefit and did not have the major importance it acquired later on.

Lopsided expansion

In 1963, for the first time after national unity governments, the Socialists entered the government coalition with the Christian Democrats, inaugurating an era of centre-left governments (*Centro-sinistra*). In the new coalition there was considerable support for more universalistic reforms of the welfare state. Also a report on social policy from the advisory council on economic and employment policy (CNEL) promoted a more comprehensive approach. Nevertheless, apart from health care, the universalist intentions failed (cf. Ferrera 1993: Ch. 7). Rather, in the wake of massive worker mobilizations, the next 10–15 years brought about a range of marked expansions that initially favoured workers with standard contracts in big industrial firms. Apart from unemployment benefits, these expansions included a pension reform in 1969, workers' and unions' rights – especially dismissal protection (*Statuto dei Lavoratori*) in 1970 – and an indexation of wage increases (aptly called *scala mobile*, i.e. 'escalator') in 1975.

A similar transformation took place in the field of unemployment compensation. The already mentioned wage supplementation fund (CIG) was in effect turned into an unemployment benefit on very generous terms. As a first step in this direction an additional CIG scheme was introduced for construction workers in 1963. At the same time, the nominal replacement rate of CIG was raised to 80 per cent and it could now be paid for a weekly maximum of 40 hours, that is to say, it could also be paid to workers who were on a short-time schedule of zero hours. This reform took place when in the wake of the Italian 'economic miracle' unemployment had fallen to an all-time low of 3.9 per cent (see Figure 4.1).

However, the industrial boom and inner-national migration from South to North had mixed up social relations, which favoured worker unrest, and the end of the boom and a new rise of unemployment were on the horizon.

The most significant reform in this phase of lopsided expansion was the introduction of a special scheme of CIG (*Cassa Integrazione Guadagni Straordinaria*, CIGS) in 1968. Ordinary CIG was applicable only when production had to be reduced for cyclical or accidental reasons. By contrast the new scheme could be employed in cases of sectoral crises or industrial restructuring. As in the case of ordinary CIG, the new benefit could include workers who were suspended completely from work without being formally dismissed. CIGS covered only industrial firms with more than 15 employees. But the employees of these firms had (and still have) no individual entitlement to the benefit (again, this is also true of the ordinary scheme). Rather, payments are granted to groups of workers after consultations between the firm, trade unions, and different government bodies (from local government to the Ministry of Labour). The replacement rate of CIGS was set at 80 per cent and a maximum duration of nine months. Initially, no social contributions were paid on the benefit income and there was no benefit ceiling. Hence, the effective benefit amount in relation to previous net income was often higher than 80 per cent. Over the course of the 1970s the net replacement rate of CIGS fluctuated between 85 per cent and 95 per cent for an average production worker.[13] In 1972 it was made potentially possible to extend the duration of CIGS payments indefinitely.

Several particularistic extensions of coverage followed. The CIG scheme for the construction sector was extended to artisan firms in 1970 and to the mining sector in 1971. In 1972 an additional CIG scheme for the agricultural sector was set up, initially with somewhat less generous conditions. Yet, in 1975 the replacement rate for all CIG schemes was fixed at 80 per cent. This, however, did not imply a reduction of the number of separate schemes, but only that the benefit levels were brought in line. At the same time, the role of trade unions in the activating procedures of CIG payments was strengthened.

Another special unemployment benefit (*trattamento speciale di disoccupazione*) was introduced in 1968 for workers made redundant due to the closing down of firms in the industrial sector (excluding construction). This benefit paid two-thirds of the previous wage for a maximum of 180 days. Special provisions helped older unemployed to bridge the gap into retirement and old-age pension. Access to the *trattamento speciale* was extended to construction workers in 1970 and to agricultural workers in 1972, again with group-specific benefit regulations. Originally for both groups somewhat lower conditions were adopted than for industrial workers, but in the following years the replacement rate for both was raised to levels similar to those applied for industrial workers. Moreover, the *trattamento speciale* was extended to agricultural part-time workers again under specific benefit conditions. These developments vividly show the extraordinary fragmentation along occupational categories in Italian unemployment compensation, and have remained typical for the Italian system of unemployment compensation up to the present day. High fragmentation and the jungle of regulations led even labour law experts to complain in a policy report: 'the legislation is so complex, stratified and particularistic that often and in some areas it ends up being absolutely indecipherable' (CNEL 2003: 21).

From 1976 to 1979, for the first time since foundation of the Italian Republic, government was externally supported by the Communist Party, while the leading government party were still the Christian Democrats. This government of National Solidarity was formed against the background of domestic terrorism and an increasingly challenging economic situation. However, while it did see to the introduction of Italy's National Health Service (*Servizio Sanitario Nazionale*) in 1978, it did not bring about any crucial changes in the field of labour market policy. Rather, some of its decisions completed the picture of lopsided benefit expansion.

Some of the already mentioned expansions of the *trattamento speciale* were, in fact, adopted by the government of National Solidarity. In addition, the applicability of CIGS was extended in 1977 to 'corporate crises with a particular social relevance', which made the scheme an even more flexible tool in addressing those situations of redundancy that were politically relevant. Moreover, procedures were set up to support those recipients of CIGS who were willing to take up a new job instead of staying on CIGS payments. This completed the transformation of the programme into a de facto unemployment benefit. It was a useful mechanism for firms to shed labour without formally dismissing workers. After all, collective dismissals were basically impossible due to strict employment regulations. This generous tool for, in effect, laying off workers remained restricted to firms in the industrial sector (including construction) with more than 15 employees. The same threshold of 15 employees applies to dismissal protection under article 18 of the above-mentioned *Statuto dei Lavoratori*.

In contrast to these marked expansions, UI or poor relief were hardly reformed at all and surely not significantly improved. Due to the new regulations and the power of the worker movement in big establishments, firms increasingly decentralized their production and made use of work-at-home. Reacting to this trend, a law in 1973 specified that coverage of UI also applies to home workers. A year later the benefit level of UI was raised from a daily amount of 400 lira to 800 lira. This made the net replacement rate rise from 10 per cent to 15 per cent (Scruggs 2004; see Figure 5.1). But over the next 14 years the benefit was not increased any more, leading again to a continuous loss in real value that was only cushioned by the entitlement to family benefits, which were regularly adjusted.

Concerning SA, the 1969 pension reform introduced a social pension for people over 65 years without pension entitlements or sufficient income, but, of course, this did not affect the situation of the unemployed. More relevantly, decentralization of government during the 1970s cleared the way for regional governments to assume responsibility for SA. Formally this power was transferred to them in 1972. In 1977 the private and church-affiliated IPAB and national welfare entities were barred from this sector. However, the use that regional governments made of their new competences depended on the initiative and capacities of each region. Thus, in the absence of national regulation, a geographically highly differentiated and variegated system of welfare assistance evolved (Fargion 1996).

Therefore, by the end of this period of lopsided expansion, and coinciding roughly with the end of the overall phase of welfare state expansion, Italy was equipped with a highly fragmented system of unemployment compensation, in which four broad strata can be distinguished (Pirrone and Sestito 2006; Porcari 2004). First, a very generous level that can be called 'industrial schemes' because it originated from the industrial sector and still principally covers that sector; these industrial schemes comprise all the CIGS above but also other CIG schemes and the *trattamenti speciali*. Second, UI, which paid only meagre benefits, had the most general coverage with respect to the other unemployment benefits but low take-up rates. Third, UI for the agricultural sector followed different rules from the general UI scheme and had the character of an additional income subsidy. Fourth, due to the lack of a national minimum income programme we find essentially a gap of protection for those unemployed persons who did not qualify for any of the existing unemployment benefits. All schemes were funded by employers' contributions that were differentiated according to sector and size of the firm, with the state covering any financial deficits. Table 4.2 summarizes the most important reforms that brought about this benefit system. Overall, its fragmentation and extreme generosity differences were in stark contrast to the German benefit system with its comprehensive benefits and moderate three-tier stratification.

Table 4.2 Important reforms of unemployment benefits in Italy, 1945–79

Provisional reconstruction and policy neglect

1945 • introduction of wage supplementation fund (CIG, d.l. 788)
1949 • coverage of unemployment insurance (UI) extended to agricultural workers in separate scheme (implemented only in 1955)
     • benefit levels changed to flat-rate benefit, not indexed to inflation (l. 264)

Lopsided expansion

1963 • coverage of CIG extended, replacement rate raised, weekly maximum hours extended to provide for complete suspension from work (l. 77)
1968 • special scheme of CIG introduced (CIGS), covers only industrial firms with more than 15 employees, nominal replacement rate 80%
     • special unemployment allowance (*trattamento speciale*) introduced for industrial firms closing down, nominal replacement rate 66% (l. 1115)
1972 • CIG and *trattamento speciale* extended to agricultural sector
     • possibility introduced to extend duration of CIGS indefinitely (l. 464)
     • responsibility of social assistance transferred to regional governments
1975 • nominal replacement rate for all CIG schemes set at 80%, duration of ordinary CIG extended, role of unions in activation procedures strengthened (l. 164)
1977 • scope of CIGS extended, procedures introduced for recipients willing to change 'jobs' (l. 675).

Note
The numbers of laws are in brackets, abbreviations: *legge* (l.), *decreto legge* (d.l.).

5 Italy and Germany

Changing trends during welfare state restructuring

The previous chapter has shown how, under favourable economic conditions, the systems of unemployment compensation diverged markedly in Italy and Germany. In Germany a comprehensive three-tier benefit system was established while Italy developed a highly fragmented benefit system with wide generosity differences. In the middle of the 1970s, both countries entered a phase of economic austerity that compelled them to abandon the path of social policy expansion and forced them to contain the costs of their welfare states.

The socio-economic conditions that challenged the Italian and the German welfare state were essentially the same as for most of the advanced industrial states (some of the national specifics are mentioned below). The reform pressures can be divided into domestic and external (for an overview see Ferrera 2008). Most of the domestic developments are related to the transition from industrial to post-industrial society. The rising economic importance of services constrained productivity growth and increased demand for low-skilled and flexible workers. It coincided with changes in household structures and higher female participation in the labour market. Population ageing and the extent of government welfare commitments were other domestic factors that strained government budgets.[1] The external pressures arise mainly from the international integration of markets. In advanced welfare states, this integration had a negative effect on the demand for labour and made it more difficult to raise the necessary revenues for social policy.[2] In the field of unemployment compensation, governments and policy experts saw mainly three reform needs as a response to these pressures: to reduce work disincentives, to cut costs, and to close protection gaps that were caused by the more flexible employment relations (Clasen and Clegg 2006).

However, in the beginning of this new phase of austerity the efforts to reform unemployment benefits in Germany and Italy were rather cautious. Only in the 1990s (Italy) and 2000s (Germany) can more decisive policy changes be noted. In Italy gradual but, taken altogether, transformative reforms were introduced since the beginning of the 1990s; while in Germany the unemployment system was radically reformed in the early 2000s. Therefore, we can distinguish two reform phases in either country. Interestingly, the reforms had different effects on the segmentation of unemployment benefits in both countries. In Germany both the incremental and, later, the fundamental reforms increased benefit segmentation (but in different ways). In Italy, by contrast, the early small-scale reforms had little impact whereas the later policy changes reduced the wide generosity gap between benefits.

Two modes of increasing segmentation in Germany

Following the first oil crisis, the unemployment rate shot up in 1974 and reached 4 per cent in 1975, a level it had not reached in almost 20 years (see Figure 4.1). For unemployment benefits, as for the welfare state in general (Alber 1989: 186–99), policy restrictions began precisely in 1975, only a year after the last expansions had been adopted. As mentioned, the reforms of unemployment benefits in Germany were at first only incremental. During a long period (1975 to end of 1990s), they consisted mainly of small retrenchments on the margins of the benefit system. Then, in the beginning of the 2000s, the benefit system was substantially reformed. These so-called 'Hartz reforms' created a new two-tier benefit system with less inclusive UI and a comprehensive but lean UA scheme.[3]

Incremental retrenchments on the margin

Retrenchment started while the governing coalition of Social Democrats (SPD) and Liberals (FDP) was still in power. In the remaining years of this coalition (1975–82), mainly the job search conditions for recipients of UI and UA and the eligibility for these two schemes were restricted. The benefit levels of UI and UA were only reduced moderately and indirectly. In 1975, for the first time government defined the meaning of 'suitable work' that beneficiaries had to accept.[4] This meant that the range of job offers that could not be declined without incurring sanctions increased. Few years later, this range of 'suitable work' was again widened and the sanctions for rejecting such job offers were tightened. Regarding eligibility, school-leavers and university graduates were excluded from directly receiving UA in 1975. Required contribution records for UI and UA were doubled in 1981 and were further increased only a year later, already under the rule of Christian Democrats and Liberals. Other changes adopted by the SPD and FDP government included the more frequent re-examination (yearly) of UA claimants' eligibility, but also a certain weakening of the means test. Conversely, benefit levels were only indirectly scaled down, by reducing their calculation basis and by lowering the pension contributions paid on behalf of recipients.

The benefit level of SA was more clearly reduced. SA benefits are defined as covering the socio-cultural minimum necessary for a dignified life. Therefore, governments cannot cut the benefit level of SA directly. One path that was embarked upon and that was followed later in the retrenchment phase was to limit or to suspend the adjustment of the benefit level to rising prices and social living standards. This was done first in 1981 when it was decided that the basic amount of SA must not rise more than 3 per cent in spite of a 5.4 per cent increase in the cost of living. At the same time, the means test for SA was tightened and supplementary payments were reduced. SA indexation was again limited in 1982 and the next scheduled rise was postponed by half a year.

Figure 5.1 compares the trajectory of the net replacement rate of UI to that of SA, taking 1975 as the reference point. The rate of SA is calculated analogously to Scruggs's (2004) replacement rate of UI but only based on the basic amount and family supplements that recipients get. The money for housing and heating is always determined depending on the individual living situation. The figure shows that the SA benefit level declined by roughly 10 per cent in the second half of the 1970s while UI benefits remained stable.[5] Also when looking at the retrenchment phase as a whole, the figure reveals how SA benefits were scaled back more strongly than UI benefits. Thus, by 2003, UI lost 5 per cent of its replacement rate in respect of its 1975 level, whereas SA lost 19 per cent.

In 1982, the 'red–yellow' government broke up in a row over liberal economic reforms demanded by the FDP, including a call for significant cuts in unemployment benefits. Indeed, soon after the new CDU–FDP government took over benefit levels of UI and UA were, for the first time, cut directly. However, the retrenchment was much more moderate than the initial proposals and affected only recipients without children. Their nominal replacement rate was cut from 68 to 63 per cent in the case of UI and from 58 to 56 per cent in the case of UA. Later in the

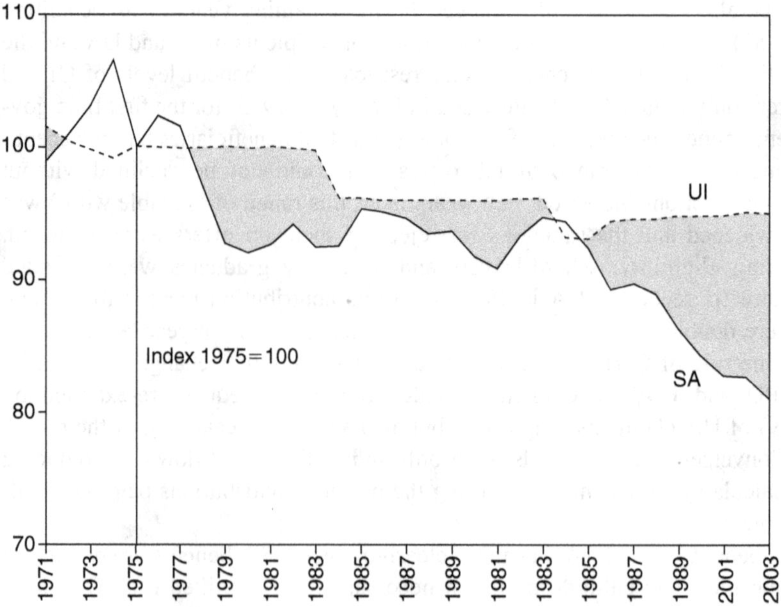

Figure 5.1 Net replacement rates of unemployment insurance and social assistance in Germany, indexed 1975 = 100 (sources: Scruggs (2004), *Bundesministerium für Arbeit und Soziales* (2007), MISSOC, own calculations).

Notes
The rates of SA are based on standard amount and family supplements not on additional payments (e.g. for housing). Both series are unweighted averages for two household types.

period of 'black–yellow' cabinets (in 1993), a second direct benefit cut was approved (UI: down to 67 per cent for recipients with children and to 60 per cent without children; UA: down to 57 per cent with children and to 53 per cent without children). This second cut was largely a reaction to the huge unemployment crisis in Eastern Germany after reunification and the related cost explosion.

In fact, reunification was the greatest challenge to labour market policy during the CDU–FDP coalition. However, the policy responses did not alter the structure of the benefit system. The West German benefit system was simply transferred to the new *Länder*. The main measures for coping with high unemployment in the East were public job creation (*Arbeitsbeschaffungs-maßnahmen*), short-time work wage supplementation (*Kurzarbeitergeld*), and early retirement. The contribution rates to UI were considerably raised to cope with the costs (Manow and Seils 2000: 284–95; Zohlnhöfer 2001: 670–8). However, the high contribution rates were increasingly seen as a problematic burden on the cost of labour. Consequently, later on in the 1990s, government attempted to reduce the costs of labour market policy. However, this led to no structural reform of unemployment benefits. Rather, job search conditions and sanctions for recipients of UI and UA were tightened (throughout the black–yellow government period, but especially in 1996 and 1997). Furthermore, the maximum duration for those UA claimants who had not previously received UI was limited to one year while for the other UA claimants the replacement rate was ruled to decrease automatically by three percentage points after every year. Therefore, the incremental cutbacks in UI and UA more clearly affected the latter benefit scheme in addition to recipients without children.

In contrast to the mentioned reductions, some groups of unemployed even profited from selective expansions during the spell of CDU–FDP governments. In particular, the maximum duration of UI was increased for elderly unemployed (in 1984, 1985, and 1987) up to a maximum of 32 months for the over 53-year-olds. Also some eligibility requirements for UI were loosened. This was part of the government's strategy to tackle unemployment by reducing labour supply. Expanded durations enabled many older unemployed to move from joblessness directly into early retirement. This contributed to the well-known vicious circle of the German and other continental welfare states. Generous unemployment benefits and early retirement encouraged firms to shed labour, but the higher number of beneficiaries made it necessary to increase social contributions. This created further incentives to shed labour and impeded job creation, thus increasing unemployment (cf. Manow and Seils 2000; Esping-Andersen 1996). In the field of unemployment benefits, the strategy of reducing labour supply was partly revised at the end of the 1990s and, more clearly, in the early 2000s (see next section). In 1997, the age thresholds for higher maximum durations were raised and eligibility requirements for UI were restricted.

Regarding SA, the retrenchment trend continued under the CDU and FDP: in 1983, housing subsidies were limited and the indexation rules were weakened; in 1990, government decided to introduce a new method for calculating the basic amount of SA that was likely to result in lower benefits; in 1993 and 1996, indexation was again constrained; also in 1993, the means test was tightened and asylum-seekers were excluded from SA. Besides this continued retrenchment, a new development was that 'activation' measures, typical for dedicated unemployment benefits (UI and UA), were adopted for SA. They comprised obligatory community work (1993) and sanctions on rejecting job offers (1996). This reflected the fact that continuing mass unemployment, a high share of long-term unemployment, and more restricted access to dedicated benefits had degraded increasing numbers of unemployed to SA. Accordingly, Figure 5.1 shows how the rate of unemployed receiving UI declined steadily right from the beginning of the retrenchment phase in 1975 (with the exception of the bump caused by reunification). Although the beneficiary rate of UA increased at the same time, until the end of the 1980s it did not make up for the decline in UI beneficiaries. At the bottom of this trend, around 1986, only 63 per cent of the unemployed received dedicated benefits.

Overall we can see that not only the differences in generosity between benefit schemes increased in this period (see Figure 5.1), but an ever greater share of the unemployed also received compensation from the less generous schemes (UA and SA; see Figure 5.2). Schmid and Oschmiansky comment succinctly on the policy development of the 1980s:[6]

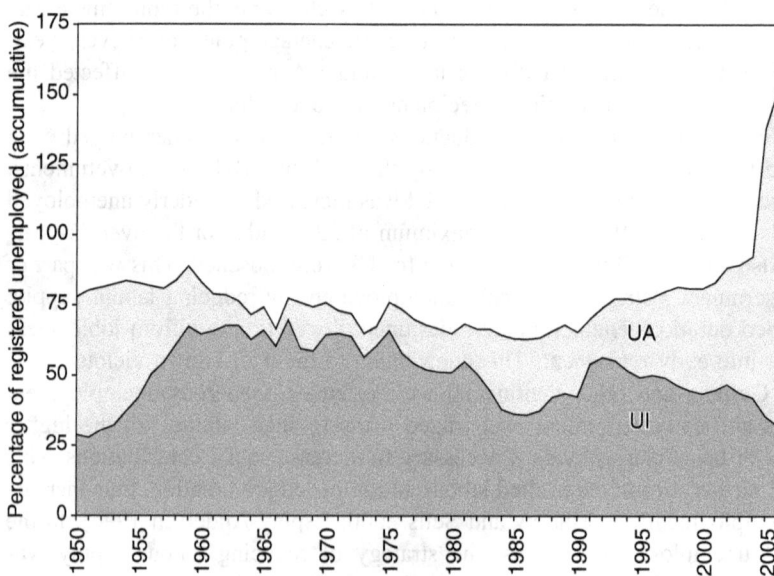

Figure 5.2 Beneficiary rates of unemployment insurance and unemployment assistance in Germany (source: *Bundesministerium für Arbeit und Soziales* (2007), own calculations).

Note
The skyrocketing UA beneficiary rate in 2005 and 2006 is explained by the fact that the new scheme also pays to persons in low-paid employment and by the inclusion of previous (unemployed) SA recipients in the new UA scheme (implemented in 2005).

To be sure, the three-fold stratified system of social protection against unemployment was accentuated: [...] unemployment insurance was hardly affected in its generosity level, but was concentrated even more on the core groups of the labour market. [...] unemployment assistance, itself moderately cut back, catered increasingly to those unemployed excluded from insurance. [...] social assistance, finally, increasingly had to shoulder those left over. [...] this burden restrained more and more the freedom of action of local authorities. Many of them started to increase the pressure on unemployed social assistance claimants.

(Schmid and Oschmiansky 2005: 281)

The last sub-phase of incremental retrenchments corresponds to the first period of office of the Social Democratic and Green government (1998–2002). Although the character of reforms was mixed, in unemployment policy this period generally displayed a pattern similar to the previous reform years. Right after the parliamentary election, the new coalition repealed some cutbacks that the black–yellow coalition had adopted, such as a reduction in the calculation basis for benefit levels and a deduction of redundancy payments from benefit payments. While mainly UI recipients benefited from these measures, the same law abolished UA for unemployed persons who had not previously received UI. Therefore, all jobless not eligible for UI could now fall back only on SA as their public support of income. On the other hand, in the context of an active labour market policy reform in 2001, an opportunity for UA recipients was introduced to avoid annual benefit reduction on the condition of participating in a training programme.

In sum, the phase of incremental retrenchments started by cutting back the inclusiveness of UI and UA, and by downgrading the generosity of SA. Benefit levels of UI and UA were subsequently also decreased, but over the whole period, SA benefits declined more strongly. By contrast, older UI recipients even profited from expansions. Clearly, even if incrementally, benefit segmentation increased in this phase due to both lower inclusiveness and sharper differences in generosity. Mainly marginal groups of the labour force such as long-term unemployed and labour market entrants were affected by the retrenchments. (For a summary of the incremental changes of unemployment benefits from the mid 1970s to 1990s, see Table 5.1.)

Fundamental reforms and dualization

In the years 2002–4, during the second term of the red–green coalition, parliament adopted a range of far-reaching labour market reforms. They were based on the recommendations of an expert commission that had been chaired by Volkswagen manager Peter Hartz, which coined their name: Hartz reforms. The reforms were divided into four legislative packages. Apart from a fundamental reform of the unemployment benefit system (the fourth reform package and, hence, 'Hartz IV'), they included an organizational reform of the Public Employment Service,

Table 5.1 Incremental changes of unemployment benefits in Germany, 1975–2001

Generosity cuts

• UI and UA benefit level:	1981 (indirect), 1983, 1993, 1996 (UA), 1997 (indirect), 1999 (*raised*, indirect)
• other restrictions – only UA:	1977, 1993
• SA – indexation limited:	1981, 1982, 1983, 1990 (new calculation of basic amount), 1993, 1996
• SA – means test, supplementary payments, sanctioned activation:	1981, 1983, 1993, 1996

Lower eligibility for UI and UA

• categorical exclusions:	1975 (UA), 1979, 1999 (UA)
• higher contribution requirements:	1981, 1982 (UI), 1987 (UI, *reduced*), 1997, 1998 (UI)

Stricter conditions for receiving UI and UA

• range of 'suitable work' extended:	1975, 1979, 1996, 1997
• severer sanctions:	1977, 1981, 1984, 1988, 1997

Expansions of UI max. duration for older unemployed	1984, 1985, 1987, *partly revised*: 1997

---

a range of new active labour market policies, and liberalization of atypical employment (especially marginal jobs, fixed-term contracts, and agency work).[7]

The most important change in unemployment compensation was the fusion of UA and SA. A completely new UA scheme was created (*Arbeitslosengeld II*) for all jobless persons who do not receive UI. Accordingly, all SA claimants capable of working (i.e. not only those actively looking for work) were included in this new scheme. Since then, SA takes care only of people in need who are not able to work and, therefore, it is no longer an unemployment benefit. The new UA pays flat-rate benefits subject to a means test and at a level of generosity essentially similar to SA.[8] At the same time, all current UA claimants were shifted from their previous earnings-related benefit to a flat-rate benefit with stricter means test, conditions of receipt and sanctions. This meant for the majority of beneficiaries being downgraded to a less generous benefit (Becker and Hauser 2006).[9] Note that the new UA scheme is not a pure unemployment benefit but is also paid to people with low work incomes. In many cases this public subsidy helped to create more low-wage jobs.

However, the Hartz IV reform cut back on UI as well. Most significantly, the maximum duration was limited to a standard of 12 months and to 18 months for over 54-year-olds. Job search requirements were tightened, mainly by enlarging the definition of 'suitable work'. At the same time, this still clearly more generous scheme was made less inclusive as the necessary contribution record for receiving UI was extended. A transitional benefit was adopted for those who exhausted their UI benefit and had to claim the new UA, in order to dampen the drop from UI to UA level.

As will be discussed in Chapter 8, the Hartz IV reform was highly controversial. The Grand Coalition of CDU and SPD that took office in 2005 re-extended the maximum durations for older claimants of UI. Those over the age of 58 can now receive the benefit for up to two years. In the down-turn of the economic crisis 2008 and 2009 German firms made massive use of short-time work, which the government supported by extending maximum durations (Möller 2010). When the economic crisis turned into a budget crisis the CDU–FDP coalition, which was elected in 2009, adopted several austerity measures. The parental leave benefit and pension contributions for UA recipients were scrapped as well as the transitional benefit for those who have exhausted UI. In early 2010 the Constitutional Court ruled that the method for determining the benefit level of the new UA scheme was unconstitutional. The main objection was that the method was unclear and poorly comprehensible so that it could not be verified whether the resulting benefit level protects the socio-cultural minimum standard of the recipients. The reform that responded to the court ruling led to an only marginal increase of the benefit level and to some supplementary benefits for child education.

The Hartz IV reform is not very straightforward to assess in terms of segmentation of unemployment benefits: first, because of the complex effect of the fusion of UA and SA; second, because not only UA recipients were affected but also benefit generosity for core groups of unemployed who had previously been spared was reduced (mainly through the cut of UI maximum durations). The new UA scheme is highly inclusive. It has integrated the previous unemployed recipients of SA and, hence, included them in the institutional realm of labour market policy, which implies better access to employment services and active labour market programmes. At the same time, the generosity of this new benefit is at roughly the same level as SA. Consequently, the majority of UA recipients were worse off while for most SA recipients little has changed in terms of benefit generosity. Although generosity of UI has also declined, the benefit remains clearly more generous although it has become harder to qualify for it.

In the end, the major effect of the Hartz IV reform was to turn the old three-tier system into a two-tier system with one relatively generous benefit and a low-paying benefit for all the rest of the unemployed. In this sense, it constitutes a dualization of the German benefit system (see also Klenk 2009). This change conforms to tendencies of dualization also in other fields of the German and other continental welfare states (Palier and Thelen 2010; Clegg 2007). Most of the minor reforms after Hartz IV hardly affected this general structural outcome. If anything, the extension of UI duration and the marginal cuts of UA reinforced segmentation. This trend was only reverted through the Constitutional Court ruling. Yet, the benefit increase that resulted from this ruling was minimal.

Hence, segmentation of unemployment compensation has increased both during the long phase of incremental retrenchments and through the more fundamental Hartz reforms. However, this occurred in two different ways: by gradually cutting the entitlements of the marginal groups of unemployed, in the first case; and by transforming the three-tier stratified system into a dual system, in the second. Apart from these different impacts on the overall system, the Hartz reforms are distinct from previous changes for two other reasons. First, terminating the old UA scheme and fusing UA with SA, constituted a structural change in the benefit system that was clearly more significant than the gradual adjustments in previous reform years (Weishaupt 2008; Eichhorst and Marx 2011). Second, the abolition of status-related UA benefits and the marked reduction of maximum UI durations affected labour market groups (including only potential beneficiaries) that had previously been spared or had even profited from selective expansions. (See Table 5.2 for a summary of important reforms in the 2000s.)

From stability to reducing generosity differences in Italy

While the segmentation of unemployment benefits increased in Germany, in Italy welfare restructuring brought about a decrease of segmentation. Again, this period can be divided into two phases: first, a phase of only incremental reform efforts that had no clear common direction (1980s); second, a phase in which generosity differences between benefits were actively reduced (1990s and 2000s).[10]

Mixed incremental reform efforts

The short period of National Solidarity governments ended in 1979 and gave way to a long phase of government coalitions coined *Pentapartito* due to the constant participation of the same five parties (DC, PSI, PSDI, PRI, PLI). In the first years of the 1980s, economic growth was slow and unemployment rose steeply. In the second half of the decade the economic situation improved, but this did not keep public debt from rising throughout the 1980s. In this period, we can observe the first efforts to restructure the welfare state. Yet, in the field of unemployment compensation, as in many other policy fields, no incisive changes were adopted during these first ten years of welfare reform.

Table 5.2 Important reforms of unemployment benefits in Germany, 2002–11

2002–3	• organizational reform of Public Employment Service, reform of active labour market policies ('Hartz I-III')
2003	• old UA scheme abolished, new UA to include also all SA recipients able to work, level of generosity basically same as SA
	• maximum durations of UI reduced
	• contributory requirements for UI raised ('Hartz IV', 24 December 2003)
2007	• maximum durations of UI for old unemployed extended (11 December 2007)
2010	• no parental leave benefit and no pension contributions paid for UA recipients
	• transitional benefit for beneficiaries who exhaust UI scrapped (9 December 2010)
2011	• following a Constitutional Court ruling, small rise of UA benefit level, additional support for education of UA recipients' children

Note
Laws are denoted by the date they were issued by the President of the Federal Republic.

Regarding unemployment benefits, the 1980s were characterized by two rather diverse developments: a reduction of CIGS benefit levels and the introduction of additional passive measures. The first of these two developments is an aspect little recognized in the literature on Italian labour market policy. Already in 1979, a government decree limited the duration and benefit levels of ordinary CIG and CIGS. At first, this decree was not fully converted into law. However, in 1980 a new law introduced a benefit ceiling for CIGS payments. In the beginning this maximum amount was set at a level slightly higher than 80 per cent of the gross wage of an average production worker. Therefore, it did not immediately have a great effect on the living of most CIGS beneficiaries. However, the law provided that the benefit ceiling should be increased yearly by 80 per cent of the indexed growth of wages (*scala mobile*). Therefore, it was clear that over time the benefit ceiling would decrease with respect to average wages and, consequently, have a more incisive effect on benefit levels. Indeed, we can observe a significant decline of the net replacement rate for the average production worker over the 1980s (see Figure 5.3).[11]

As in Germany and other European countries during the 1980s, the Italian government tried to tackle unemployment by reducing labour supply. Accordingly, in 1981, early retirement was introduced. Once more, this was a measure that was restricted to the industrial sector (excluding construction). Under

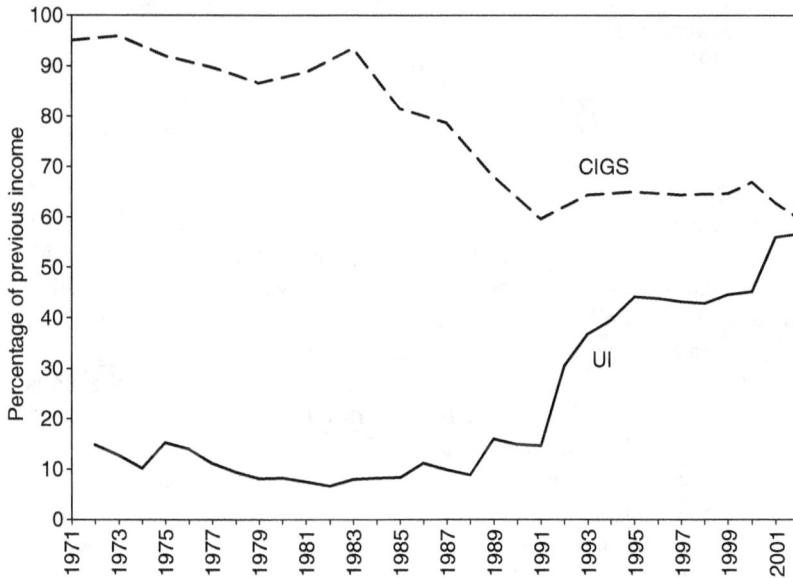

Figure 5.3 Net replacement rates of CIGS and unemployment insurance in Italy (sources: Scruggs (2004), INPS circulars, own calculations).

Notes
Replacement rates are unweighted averages for two household types and are based on the average production worker's wage. CIGS data is partly interpolated.

specific conditions and after government authorization, firms could give male workers aged 55 or above, and female workers aged 50 or above, the opportunity to retire. This was intended as a temporary policy but its expiration was repeatedly extended. Another passive measure, called 'solidarity contracts', was introduced in 1984. It gave workers the possibility to reduce their working hours in order to avoid dismissal or to enable the hiring of new workers. The forgone wages were partly replaced by the state. In addition, a new public works programme was introduced (*Lavori Socialmente Utili*, LSU) in 1981. Formally, this was an active measure to create work for the unemployed, but in practice, it functioned as a 'passive' policy that mainly provided income support to the jobless. Initially, it was intended for workers affected from the closing down of public infrastructure projects in Southern Italy, although later it was extended to the rest of the country.[12] However, among the passive measures mentioned, only early retirement was taken advantage of straight away in any great number. Solidarity contracts and LSU initially had no big impact.

The benefit ceilings for CIGS imposed restrictions on the most generous unemployment benefit; but their impact emerged only over time. Early retirement, solidarity contracts, and LSU went in a different direction. Again they mainly favoured the insiders of the labour market (except maybe for LSU). Therefore, no clear change can be recorded for segmentation of unemployment benefits during the 1980s. However, towards the end of the decade two court decisions set the stage for more distinct reforms that were then adopted in the 1990s and 2000s.

First, in 1987 the Constitutional Court ruled that the benefit level of UI was inadequate for the needs of the insured. In fact, since 1974 the benefit had remained at a lump sum amount of 800 lira per day. The government reacted in the following year and converted benefit calculation to a nominal replacement rate that was initially set at 7.5 per cent. This still rather low rate was then gradually raised in the 1990s and 2000s (see below). The same law of 1988 also introduced an additional UI scheme for workers fulfilling only lower qualifying conditions than those required for full UI. This new scheme was – and still is – governed by rules similar to the agricultural scheme. Accordingly, it actually falls into the category of income support rather than UI.

Second, a decision by the Constitutional Court in 1988 ruled that the old law from 1890, which was still the basic framework for the field of SA, was unconstitutional. This finally opened up the way for a substantial reform of the SA sector, yet, it took another ten years until the task was tackled. At the end of the 1980s two court rulings helped to initiate some progress regarding UI and SA. However, it was only in the subsequent decade that politics took up the lead and introduced improvements at the bottom end of the benefit system. (For a summary of the reforms of unemployment benefits during the 1980s in Italy, see Table 5.3.)

Table 5.3 Important reforms of unemployment benefits in Italy, 1979–89

1980	• benefit ceilings introduced for CIGS, indexed at 80% of wage rises, therefore becoming gradually more restrictive (l. 427)
1981–4	• various passive measures introduced: early retirement (l. 155/1981), *Lavori Socialmente Utili* (l. 390/1981), solidarity contracts (l. 863/1984)
1988	• following a ruling by the Constitutional Court, UI benefit level is converted from flat rate to a nominal replacement rate of 7.5%
	• introduction of a UI scheme with lower qualifying conditions (l. 160)
	• old SA law ruled unconstitutional by Constitutional Court

Note
The numbers of laws are in brackets.

Reducing the gap

In the 1990s and up to the beginning of the 2000s several important welfare reforms were adopted that concerned the areas of pension, health care and labour market regulation (cf. Ferrera and Gualmini 2004). At the beginning of this period the old party system broke down, triggered by the collapse of state communism in Eastern Europe and by a big corruption scandal (*Tangentopoli*). As a consequence, from 1992–6 several non-partisan governments ruled the country – except for the interlude of a government headed by Silvio Berlusconi in 1994. The non-partisan governments were followed by alternating centre-left and centre-right coalitions. The unemployment benefit system changed more significantly since the end of the 1980s than in the previous period. In particular, two developments have to be highlighted: first, the gradual increase of UI benefit levels; second, the attempt to establish a minimum income scheme.

As mentioned, following a court ruling, the government in 1988 transformed UI from a flat-rate benefit to an earnings-related benefit, but on a nominal replacement rate of only 7.5 per cent. Starting from the beginning of the 1990s this nominal replacement rate was raised gradually but significantly: in 1991 to 20 per cent, in 1993 to 25 per cent, in 1994 to 30 per cent, in 2000 to 40 per cent, in 2005 to 50 per cent, and in 2007 to 60 per cent. Taking account of taxes and family benefits, this meant that within less than 15 years the net replacement rate of UI rose from 9 per cent (flat-rate benefit still effective in 1988) to 57 per cent in 2002 (see Figure 5, remember that it increased further after 2005 and 2007).

In addition to the benefit level, the reforms in 2000, 2005, and 2007 augmented also the maximum durations of UI, differentiated by age. Thus, by 2007 the maximum duration was eight months and, for the 50 year-olds and above, 12 months. At the same time, the nominal replacement rate was set to decrease gradually with longer durations: 60 per cent in the first six months, 50 per cent in the next two months, and 40 per cent thereafter. Initially, the benefit levels for the income support schemes (UI in agricultural sector and UI with reduced requirements) were raised identically as for ordinary UI. Only starting from the reform in 2000 they were not expanded to the same degree.

Today, the UI scheme with reduced requirements has a maximum duration of 180 days and a replacement rate of 35 per cent for the first 120 days and 40 per cent after that.

Therefore, UI in the 1990s and 2000s was restored from being a meagre benefit, relevant only as income supplement for poor families in the South, to a standard insurance benefit similar to UI in other European countries. The more generous benefit levels of UI also affected its take-up rate. Previously, many people who were entitled to UI did not bother to apply, but by the middle of the 2000s UI payments had become much more attractive (the effect on beneficiary rates is reported below). Along with this expansion of UI, some steps were undertaken to verify more effectively the required conditions for receiving the benefit. In 1998, parliament decided that the unemployed who had voluntarily left their previous job were no longer eligible for UI payments, and in 2000 and 2002 the status of being unemployed was tied to conditions such as the participation in training courses. However, these efforts to increase conditionality, which were similar to activation measures in other European countries, remained relatively ineffective because benefit administration (by *Istituto Nazionale Previdenza Sociale* – INPS) is not administratively linked to Public Employment Services.

Apart from the expansion of UI, this period saw notable progress in the field of SA, even though in the end it did not last. As mentioned, a court ruling in 1988 repealed the old legislation of the sector. In 1997, the centre-left government under Romano Prodi convened a commission to review welfare policies (called 'Onofri commission' after its chairman). The following year, government presented a proposal for a national framework law of SA that took up many of the recommendations of the commission. At the same time, a minimum income scheme was launched in 39 municipalities on an experimental basis for two years. This scheme (*reddito minimo di inserimento*, RMI) combined monetary transfers with so-called insertion contracts that were meant to promote the labour market inclusion or, more generally, social inclusion of recipients. Two years later, the new framework law was adopted. It substituted the old 1890 legislation and tried to establish a universal safety net at the national level. Thus, the law defined minimum standards and procedures to guide the multi-level governance in the policy arena. Furthermore, with the budget law for 2001 the experimental RMI was extended for two more years and to a total of 306 municipalities (Sacchi 2007).

The new framework law constituted a major innovation. Yet, it was practically blocked only one year later by a constitutional reform that, among other things, granted exclusive competence in the field of SA to the regions. Consequently, the law was no longer binding for regional governments. The RMI experiment did not fare well either. The new centre-right government under Silvio Berlusconi that came to power in 2001 did not extend the RMI effort. Instead, it proposed a weaker programme under the name 'income of last resort'. However, in 2004 a ruling of the Constitutional Court rejected the initiative as interfering with the competence of the regions.

The increase of UI benefits and the progress within SA were complemented by efforts to contain the generous industrial unemployment benefit schemes and, more particularly, to reverse the anomaly of CIGS. During the 1980s, as we have seen, the benefit level of CIGS had been gradually but clearly reduced (Figure 5.3), but this did not change the structural role of the benefit. An important step towards redefining the function of CIGS was, instead, a reform in 1991 that limited the duration of CIGS payments and introduced the so-called mobility benefit (*Mobilità*) for workers who were laid off from firms eligible for CIGS. This was meant to reduce the number of de facto unemployed workers who were formally still employed and to transfer them into an 'explicit' unemployment benefit scheme. At the same time the mobility benefit paid the same benefit levels as CIGS (80 per cent with benefit ceiling). The maximum duration of the new benefit varied between 12 and 36 months depending on age. Moreover, the mobility scheme replaced the *trattamenti speciali*. The 1991 reform intervened also in several other respects. It extended the benefit ceiling of CIGS to the other CIG schemes (with some exceptions) and it increased coverage of CIGS to commercial enterprises with more than 200 dependent workers and coverage of ordinary CIG to white-collar workers. Most of the exceptions to the benefit ceiling that were left for specific CIG schemes were repealed in 1995. Hence, the reform introduced further restrictions on the top-level benefits and made an effort to unify regulations (Tronti 1991).

However, a change to the benefit ceiling rules became necessary when an agreement of the Amato government with trade unions and employers abolished the wage indexation mechanism (*scala mobile*) in 1992. CIG ceilings had been coupled to wage indexation by 80 per cent. Consequently, a new mechanism for the indexation of benefit ceilings was adopted. Since 1994 ceilings were to rise by 80 per cent of the consumer price index of the Italian Statistical Institute (Istat) for blue- and white-collar families. Given the union moderation in wage bargaining in those years, the effect was that the automatic decrease of the maximum benefits in relation to wages was stopped (see Figure 5.3). Moreover, in 1994 a second and higher benefit ceiling was established for the unemployed whose previous income exceeded a certain threshold.

The main change in the beginning of the 1990s, however, was the limitation of CIGS and the introduction of an explicit unemployment benefit (*Mobilità*). Fargion (2001: 47–8) shows that, although some of the restrictions in the 1991 reform were almost immediately watered down, the overall aim to restrict use of CIGS was successful. Still, coverage of *Mobilità* was the same as for CIGS and, hence, very narrow. Consequently, an attempt was made in 1996 to increase the coverage of more generous unemployment benefits by giving social partners the possibility to set up bilateral funds for this purpose. These funds were regulated and administratively supported by government. However, the approach remained within a particularistic framework and could only bear fruits in sectors with strong industrial organizations. Hence, only a few sectors made use of this possibility: banking, cooperative banking, ex-state monopolies, and insurance (CNEL 2003).

Another way to deal with the limited coverage of the industrial benefit schemes consisted of discretionary extensions that were provided for in the annual budget laws or governmental decrees. This discretionary practice came to be known as 'waiver CIG' (*CIG in deroga*).[13] It made it possible to disburse CIGS, *Mobilità*, or special UI benefits beyond the limits regarding duration and coverage that the 1991 reform had introduced. As was the case with ordinary CIG, employers had to reach an agreement with unions and, then, apply to the regional government in order to activate payments. Together with the standard CIG schemes it was massively taken advantage of in the wake of the global economic crisis (Sacchi *et al.* forthcoming). Obviously, this way to extend coverage of the more generous benefits is again ad hoc and particularistic.

Figure 5.4 displays the beneficiary rates of unemployment benefits, i.e. the proportion of unemployed receiving benefits, since 2000. Benefit schemes are aggregated into the categories identified above, resulting in three data series. The series are accumulative in order to indicate the overall proportion of unemployed receiving unemployment benefits. In 2000, the overall beneficiary rate was at a very low 20 per cent. During only six years it had increased by about 20 percentage points. Yet, this still left only 40 per cent of the unemployed receiving benefits (see Figure 5.4). Some of the rise in these shares was facilitated by falling numbers of unemployed, but also the absolute number of beneficiaries in industrial schemes and UI has increased. In the case of the industrial schemes this may have been caused by the mentioned particularistic ways of extending coverage. In the case of UI it is partly explainable by the increased attractiveness and duration of the benefit, which previously was too low for many workers – particularly in the North – to bother applying for. In any case, the inclusiveness of the more generous schemes has improved but many unemployed are still left outside (cf. Jessoula *et al.* 2010).

Furthermore, it is important to note that the decline of unemployment was to some extent enabled by labour market flexibilization. Two important reforms, in 1997 and 2003, had deregulated the use of non-standard contracts. Some of the non-standard workers are categorically excluded from access to unemployment benefits (e.g. project workers). Others have considerably lower chances of acquiring the necessary contribution and employment records for receiving unemployment benefits (Berton *et al.* 2009). Therefore, with the rising numbers of atypical workers a lower proportion of the employed has access to financial support in case of becoming unemployed.

Overall, the 1990s and 2000s have seen significant government interventions to reduce the segmentation of unemployment benefits in Italy. The benefit level of UI has been raised from a negligible lump sum at the end of the 1980s to a net replacement rate of about 57 per cent in 2002 (which was further raised afterwards). Also, government almost succeeded in introducing a minimum income scheme that would have filled the protection gap for those not eligible for dedicated unemployment benefits. At the same time, efforts continued to limit the generosity of CIG and in a more structural reform it was attempted to contain the deviated role of CIGS. The UI net replacement rate for the average production

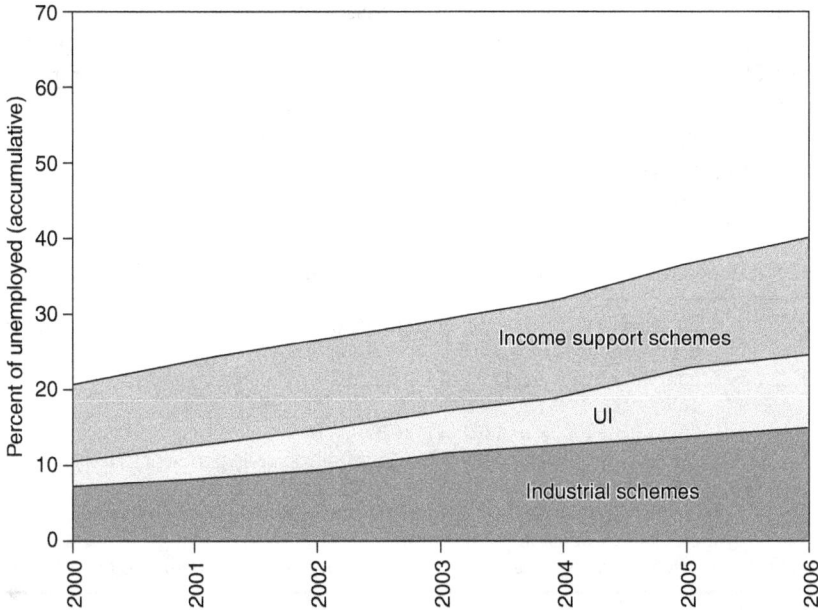

Figure 5.4 Beneficiary rates in Italy – aggregated into three groups of benefit schemes (sources: *Ministero del Lavoro e della Previdenza Sociale* (various years), OECD (2010b), own calculations).

Notes
Lines are accumulative. Income support schemes include: UI reduced requirements and UI agricultural sector. UI includes normal UI and UI for construction sector. Industrial schemes include: CIG, CIGS, Mobility, special benefit construction sector, and bilateral funds.

worker increased by 40 percentage points over the course of the 1990s and early 2000s and the net replacement rate of CIGS decreased by about 30 percentage points since the beginning of the 1980s (see Figure 5.3). This constitutes a considerable narrowing of the generosity gap that was one of the main aspects of unemployment benefit segmentation in Italy.

Nevertheless, in other aspects the Italian system of unemployment compensation remains highly segmented. Fragmentation along categorical lines persists, access to the upper strata of benefits (industrial schemes) is still limited, and a minimum income scheme, which would protect the consistent numbers of unemployed who do not qualify for any dedicated unemployment benefit, is still lacking. In addition, the efforts at widening the coverage of the generous industrial schemes follow a particularistic logic. Most analysts of the Italian labour market emphasize these continuing policy problems and point out that no structural reform has taken place in spite of a high awareness among political actors for the need of more fundamental reforms. In fact, since 1988 many legislative measures in this field are introduced by the phrase 'In the expectation of a comprehensive unemployment benefit reform [...]'.[14] So, it is true that the lack of a structural reform is palpable but this should not lead us to overlook the changes that did take place. They may be easily missed because of their incremental nature, but this does not make their accumulative effect less real (Streeck and Thelen 2005). Table 5.4 summarizes the most important reforms of unemployment benefits during the 1990s and 2000s. In comparison, we can note that the severe segmentation in Italy was reduced after an initial phase of unclear vacillating reforms, whereas in Germany the originally moderate segmentation increased; first through marginal, and later through more radical reforms.

Table 5.4 Important reforms of unemployment benefits in Italy, 1989–2007

1991	• duration of CIGS limited, unemployment benefit (*Mobilità*) introduced for firms eligible for CIGS (l. 223)
1991–2007	• nominal replacement rate of UI successively increased to 20% (l. 169/1991), 25% (l. 236/1993), 30% (l. 451/1994), 40% (l. 388/2000), 50% (l. 80/2005), and 60% (l. 247/2007)
1998	• Minimal Insertion Income (RMI) introduced on experimental basis for two years, later extended for two more years (l. 237)
2000	• new SA framework law setting minimum standards and procedures, but blocked by constitutional reform in 2001 (l. 328)
since 2001	• discretionary extensions of CIG gradually become established practice

Note
The numbers of laws are in brackets.

Part III

The impact of party competition

6 Explaining labour market reforms in Italy and Germany

Part II has shown how the Italian and German unemployment benefit systems clearly diverged after the Second World War and how the segmentation in both benefit systems changed over time during welfare state restructuring. Since the 1970s the German government first adopted incremental retrenchments on the margins of the system and, then, more fundamental reforms that led to a dual structure of unemployment compensation. In Italy, no clear reforms were adopted at the beginning of the reform phase. Only later gradual reforms added up to an overall significant reduction of generosity differences.

In order to explain these policy developments I will focus on the Italian and the German party systems and analyse how they shaped competition between parties and, in consequence, policy decisions. As set out in Chapter 1, party competition should be taken into consideration as an explanatory variable in welfare state research because it has its own dynamic, which makes it partially autonomous from socio-economic structures and the institutional context (Sartori 1990 [1968]; Ferrera 1993; Kitschelt 2001). The characteristics of this dynamic of competition depend largely on the party system.

If the party system contains many parties we expect each to focus on narrower interests which, in turn, lead to more fragmented policies. If the party system is ideologically polarized, anti-system parties do not participate in normal programmatic competition and can block the political process, which gives rise to bargaining over small-scale policy changes targeted on party constituencies. In this way the anti-system parties, although excluded from government, can still exert significant policy influence. By contrast, in non-polarized party systems programmatic competition prevails. As a consequence, the policy preferences of the voters on which party competition concentrates are likely to be reflected in policy reforms. However, the groups of voters, on which voter competition focuses, are determined by the spatial configuration of the party system (see Chapter 1).

Before we apply this theoretical framework to explaining the policy developments described in Part II, we first have to take a look at alternative explanations of labour market reforms provided in the country-specific literature on Italy and Germany. Regarding the German case, institutional explanations prevail in the literature on labour market policy while party competition is largely neglected.

The literature mainly predicted policy stability and, therefore, had trouble accounting for the recent fundamental reforms. As I will show, an argument based on party competition, by contrast, can help to explain these reforms. Studies of Italian labour market policy have employed mainly arguments based on union power as well as policy feedbacks. The relevance of party competition for the development of the Italian welfare state has been recognized. However, a party system framework has not yet been applied systematically to labour market policy.

Germany: institutions and the challenge posed by the 'Hartz reforms'

In the literature on German labour market policy, party competition rarely figures as an explanatory variable. Analyses of labour market reforms in Germany mostly underline the role of institutions. Insofar as they address electoral competition, they focus more on policy demand. Consequently, most studies ended up predicting high stability in German labour market policy. For this reason, established approaches face serious problems in accounting for the fundamental changes that the recent Hartz reforms brought about. The only recurrent argument that can be found in this respect points out that a window of opportunity opened up when irregularities in the German Federal Employment Office (*Bundesamt* [now: *Bundesagentur*] *für Arbeit* – BA) were uncovered.

Institutional arguments can be found with regard to both the German political system and labour market institutions. Katzenstein's classic book on *Policy and Politics in West Germany* (1987) already elaborated how German politics is characterized by fragmented state structures and centralized social interest organizations. These two sides interact in three policy nodes: political parties, cooperative federalism, and parapublic institutions of policy administration. The structure of this policy process impedes radical reforms. Katzenstein does consider the role of parties. However, he focuses on their 'catch-all' character and on the exigencies of coalition government rather than on the logic of competition generated by the party system. Above all, his book emphasizes the institutional constraints on the policy process.

This core argument is shared by M.G. Schmidt (2002). He argues that the number and leverage of institutional veto points in Germany limit the impact of partisan politics (i.e. of left parties introducing pro-labour policies and right parties introducing pro-capital policies). The most important veto points in the German legislative process are the upper chamber of parliament (*Bundesrat*), coalition government, and the Constitutional Court. Schmidt stresses that this institutional framework often makes cooperation between the two largest parties (CDU and SPD) necessary. Somewhat in contrast to Schmidt's emphasis on cooperation, Lehmbruch (2000) highlights the strong competition between the two biggest parties. Lehmbruch finds this bipolar logic of competition in conflict with the cooperative logic of German federalism. The consequence is that the policy process can easily be blocked.

More specifically for the field of labour market policy, scholars have argued that reforms are restrained and shaped by institutional features such as the semi-autonomous position of the BA, which administers UI and UA (it is only partly responsible for the new assistance scheme); the participation of unions and employers' association in the tripartite governance of the BA; and the funding of unemployment insurance through social insurance contributions. These factors gave strong actors a stake in defending the status quo. The interest of collective actors in UI is particularly articulate, whereas the assistance benefits (UA and SA) have fewer institutional safeguards (Clasen 1994; Clasen and Clegg 2006; G. Schmid 2006; J. Schmid and Picot 2001).

Zohlnhöfer (2001) points out that in the field of labour market policy some of the constraints imposed by political institutions apply to a lesser extent than in other policy fields. Above all, most labour market reforms do not affect the responsibility of the German *Länder*. For this reason, the *Bundesrat* has little veto power in this field. However, SA falls under the jurisdiction of municipalities and, consequently, under the responsibility of the *Länder*. Just this benefit scheme did play a role in the Hartz reforms. Therefore, the adoption of those reforms is even more of a puzzle from the institutionalist point of view. In his study of labour market policy in the Kohl era, Zohlnhöfer (2001) starts, as does Schmidt, from a partisan politics hypothesis. Yet, differently from Schmidt, he does not see institutions as the main obstacles to reform but emphasizes intra-party factions and party competition. However, his concept of party competition differs from the approach of the present study. Zohlnhöfer refers mainly to problem pressure that raises concern in the electorate and, hence, increases party competition around a certain issue. He is less concerned with the structures of party systems.

More similar to the approach taken in the present contribution, Herbert Kitschelt (2001) emphasizes how the strategic configuration of a party system influences the chances of introducing social policy reforms. As mentioned in Chapter 1, he proposes four factors that increase the probability of welfare state retrenchment: (1) low credibility of welfare state-defending parties; (2) low electoral trade-offs, i.e. only weak or no rival parties to the immediate left of governing parties; (3) party organization that favours strategic flexibility; (4) salience of the socio-economic political dimension for party competition. In the German case, Kitschelt argues, political competition on the socio-economic axis is condensed and two welfare state-defending parties keep each other in check with respect to welfare reforms. His period of analysis ends in 1998 and predicts only limited restructuring efforts for the future. He adds, 'If, however the [CDU] moved to the market liberal right, then the new red–green coalition enjoys more leeway to enact retrenchment without having to fear that dissatisfied voters will turn to the main opposition party' (2001: 295). As will be shown below, this qualification was long-sighted.

However, in a later analysis of the German party system, Kitschelt (2003a) does not follow up on this argument. Rather, he focuses on a realignment of voters driven by macro structural changes and increasingly dividing the electorate into a market liberal and a social protectionist camp. Therefore, in contrast to his earlier article, he concentrates on policy demand. From this perspective, he sees the considerable social protectionist component of policy demand in Germany as still blocking welfare reforms in the short- and medium-term. This prediction proved to be at odds with the Hartz reforms that soon followed. In a similar vein, Stephen Padgett (2004) attributes the lack of decisive welfare reforms up to 2002 to the pro-welfare consensus among German voters and the diffuse distribution of this preference across party constituencies. At the same time, he finds some evidence for a slow opinion shift in favour of reform but argues that this shift by itself is not sufficient to encourage parties to adopt stronger measures. As I will argue below, Padgett was right in saying that the public opinion shift by itself was not large enough, but the structure of the party system directed the attention of parties (and in particular of the Social Democrats) on exactly those voters who started to demand more ambitious reforms.

By and large, most studies of German labour market policy predicted high stability. This was particularly true for the dominant institutionalist approach but also for the fewer studies considering electoral competition. Consequently, the available theoretical toolkit left scholars in dire straits when faced with the more radical Hartz reforms. Most authors have chosen either or both of two arguments to remedy this problem: a window of opportunity and the impact of ideas. The first argument points to a public scandal about mismanagement in the BA that is said to have opened a window of opportunity for the government to reform the BA and the unemployment benefit system (e.g. Schmid 2006: 369–70; Weimar 2004: 46–7). This is a typical 'punctuated equilibrium' argument as it is used in many institutionalist accounts for explaining change. While the point is well taken, it is insufficient to explain the occurrence and, even more so, the direction of the Hartz reforms. There has to be an actor with the political will and capacity to make use of a window of opportunity (or rather, to turn the incidence of an administrative irregularity into a window of opportunity). Moreover, taking advantage of an opportunity does not pre-determine the kind of action that is then taken. The second of the two mentioned arguments sees labour market reforms caused by a change in 'interpretative patterns' (see e.g. Bleses and Seeleib-Kaiser 2004: 119–27). Here, however, two questions remain: what determines which policy ideas become dominant, and what determines whether and when a dominant interpretative pattern is translated into policy?

In contrast, I argue that in order to understand why the government took advantage of the BA scandal we have to look at the interaction between the limited shift in policy demand (that was indentified already by Padgett 2004) and the configuration of the party system. During the 1990s public opinion shifted to some extent in favour of restructuring. This increase of supporters of liberal reforms constituted an electoral advantage for the Christian Democrats who actively pursued this demand shift; but, while in power, they were restrained by the competition of the Social Democrats on their left. On the other side, the Social Democrats had to react to this demand shift in order to return to power and, later, stay in power. In addressing this more liberal policy demand, they were not held back by a credible left-wing competitor. Thus, the structure of the party system made it possible that a small change in electoral demand had a big impact. However, the Social Democratic shift to the centre opened up enough space on the left for a new competitor to emerge. This changed the spatial configuration of the party system and again had an effect on the policy level.

In the earlier phases, the development of German unemployment benefits was shaped by the much more stable centripetal competition between SPD and CDU and, to some extent FDP as a right-wing competitor to the CDU on socio-economic issues. During welfare state expansion this dynamic led to a credit claiming competition over the core groups of workers and employees in the labour market while social protection was only gradually extended to more marginal groups. In the 1980s and 1990s the challenge of high unemployment made reforms necessary, but the pro-welfare consensus in the electorate and, again, centripetal competition impeded retrenchments of the core benefits. Accordingly, cutbacks were targeted on the margins of the benefit system.

Italy: class power, institutions, and the recognized role of party competition

There are not many studies that try to explain the development of labour market policy in Italy. Some older works tend to emphasize the relations of power between workers and employers in order to account for the emergence of the post-war labour market regime. With respect to the persistence of this regime others have emphasized the role of policy feedback. At the same time, the importance of party competition for explaining Italian social policy has been recognized. However, this was not yet systematically applied to the field of labour market policy.

In an important early article on labour market policy Regalia (1984) emphasized how two class-based factors have influenced the post-war development in this field: the relation between labour supply and demand in the market and the political representation of the working class on the political level, in other words, the economic and the political power of the working class. Similar arguments on class power have been sustained by Reyneri (1987) and, for the period up to the end of the 1970s, by Gualmini (1998: Ch. 3). In this perspective the failure to establish adequate unemployment benefits at the end of the 1940s, and 1950s appears, above all, as a result of the relative weakness of unions and left parties in this period. Conversely, the following unbalanced expansion of unemployment benefits in favour of core industrial workers is seen as a result of the particular strength of the worker movement in the 1960s and 1970s.

In order to explain the persistence of the segmented system of unemployment compensation in spite of rising reform pressures during the 1980s and 1990s Gualmini (1998: Ch. 3; see also Gualmini 1997) highlights the impact of policy feedback. In particular, she shows how both the process of activating CIG payments and the short-term economic implications of CIG are beneficial for the central political actors. Both aspects, therefore, reproduce interests in maintaining this core policy of Italian unemployment protection. Initializing *Cassa Integrazione* transfers requires a request by the employer, the consultation and active support of the union, additional political support from local politicians and notables, and the final approval by the Labour Ministry. Hence, the process allows many actors to claim merit for the CIG payments that redundant workers finally receive. The economic effects of the CIG are, obviously, convenient for unions and workers because of the high level of protection that the scheme offers – but employers appreciate the advantages of CIG too. After all, it yields numerical employment flexibility without the risk of intense social conflict.[1] Negative long-term consequences of the policy (e.g. employment rigidity and labour market dualism) are less tangible for the individual actors. Therefore, the process of activating CIG payments and the economic effects of the scheme have endowed many actors with vested interests in its maintenance, leading to a self-reinforcement of this policy.

In a nutshell, the main argument in the literature on the development of labour market policy can be summarized by the following sequence: weakness of labour movement (1948–50s), strength of labour movement (1960s, 1970s), and path dependence due to institutionalization (1980s, 1990s). These are all relevant aspects, of course, yet, there are some ambiguities. Concerning the first phase, it is not clear that the missing introduction of a comprehensive unemployment benefit system owed to the fact that a weak left failed to impose its will. As I will show in the next chapter, a comprehensive system of unemployment compensation was not actually on the agenda of the radical left, which focused rather on employment creation and labour market administration. In addition, it is true that the left was weak compared to the years at the end of the war (1943–8) and compared to the mobilizations of the 1960s and 1970s. However, at least in the first half of the 1950s and in the rural areas, the unions still proved to have a high capacity of social mobilization, and after 1948 the Communist Party (*Partito Comunista Italiano,* PCI) continuously increased its share of the votes.

The lopsided expansion of unemployment benefits in the 1960s and 1970s was surely related to the strength of the left in those years. Yet, mere reference to the strength of the left begs the tongue-in-cheek question why no Scandinavian welfare state was established. Apart, of course, from economic and institutional differences, the point here is to acknowledge what kind of left (social democratic, socialist, or communist) we are talking about and what role it had in the wider constellation of political forces. Traditional partisan theory does not help us here because the strong part of the left, the PCI, did not participate in government. In addition, the PCI, at least initially, was not on top of massive worker mobilizations but rather had to struggle in order not to lose touch with popular activism.

Finally, the institutionalization argument surely points out some of the factors that have impeded incisive reform of the benefit system. In this respect, I will, however, add two observations. First, an additional reason for policy persistence during the 1980s was the continuing polarization of party competition, which blocked major reforms. Second, I argue that over the 1990s Italian unemployment compensation changed more clearly than the path dependency argument can account for. This change was made possible by the drastic transformation of the party system, in particular, the moderation of anti-system parties.

Party competition was already identified by Ferrera (1993: Chs 6–7) as a relevant framework for explaining the development of the Italian welfare state. However, his analysis included only pensions and health care, not labour market policy. In the field of pensions, the universalist ambitions of the centre-left governments of the 1960s were thwarted by the polarized party system, in particular, the opposition of the Communist Party. Conversely, the very same party system enabled a nationalization of health care. Due to the decentralization of government the Communist Party had an institutional interest in this reform because it governed some of the regions. In addition, it saw the health sector from the start as a citizen rather than a worker issue.

In their book on the reforms of the 1990s Ferrera and Gualmini (2004) consider labour market reforms (but not very specifically unemployment benefits). Party competition also figures prominently in this account, but to some extent *ex negativo*. Again, the authors note that polarized pluralism has obstructed many reforms up to the 1980s. In the middle of the 1990s, by contrast, two factors facilitated a number of welfare reforms. First, the commonly recognized desirability of entering the European Monetary Union and the economic constraints of the Maastricht process altered the policy preferences of political actors. Second, the collapse of the First Republic, particularly of the old party system, created a political void that was filled by technical governments, social concertation, and a more consensual approach to policy-making.

How, exactly, did these two factors affect party competition? Two different interpretations seem possible. The first would be that party competition was partly suspended, thus enabling a process of policy learning as opposed to political confrontation. This interpretation is somewhat more visible in the book and is justified by the temporary breakdown of the party system. The second interpretation would be that the two mentioned factors changed the nature of party competition and helped to make party competition itself less confrontational and less polarized. This interpretation is, in any case, consistent with the more general theoretical framework of the book that considers how internal developments (transition from First to Second Republic) and external developments (Maastricht process and globalization) have changed the actor constellation, which in turn generated a different policy-making process. The analysis of the 1990s in the present study is closer to the second interpretation. To be sure, when the party system was in complete disarray and technical governments took over, party competition was partly suspended. However, I argue that after the elections in 1996 we can see a new configuration of party competition emerge that shaped unemployment benefit reforms.

In sum, the literature on the Italian welfare state recognizes party competition as a relevant factor for explaining social policy. However, so far only one study has directly analysed the effect of party competition in the field of labour market policy. In that study the concept of party competition refers mainly to different kinds of party-voter linkages (programmatic or particularistic) and not to the role of the party system. In her book on the distribution of social spending on different age groups, Lynch (2006) examines unemployment benefits in Italy in more detail as part of her case studies. She focuses on the clientelism of the Christian Democrats, which, she argues, has conditioned the policy demands of the left, which otherwise may have promoted more universal policies (Lynch 2006: 109–10 and 134–5). The point is plausible. However, as with the class power arguments reported above, the weak spot is the assumption on the left's original preferences. Is it likely that a communist party that is in fundamental opposition to the system in which it operates would advocate the same universal policies that social democratic parties at the head of national governments have implemented in other European states? Certainly, the Italian Communist Party adapted to the political system over the years and was not a revolutionary renegade, but its principles and the principles of its voters remained based on the vanguard historical role of the working class and on the objective of overcoming capitalism. Universal unemployment compensation was not a priority because it presupposes the power of employers to fire workers.

Up to the end of the 1980s the post-war party system was characterized by a high number of parties and by ideological polarization through a strong Communist Party and a smaller, but still significant, neo-fascist party. Polarization blocked programmatic reform efforts and provided the Communist Party with bargaining power. As a consequence, the preference of the Communist Party (initially for employment creation, later for employment protection) conditioned the neglect of unemployment benefits and, later on, the unbalanced growth of benefits for the core industrial working force. In the context of economic austerity, polarized pluralism continued to block any significant reforms. The party system change in the early 1990s introduced a centripetal dynamic of competition between pre-electoral coalitions into Italian party politics. This enabled the reduction of the wide disparity between benefits. Yet, a high number of parties and centrifugal tendencies within party coalitions continued to mark political competition and prevented more structural reforms of unemployment compensation.

7 Italy and Germany

Political driving forces behind different post-war paths

Chapter 4 has shown how Italy and Germany developed markedly different systems of unemployment benefits under similar economic conditions of rapid growth and falling unemployment. In this chapter, I will explain how these two policy trajectories were influenced by the very different party systems in both countries. The German post-war party system, consisted (after a phase of consolidation) of only three parties. Ideological distances were moderate and centripetal competition prevailed. By contrast, Italian party politics was characterized by a high number of parties, ideological polarization, and centrifugal competition. These various political dynamics left their mark on the reconstruction and expansion of unemployment benefits after the war.

Germany: centripetal competition and comprehensive benefits

After military defeat of the Nazi regime, the division of occupied Germany into West under control of the Western Allies, and East under Soviet control, had a profound impact not only, of course, on the new political system but also on the party system in both parts of the country.[1] Explaining the configuration of party systems is not a task of this study as I use party systems as a causal variable. Nevertheless, for the comparison between Germany and Italy it is interesting to point out some general historical reasons for their widely different post-war party systems.

The German party system was historically shaped by the cleavage between labour and capital as well as the cleavage between the state and its protestant elite and the considerable Catholic minority. In addition, under the influence of the October Revolution in Russia, and wartime politics in the First World War, the left of the Weimer Republic had been divided into Social Democrats and Communists (Lipset and Rokkan 1967; Lees 2005; Lösche 1994; Rohe 2001).

The division of Germany helped to simplify the emerging West German party system in mainly two respects (Niedermayer 2006: 111–12). First, the ideological conflict between capitalism and communism was projected on the national division and the Communist Party disappeared from domestic party competition. As is well known, the ideological conflict between the Western

Allies and the Soviet Union had already started to emerge towards the end of the war and escalated with the Truman Doctrine in 1947 and the blockade of West Berlin by the Soviet Union in 1948. During occupation Western Allies as well as the Soviet Union (although, of course, to a varying extent and by different means) directly influenced political development, later they retained a more indirect influence. When the German Communist Party (*Kommunistische Partei Deutschlands*, KPD) returned from exile, the Soviet occupied East of Germany was naturally its main focus of activities. At the same time, communism was soon discredited among large parts of the West German population. Nevertheless, at first, the KPD was also active in West Germany. It entered the lower house of parliament (*Bundestag*) in the first national election with 5.7 per cent of the votes and was represented in all regional parliaments. Yet, it was neither relevant for coalition-building nor was it strong enough to generate a centrifugal dynamic of competition. After 1953 the KPD became marginal in electoral terms and in 1956 it was banned by a ruling of the Federal Constitutional Court.

Second, during the Wilhelmine Reich and the Weimar Republic one of the biggest parties had been the *Zentrumspartei*, scoring between 11 per cent and 20 per cent of the votes in the Weimar Republic. It was the political representation of the Catholic minority. The separation of West Germany from the prevalently protestant territories and from the former Prussian state-centre, fundamentally altered the position of Catholicism in the state. It no longer faced a daunting Prussian-protestant dominance. This enabled the emergence of a new Christian Democratic Party that replaced the Zentrum. The newly founded CDU (*Christlich Demokratische Union*; in Bavaria – *Christlich Soziale Union*, CSU)[2] was different from the Zentrum in that it was explicitly inter-confessional and less focused on its religious identity. Thus, it managed to gather support from a wider Christian, centrist, and bourgeois spectrum.

The National Socialist regime had been a one-party-state that suppressed other political parties. Hence, after the war old political parties re-established themselves or returned from exile and new parties were founded. This early stage of the West German party system was characterized by a high degree of fragmentation and polarization. However, a process of concentration and depolarization set in almost immediately (Lehmbruch 2000: 37–44; Alemann 2003: 41–62). After the first election to the *Bundestag* in 1949 ten parties entered parliament, in 1953 six parties, in 1957 four parties, and in 1961 three parties. To some extent, this reduction was caused by changes in the electoral system: a mixed system in which the proportional element was decisive for the distribution of seats between parties. Yet, the entry threshold of 5 per cent was applied at the national level only in the election of 1953.[3]

Using Sartori's rules for counting parties (see Chapter 2) the number of actually relevant parties was, of course, smaller. Between 1949 and 1966 the Christian Democrats formed in varying combinations governing coalitions with the FDP and two smaller conservative parties that disappeared after 1961. At the same time, the only relevant opposition party, i.e. one having an influence on the direction of competition, was the SPD. Therefore, between 1949 and 1961 there were five relevant parties. However, after the election in 1961, and up to the 1980s, Germany had a very stable three-party system consisting of CDU, SPD, and FDP.

Regarding polarization, an extreme left (KPD) and an extreme right party (DKP–DRP) were also represented in the first parliament of the Federal Republic. But neither of them was relevant for party competition and in 1953 they did not re-enter the *Bundestag*. More interesting was the relative polarization between the CDU and SPD. Already during the occupation period these two parties started to establish themselves as the two main poles of party competition (Lehmbruch 2000: 41). In these early years of West German party competition they were divided by a notable ideological distance. Actually right after the war many Christian Democrats embraced ideas of 'Christian socialism' (e.g. in the *Ahlener Programm*, 1947). But soon the dominant party ideology became the 'social market economy' (*Düsseldorfer Leitsätze*, 1949). The way this concept was designed by its founders (Ludwig Erhard, Alfred Müller-Armack, and the school of 'ordoliberalism'), the 'social' component was to come from a free market that raised the level of welfare for everyone. The state was meant to ensure free competition in the market, but not to intervene in the outcome of the market. Hence, this was essentially a 'free market' ideology. However, other sections of the party upheld social protection as a part of Catholic social doctrine. Overall, the CDU was rather pro-welfare but it favoured social policies that did not interfere strongly with the market.

The SPD, on the other hand, in the early post-war years adhered to the idea of democratic socialism, which implied economic planning and the socialisation of core industries. However, the subsequent electoral defeats that it suffered – particularly in 1949, 1953, and 1957 – led to a questioning of its socialist principles. The party showed the first signs of relaxing its left-wing ideology in 1952 in its *Dortmunder Aktionsprogramm* and its following revision in 1954, when the policy formula 'as much market as possible, as much planning as necessary' was adopted (Walter 2002: Chs 9–10). This revision process culminated in the famous Bad Godesberg party convention in 1959 where a new party programme was adopted in which the party came out in favour of market economy. Socialisation of industries was not mentioned any more. Quite consciously, the party tried to transform itself from a labour party into a party that appealed to broad sections of the electorate (*Volkspartei* or 'catch-all-party'). Right at the next election (1961) the SPD increased its vote share by almost five percentage points up to 36 per cent and it continued to gain electoral support in the following federal elections (see Table 7.1).

In sum, from the early post-war years onwards ideological differences and the number of parties in the West German party system decreased. By 1961, the party system was consolidated. Its basic features remained stable up to the 1980s and conformed to Sartori's (1976) concept of moderate pluralism. It consisted of three relevant parties and ideological polarization was low. On the socio-economic political dimension, the SPD was situated on the centre-left, the CDU on the centre-right, and the FDP to the right of the CDU. In addition, the German

Table 7.1 German parliamentary election results, 1949–2009

	PDS/Linke	Greens	SPD	CDU/CSU	FDP	Others	Turnout
1949			29.2	31.0	11.9	27.9	78.5
1953			28.8	45.2	9.5	16.5	86.0
1957			31.8	50.2	7.7	10.5	87.8
1961			36.2	45.3	12.8	5.7	87.7
1965			39.3	47.6	9.5	3.6	86.8
1969			42.7	46.1	5.8	5.5	86.7
1972			45.8	44.9	8.4	0.9	91.1
1976			42.6	48.6	7.9	0.9	90.7
1980		1.5	42.9	44.5	10.6	0.5	88.6
1983		5.6	38.2	48.8	7.0	0.4	89.1
1987		8.3	37.0	44.3	9.1	1.3	84.3
1990	2.4	5.0	33.5	43.8	11.0	4.3	77.8
1994	4.4	7.3	36.4	41.5	6.9	3.5	79.0
1998	5.1	6.7	40.9	35.2	6.2	5.9	82.2
2002	4.0	8.6	38.5	38.5	7.4	3.0	79.1
2005	8.7	8.1	34.2	35.2	9.8	4.0	77.7
2009	11.9	10.7	23.0	33.8	14.6	6.0	70.8

Sources: www.bundestag.de; *Statistisches Bundesamt Deutschland* (2006).

Note
Party results are per cent of party list votes (*Zweitstimmen*). Turnout is per cent of those entitled to vote.

party system was structured by a socio-cultural dimension (Benoit and Laver 2006; Kitschelt 2003b). On this dimension the SPD was situated moderately on the 'libertarian' side (which is perceived as left-wing in Germany) and the CDU moderately on the 'authoritarian' (right-wing) side. The position of the FDP was split with respect to the two axes. The Liberals were associated with a 'left' position on the socio-cultural dimension and a right position on the socio-economic dimension. Consequently, up to the 1980s the FDP was generally regarded to be in the centre of the political space and it had the chance to enter a coalition with either of the two big parties. This German three-party system is illustrated in Figure 7.1.[4] The data for the figure refers to the beginning of the 1970s, but the basic structure of the party system hardly changed between 1961 and the beginning of the 1980s.

The main competition in this party system was between the SPD on the centre-left and the CDU on the centre-right. Hence, the two dominant parties competed over the centre of the political spectrum. Although both parties had their core constituencies (churchgoing Catholics and union-affiliated workers; see Weßels 2000), to a large extent the voters they tried to attract overlapped (Kirchheimer 1966). How did this affect the development of unemployment benefits? Right after the war social protection was generally at a modest level. As the economy started to grow, rising living standards also raised the expectations regarding public support in case of a loss of income (M.G. Schmidt 2005: 78–9). Accordingly, there was widespread demand for better social protection.

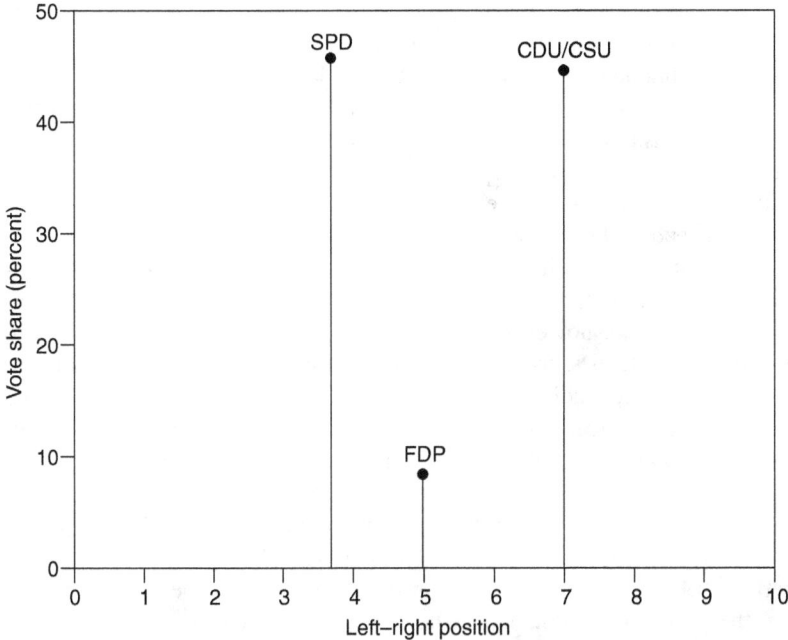

Figure 7.1 German party system in 1973 (sources: Rehm and Reilly (2010), www.bund-estag.de).

Note
Party positions are the average self-placement of each party's voters. Vote shares are from the national election in 1972.

The two big parties competed over who would best meet this demand and could claim credit for expanding the welfare state. The existence of only three parties and the focus on the political centre meant that each of the two large parties tried to make comprehensive proposals that appealed to broad sections of the elector-ate. For CDU and SPD, privileging narrowly defined groups was not an option for winning elections. Neither would it have been helpful to advocate radical policies – of the 'free market' or of the socialist kind – as this would have deterred the moderate voters in the centre. The CDU was better equipped for this competition as the broad social basis was part of its founding principles. However, the SPD learned only after three electoral defeats that it was bound to stay in opposition if it only focused on its electoral base among the workers (cf. Przeworski and Sprague 1986).

Two minor qualifications have to be added to this prevailing logic of centrip-etal competition. First, the expansion of social policy was to some extent con-strained by the presence of the FDP, and especially the CDU had to avoid losing market liberal voters to the FDP. The SPD, in turn, had to make compromises when it governed in coalition with the Liberals (1969–82). Second, to say that both dominant parties focused on the political centre does not mean that we cannot distinguish the policies pursued by either of them. The tendency of their policy proposals was strongly determined by the logic of competition, but the ideological starting point of each party could still be recognized.

We can also find the effect of this centripetal dynamic in the field of unemployment compensation. One of the first important post-war decisions in this field, however, was largely independent of party competition because it was made in the years of post-war emergency and under the occupation regime. Right after the end of the war, when the tensions between the Western Allies and the Soviet Union were still limited, the Allied Control Commission had contemplated introducing a unitary social insurance along the lines of the British Beveridge Plan. This idea, however, was met with scepticism and resistance from various domestic interests, 'ranging from private insurance companies, occupational groups and the traditional insurance funds to sections within the trade union movement who feared that a universal scheme would involve low benefit rates' (Clasen 1994: 62). With the aggravation of the conflict with the Soviet Union, the Western Allies lost interest in the plan and left the decision to domestic forces. In the field of unemployment compensation, this led in 1947 to the re-introduction of UI and UA on the basis of the 1927 legislation.

Apart from the mentioned pressure from interest groups, the decision to fall back on the previous legislation was influenced by the emergency situation of the post-war years. Those conditions did not leave room for an ambitious reform project such as integrating UI into a unitary social insurance and re-designing its features on the basis of more universal rather than employment-driven principles. For this reason, path dependency played a role here: the authorities re-established the inter-war legislation and institutions of unemployment compensation because they were the easiest solution at hand.

The re-introduction of the 1927 legislation was intended as a provisional measure. Of course, after the foundation of the Federal Republic of Germany, the existence of these policy schemes conditioned subsequent reform decisions. Nevertheless, the new situation left room for different paths of development. Above all, German governments could have failed to update and expand UI and UA and instead could have resorted to discretionary public work programmes and specific generous benefits for narrowly defined groups, as happened in Italy. As shown in Chapter 4, this did not take place. Rather, German parties promoted higher benefit levels of UI and UA, making them accessible to a wider range of workers. Hence, both schemes became part of a stratified but comprehensive system of unemployment benefits.

By the time that the foundations for this benefit system were laid in 1956, centripetal competition was well under way. In 1952, the SPD still championed a unification of benefit schemes. This position was gradually abandoned in favour of maintaining but expanding the existing schemes. In 1954 the Social Democrats set the governing coalition under pressure by submitting three legislative proposals that aimed at extending coverage and benefit levels of UI and assistance.[5] These proposals were closer to the position of the Christian

Democrats and, hence, suitable to attract CDU voters. The government reacted by putting forward its own proposal that went in a similar direction, i.e. maintaining both benefit tiers, but increasing their coverage and generosity. In the end, this bill was approved by all parties in parliament (Schmid *et al.* 2005: 289–92). The process illustrates not only the reciprocal rapprochement of policy positions but also how the CDU-led government reacted to competition by the SPD by accelerating the reform of unemployment benefits.

That competition between the two big parties and electoral considerations influenced social policy reforms in this period has been reported by many observers with respect to the important pension reform of 1957, but without drawing conclusions on the relevance of the party system structure. In that case the SPD again started from Beveridgean ideas of unified insurance, but in 1956 submitted a proposal for pension reform that was much closer to the ideas of the Christian Democrats. This put the CDU under pressure to act: shortly afterwards, the government submitted its own draft legislation that was in many respects similar to the SPD bill. Observers agree that Chancellor Konrad Adenauer endorsed this highly expansionary reform despite contestation by the CDU's coalition partner FDP and the market liberal wing of the CDU for three interrelated reasons: because elections were imminent, because it was suitable to attract voters who might also vote for the SPD, and because generally the reform was highly popular in the electorate. Indeed, the reform helped the Christian Democrats to win an absolute majority in the election of 1957 (M.G. Schmidt 2005: 79–83; Abelshauser 2004: 194–200; Hockerts 1980).

Schwarz (1981) reports, in fact, that in 1956 a so-called 'cake commission' was founded by the CDU, which devised a plan of how to spend the substantial surplus in the public budget. The objective was to take care of all groups that could be decisive at the polls: 'The procedure followed the principle of satisfying the party's own voters and, furthermore, to disburse election presents such that population strata as broad as possible could have a part' (ibid.: 325–6). This underlines the strategy of the government party to design comprehensive policies in order to appeal to many voters at once. In addition, Schwarz mentions the intention to attract support from low and middle income groups and the role of social policy to this end. The backdrop of financial surpluses also explains why the expansion of social protection had to face only little resistance. More generally speaking, economic growth, rising wages, and full employment made it seem unproblematic – to political parties and to voters – to introduce and expand generous programmes of unemployment compensation.

M.G. Schmidt (2005) has argued that after the 1957 pension reform the objectives of welfare state expansion changed. Social policy was no longer concerned with 'combating the most urgent needs' but with an 'extension and consolidation of social policy under the sign of the prosperity that had recently been achieved' (ibid.: 76). In political terms, this implied that the demands of the most important sections of the electorate and interest groups had been taken care of and that the two catch-all-parties now had the chance to promote reform projects that would broaden and consolidate their social consent. The small number of parties was important in this context: the need of large parties was to address broad sections of the electorate. Given the proportional logic of the German electoral system, by addressing more narrow interests small parties also had a chance to succeed – but the larger parties tried to absorb the electoral potential of these smaller parties.

The introduction of comprehensive SA in 1961 has to be seen in this light. In fact, the reform was adopted only several months before a parliamentary election. Commentators at the time interpreted the bill as one in a series of 'election presents'.[6] Social assistance took care of a very heterogeneous group of people that did not profit from the already established social insurance programmes. Among many other beneficiaries, it was particularly relevant for the constituency of the GB/BHE, a party representing those expelled from former German territories in the East. Many of the expellees had insufficient means to sustain themselves and, consequently, had to rely on public assistance, which was considerably improved by the SA reform. The GB/BHE was a coalition partner of the CDU from 1953 until its two ministers and some other parliamentarians became CDU members in 1956. In 1957 the party failed to re-enter parliament, but only by a close margin. Hence, for the 1961 election it still had some electoral potential, which it tried to bolster by fusing with another small conservative party. Yet, it lost the 1961 election and disappeared thereafter. Quite clearly, the CDU managed to absorb the electorate of the GB/BHE through the integration of some of the GB/BHE party leaders as well as through the introduction of SA, which provided valuable support to many expellees (cf. Wolfrum 2007: 60–1).

Due to full employment public support for the unemployed was a low political priority during the 1960s (Schmid and Oschmiansky 2008a). When, however, in 1967 a small but sharp recession briefly augmented unemployment this was immediately perceived as potentially undermining political legitimacy and the replacement rate of UI (about 44 per cent for average earners) was deemed inadequate. The Grand Coalition of CDU and SPD that had taken office in 1966 quickly approved an increase of UI and UA. The FDP did not contest the fact that benefit levels were raised but considered the rise as too steep. In its role as a right-wing competitor it strengthened the cause of the market liberal wing of the CDU who also favoured a more limited increase. Thus, the original proposal of the Christian Democratic Labour Minister of lifting the replacement rate by 20 percentage points was scaled down to 15 percentage points (Clasen 1994: 95–7).

A similar constraining role, even if modest, was played by the FDP when the Labour Promotion Act (AFG) was adopted in 1969. However, while this bill again made UI and assistance more generous, the main contested issue was how to finance the newly introduced active labour market programmes (from the contribution-based funds of the Employment Agency or from general revenue). Previously, the Grand Coalition had successfully introduced several important innovations in economic and social policy due to its numerical strength. Nevertheless, coalitional cohabitation was uneasy and also among voters the Grand Coalition was regarded from the beginning as somewhat anomalous because of the entrenched bipolar competition of the party system (Lehmbruch 2000: 43–4). Towards the end of the legislative period, tensions within the coalition increased and it was not expected to be renewed. Therefore, in the debate on the AFG, the imminent election reinforced the position of the market liberal CDU faction that worried about losing market liberal voters to the FDP. This contributed to the adoption of the preferred option of the market liberal wing, i.e. financing through contributions (Mätzke 2004: 30–6).

It would be expected that the following government coalition, between Social Democrats and Liberals (1969–82), found it impossible to reach agreements in the field of social policy due to the great political differences on these issues between the two parties. However, as long as favourable economic conditions prevailed, both found a *modus vivendi* that enabled the SPD to go ahead with extending social security, which in some cases benefited the constituencies of the Liberals (especially the self-employed). This compromise was made possible by a certain moderation of both sides. On the one hand, the SPD promoted an interventionist approach in economic and social matters, but did not set its sights on more severe redistribution. On the other hand, the FDP was more flexible with respect to social measures that supplemented the market. In addition, a partisan division of policy areas conceded relative autonomy to the Social Democrats in the field of social policy. Only some projects, such as an amplification of workers' participation in corporate governance, were vetoed by the FDP (M.G. Schmidt 2005: 91–2).

When in 1974 unemployment rose again as a consequence of the economic crisis, it became immediately a political issue. The number of unemployed people rose from a very low level, but it rose steeply. The government reacted with three measures: it introduced a benefit that secured for three months the wages of workers whose employers went bankrupt (*Konkursausfallgeld*); it raised again the benefit levels of UI and assistance; and it enhanced SA (Clasen 1994: 124–6). In order to ease people's worries and, at the same time, claim the credit for the recent expansions of unemployment compensation, the SPD printed more than a million copies of a leaflet that was distributed in front of office buildings and factories. The leaflet asked workers not to be anxious in the face of rising unemployment and reassured them that thanks to the recent reforms, adopted during SPD spells in government, 'the employee in the Federal Republic is better protected than most of his colleagues in other countries of the world'.[7] Hence, at the very beginning of the phase of austerity, when the continuation of tight economic conditions was not yet recognized, the SPD reacted the way both major parties had done in the recent decades when they were in government. They swiftly met social demands and claimed the credit for it in order to increase electoral consent. Not doing so would have left either party vulnerable to competing proposals from the respective other major party.

In sum, the expansion of unemployment benefits after the Second World War was clearly shaped by two factors: first, the fact that competition was dominated by two catch-all parties favoured the introduction of comprehensive benefit schemes. Second, the centripetal competition between these two parties, one on the centre-left and the other on the centre-right, facilitated programmatic competition for electoral support. At the very beginning, the provisional re-introduction of the benefit system in the early post-war years was still influenced by the emergency conditions and path dependency. However, the foundational reforms of UI and UA were driven by the need of the governing CDU to cover politically salient social demands that the Social Democratic opposition threatened to exploit for its own electoral purposes. The adoption of SA was less salient but helped to stabilize the electoral consent of the Christian Democrats. During the subsequent linear expansion of the benefit system the governing parties repeatedly reacted to rising public concern about unemployment by increasing benefit levels. Not to take care of these social concerns would have made either party vulnerable to the other party exploiting the issue. This expansionary path was only to a limited degree constrained by the Liberal Party.

Italy: centrifugal competition and benefit disparity

In Italy domestic politics and the party system took a very different direction compared to Germany after the Second World War.[8] This difference resulted largely from the strength of the Communist Party. In contrast to Germany, the ideological conflict between capitalism and communism was not externalized but ran through domestic politics. In 1943 the fascist government of Benito Mussolini fell. As German military occupied Northern Italy various political groups organized partisan resistance. At the national level this resistance was coordinated by the Committee of National Liberation, which comprised all major anti-fascist parties: the Communists (PCI), the Socialists (PSI, at the time called PSIUP), the Actionists (a small party of the left that played a relevant role in the resistance, but lacked a mass following), and the Catholic party (*Democrazia Cristiana*, DC). The Committee of National Liberation focused explicitly on combating the external enemy and intended to postpone decisions on the new institutional order of the state to the period after victory. Therefore, very different political forces, from Communists to Catholics and Liberals, were united by the common enemy.

The anti-fascist alliance formed the government from 1944 to 1947. However, from the moment of military victory in 1945 the first cracks started to show. Just like the Allies at the international level, the anti-fascist political forces in Italy could no longer contain the ideological confrontation between capitalism and communism once their common enemy was defeated. Moreover, international politics intervened in domestic politics. In particular, the US supported the pro-capitalist and pro-Western parties, especially the DC, while the Soviet Union backed the PCI.

The fact that the DC cooperated with the Communists during the first post-war years was increasingly criticized by the US and the Catholic Church. Moreover, it lost electoral support to the parties on its right – the *Partito Liberale Italiano* (PLI) and the populist *Uomo Qualunque* – because of this cooperation. Nevertheless, the DC hesitated to break the coalition with the left. Due to the

dire social and economic situation, social unrest was widespread. In spite of dis-
armament, many partisans had retained their weapons. Under these conditions,
the DC worried that ending the alliance with the left could trigger a civil war.
Conversely, the PCI under its leader Palmiro Togliatti shied away from attempt-
ing a revolution even though this was certainly what many of its supporters
expected. One of the major reasons for Togliatti's reluctance was the military
presence of the Western Allies.

In 1947, DC Prime Minister De Gasperi eventually excluded the left from
government.[9] Obviously this increased tensions in the Constituent Assembly,
which had been elected in 1946. Due to the ideological confrontation, the compromise on the constitution was in parts ambiguous. Its interpretation and implementation depended largely on the political forces that would come to power
(Bull and Newell 2005: Ch. 1; Guarnieri 2006: Ch. 2). This intensified political
competition, as did the fact that the electoral outcome of the first regular parliamentary election in 1948 was far from clear beforehand. The left parties were
optimistic to have the majority of the popular vote on their side (Ginsborg 1990:
Ch. 3). In the election to the Constituent Assembly in 1946 PCI and PSI had
obtained together 39.7 per cent of the vote (see Table 7.2). For the 1948 election
they joined forces in the Democratic Popular Front. However, parts of the PSI
disagreed with the radical stance that the alliance with the Communists implied.
Consequently, they broke away and formed the Italian Social Democratic Party
(PSDI). This centre-left competitor imposed losses on the Popular Front and in
particular on the PSI. In the end, the Popular Front obtained only 31 per cent of
the votes, while the DC achieved with 48.5 per cent its best result of the whole
post-war period.

After 1948 the Italian party system slowly consolidated. On the extreme right,
the neo-fascist Italian Social Movement (MSI) had emerged from the ashes of
the Italian Social Republic (the Mussolini regime in Northern Italy during
German occupation). Electoral support for the MSI was reinforced when the
populist *Uomo Qualunque* disappeared soon after the 1948 elections. Many
years later, in 1972, the Monarchist party joined the MSI, which at that point
reached its highest election result (8.7 per cent of the votes). On the extreme left,
the Popular Front was dissolved as a consequence of the 1948 defeat. The dominant party on the left and second largest party overall was the PCI. In the following election, 1953, it received 22.6 per cent of the votes. Thereafter its electoral
support rose continuously until 1976. The PSI at first maintained an informal
alliance with the PCI, which is why the united left opposition of the time was
sometimes called 'social-communist'. Only after the Soviet repression of the
Hungarian uprising in 1956, the PSI distanced itself from the Communists,
moved slowly towards the centre-left, and opened to the possibility of cooperating with the DC.

The DC was the largest party overall and the dominant party in the centre of
the political space. In varying combinations it formed governing coalitions with
the smaller moderate parties: on the centre-left with the PSDI and the republican
PRI as well as on the centre-right with the PLI. However, these governing

Table 7.2 Italian parliamentary election results, 1946–76

	PCI	FDP/PSIUP	PSI	PSDI	PRI	DC	PLI	UQ	Mon	MSI	Others	Turnout
1946	19.0		20.7	1.5	4.4	35.2	6.8	5.3	2.8		4.5	89.1
1948		31.0		7.1	2.5	48.5	3.8		2.8	2.0	2.4	92.2
1953	22.6		12.7	4.5	1.6	40.1	3.0		6.9	5.8	2.7	93.8
1958	22.7		14.2	4.6	1.4	42.4	3.5		4.9	4.8	1.6	93.8
1963	25.2		13.8	6.1	1.4	38.3	7.0		1.8	5.1	1.3	92.9
1968	26.9	4.5	14.5		2.0	39.1	5.8		1.3	4.5	1.5	92.8
1972	27.2	1.9	9.6	5.1	2.9	38.7	3.9			8.7	2.1	93.2
1976	34.4		9.6	3.4	3.1	38.7	1.3			6.1	3.4	93.4

Source: Ministero Dell'Interno.

Notes
Party results are per cent of party list votes for the Lower House (*Camera dei Deputati*; 1946: Constituent Assembly). Turnout is per cent of those entitled to vote. 'Mon' stands for Monarchists.
1946: PSDI column reports result of *Partito d'Azione*, PSI under the name PSIUP, PLI under the name *Unione Democratica Nazionale*, Monarchists (Mon) under the name *Blocco Nazionale della Libertà*.
1948: UQ and PLI present a joint list called *Blocco Nazionale*, FDP/PSIUP column reports result of FDP (electoral coalition of PCI and PSI), PSDI under the name *Unità Socialista*, Monarchists under the name *Partito Nazionale Monarchico*.
1958: result for Monarchists is sum of two party lists.
1968: PSI and PSDI present the joint list PSU, FDP/PSIUP column reports result of PSIUP (same in 1972).
1976: others include DP 1.52 per cent and PR 1.07 per cent.

coalitions were notoriously unstable: first, because the centre parties competed between themselves in order to retain distinct party profiles; second, because the overall parliamentary majority of the centre block declined over time so that the DC had to look for support beyond the centre: first, in 1960 on the right with the MSI, thereafter, on the left with the PSI (Bull and Newell 2005: Ch. 3; Cotta and Verzichelli 2007: Ch. 2; Guarnieri 2006: Ch. 2; Hine 1993: Ch. 3).

All in all, after the first years of consolidation, the Italian party system consisted of seven parties: four that participated in government coalitions (DC, PSDI, PRI, PLI), two anti-system parties (PCI, MSI), and one that changed over time from anti-system to government party (PSI). Through the presence of anti-system parties, the system was ideologically polarized. Therefore, it was a case of polarized pluralism (Giovanni Sartori 1982; 2005: 116–54). Some authors have objected to the categorization of the PCI as 'anti-system' by pointing out that this party collaborated in parliament and that the majority of new legislation has been adopted with the consent of the Communists. However, as stressed by Sartori, anti-system parties are not necessarily outside of the system. What makes them 'anti-system' is that they openly reject basic principles of the existing system and, consequently, undermine its legitimacy. Precisely for this reason, it is important to distinguish between a party's inner-institutional collaboration, which does not change its anti-system character, and the party's stance in the public arena (Sartori 2005: 117–18; 1982: 221–6).

Characteristic of the Italian party system was, furthermore, the occupation of the centre. The DC (to a lesser extent also its smaller coalition partners) was situated squarely in the middle of political space. In fact, the existence of anti-system parties on the left and the right to some degree forced the DC into this role of the system-preserving party. Accordingly, the party system had a tripolar structure in terms of party weights: the DC in the centre, next the PCI on the radical left, and the MSI on the radical right. The MSI was smaller but can still be recognized as a distinct pole. This is illustrated in Figure 7.2.[10] It also shows nicely the location of the PSI in the middle between PCI and DC and the positioning from left to right of the three small centrist parties (PSDI, PRI, PLI). The tripolar structure of the party system created a centrifugal mode of competition. Party competition could not focus on the centre of the political space as in Germany and many other party systems because the centre was occupied by a major party. Rather, the centre party faced on both sides competition from anti-system parties that did not move themselves towards centre.

'Social-communist' opposition and the neglect of unemployment benefits

From the expulsion of the left from government up until 1960 the DC governed the country in coalition with the small centrist parties (hence, this period is called *Centrismo*). The DC had won a comfortable majority in 1948, but as early as 1951 and 1952, local elections showed that it was losing electoral support (Ginsborg 1990: 141–2). Accordingly, party competition was acute. As shown in

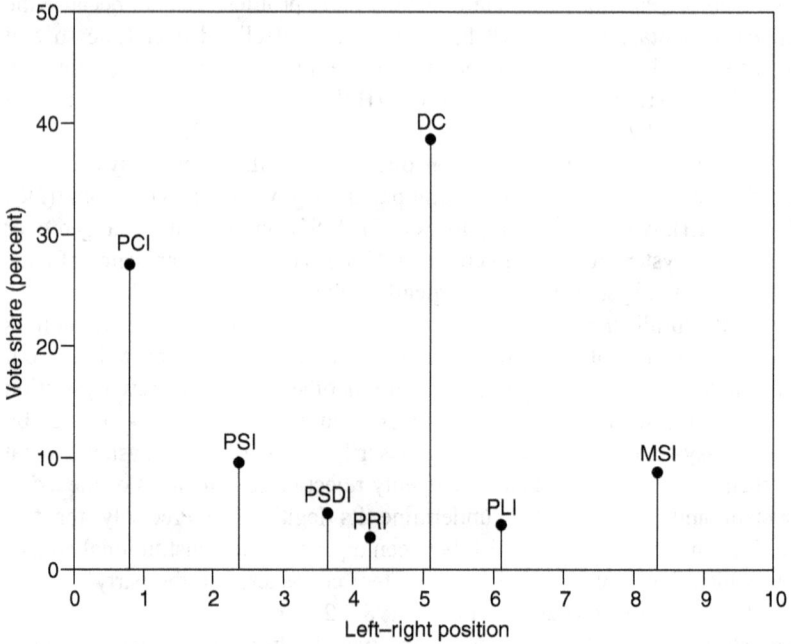

Figure 7.2 Italian party system in 1973 (sources: Rehm & Reilly (2010), *Ministero Dell'Interno*).

Note
Party positions are the average self-placement of each party's voters. Vote shares are from the national election in 1972.

Chapter 4, unemployment benefits did not play a major role in government policy during this early period despite the post-war economic crisis and high levels of unemployment. The only major reform was the extension of UI to the agricultural sector. For the rest, government focused on public work programmes, labour market administration, and agrarian reform.

This approach to labour market policy was strongly influenced by the radical opposition from PCI and PSI. The left approached the problem of unemployment not so much in terms of providing financial help to the unemployed but focused on combating unemployment altogether by creating employment. Hence, in its manifesto for the election to the Constituent Assembly in 1946, the principal demand of the PCI in the field of social and economic policies was to confront unemployment and the economic crisis by setting up 'a very vast [*vastissimo*] programme of public works in the cities and on the countryside and, above all, the systematic reconstruction of houses'.[11] Moreover, the party demanded a reform of the agrarian sector to 'make chronic unemployment disappear' (ibid.). To be sure, the same manifesto also called for 'the introduction of an effective unemployment subsidy' (ibid.). However, this shows up only as a secondary point in a list of proposals on salaries and social protection. The emphasis on eradicating unemployment is also confirmed by successive party programmes of the radical left. Thus, in 1953 when it was still closely allied to the PCI, the PSI stated in its manifesto:

> In the economic-social field the socialist alternative starts from the premise that it is necessary and possible to provide work to every Italian, a sufficient remuneration to every worker, an adequate assistance to children and to the old, to the disabled and to the mutilated.
>
> (*Il PSI agli elettori* 1953)[12]

The quotation makes explicit that an economy without unemployment was a crucial objective for the radical left. Moreover, it is significant that the unemployed are not mentioned among the main target groups for social protection – despite the fact that unemployment was still a widespread problem at the beginning of the 1950s. It is also clear why unemployment benefits were not an attractive option from the point of view of the radical left. After all, the idea of unemployment benefits implied the acceptance of the idea that having work depends on employers who are free to recruit and dismiss workers.

This approach of the left to the unemployment crisis in the early years of the Republic can also be seen from the Employment Plan (*Piano del Lavoro*) launched in 1949 by the biggest trade union federation, *Confederazione Generale Italiana del Lavoro* (CGIL), which was closely associated to PCI and PSI. With this plan the union demanded from government to embark on a huge spending programme in three areas: electric power supply, land reclamation for agriculture, and housing. This was intended to create 600,000–700,000 new jobs. The CGIL pursued this campaign for the next two and a half years. The DC-led government rejected the plan. However, it is clear that in a situation in which more than two million people were registered as unemployed, the DC had to react to the public proposals of the opposition (Ginsborg 1990: 187–90). More to the point, it had to react in similar terms, that is, by creating work and not by offering subsidies to the unemployed.

Consequently, the governmental response consisted mainly of public work programmes and agrarian reform. Mariuccia Salvati (1982: 401–2) reports how the DC-led executive prepared the legislative proposal for the public work programmes while unions were out on the streets against unemployment. The government felt under pressure to make progress on the issue. In a note to the Prime Minister, the Minister of Labour rejected explicitly the option to simply pay transfers to the unemployed. Rather, cash benefits should be connected to public work programmes and get as close as possible to being a salary (ibid.: 401; see also Ferrera *et al.* forthcoming: Ch. 3).

Ideological polarization generated an intense struggle over the control of institutions. In the first place, DC and CGIL engaged in a bitter struggle over the administration of job placements, which had been largely in the hands of trade unions. Now, as the biggest union was affiliated with the PCI and PSI, the DC tried to exclude unions from this important task. The matter was tackled in the same law that also reformed UI and overshadowed the question of unemployment benefits (Musso 2004: Ch. 10; Ferrera *et al.* forthcoming: Ch. 3). While the DC strove to keep the left out of important administrative positions, it extended its own control over state institutions and resources. It then used many of these resources in order to secure electoral support. The same pattern applies to the public work programmes that were administered at discretion of the Ministry of Labour (Ginsborg 1990: 162; Ferrera *et al.* forthcoming: Ch. 3). Furthermore the UI scheme in the agricultural sector soon became a currency of clientelism (Ferrera 1984: 207–10).

The DC used particularistic means to secure electoral support because, in the context of ideological confrontation, a programmatic competition between parties was not possible. The DC was constrained in making policy concessions because it faced radical opposition parties on both sides. When it intensified efforts to move in one of the two directions it risked triggering a violent response from the other side. Either it could lead to militant demonstrations by left-wing workers (e.g. the reaction to a DC government in 1960 whose parliamentary majority included the MSI) or it could lead to an authoritarian coup (e.g. the 'Solo plan' of a coup one year after the first centre-left government took office, or the attempted 'Borghese coup' in 1970 following labour mobilizations and government concessions). However, the anti-system parties had little motivation to moderate their standpoint. Their social basis and electoral strength was built around an anti-system ideology, and being excluded from government they could advance far-reaching policy proposals without having to implement them (Sartori 1982). Hence, the popular demand by the PCI and its allies to abolish unemployment rather than subsidizing it led to the two-pronged response by the DC: to assimilate the left-wing demands, and to use the corresponding measures as well as other institutional resources in order to secure electoral consent by particularistic means.

A divided left and lopsided expansion

As mentioned, the PSI had maintained an informal alliance with the PCI after the defeat of the Popular Front in 1948. However, in this role the Socialists were perceived as subordinate to the PCI and lacked an independent profile. Therefore, starting from 1956 they tried to occupy consciously the political space between PCI and the social democratic PSDI. This was also motivated by the hope to gain some control over state policies. The DC, on the other hand, was in need of a new coalition partner. In the elections of 1953 and 1958 the centrist parties had received only around 50 per cent of the vote, which the highly proportional electoral system translated into minuscule parliamentary majorities. Moreover, the DC hoped that a coalition with the PSI would isolate and weaken the PCI. From these motivations, the first government coalition including the PSI was born in 1963. Apart from some fluctuations and a break in 1972–3, this centre-left coalition prevailed until 1976 (Tamburrano 1990).

By the beginning of the 1960s, the two biggest parties, DC and PCI, had entrenched the relations with their respective electorates. On the one hand, this was based on organizational and cultural ties that in some areas had the character of partisan ('red' or 'white') subcultures. On the other hand, these ties were often based on material advantages that were offered to narrow electoral groups or individual voters in return for their support. Patronage and clientelism were used especially by the DC due to its superior access to state resources. To a lesser extent, the PCI used material benefits to motivate its voters, e.g. through local government or through union influence. By contrast, party-electorate linkages based on programmatic competition played only a subordinate role (Parisi and Pasquino 1977). Again, this entrenchment of party-electorate linkages was a consequence of a party system where competition by programmatic policy proposals was blocked due to ideological polarization. Of course, some voter movements did occur, but these often depended on outbidding by material incentives or on the attractiveness of ideological-cultural claims as well.

The PSI was caught in the middle between the two major parties (see Figure 7.2). It had its own institutionally rooted social base but risked to alienate many of its traditional left-wing voters by cooperating with the 'class enemy'. Accordingly, the left wing of the PSI disagreed with the party's entrance into a government coalition with the DC. In 1964, this wing broke away and formed the *Partito Socialista Italiano di Unità Proletaria* (PSIUP), which competed for election on the left of the PSI in the next two electoral rounds. The breakaway of the PSIUP also weakened the PSI's links to the CGIL as most of the Socialist union leaders joined the left-wing splinter party. Conversely, in 1966 the PSI attempted a reunification with the PSDI, which was facilitated by the party's move to the centre-left and the common experience in government. The reunified party stood for the 1968 election under the name *Partito Socialista Unitario* (PSU) but clearly lost support, receiving 5.4 percentage points less than the sum of votes for both parties in the previous election.

Hence, the reunification with the PSDI was revoked only two year later, but the PSI remained weakened, receiving only 9.6 per cent of the votes in the following two elections as opposed to 13.8 per cent that it had received in the election of 1963. It was mainly the PCI that profited from the weakness of the PSI. It continuously increased its vote share and reached an all-time high of 34.4 per cent in the election of 1976. On the other side of the political spectrum, the DC lost votes on the right because of its coalition with the PSI. Thus, especially PLI, but also MSI gained in the 1963 election (the formation of the centre-left coalition was already clear before that election, see Tamburrano 1990). In the following elections, however, the DC managed to maintain its electoral consent (see Table 7.2).

As shown in Chapter 4, the period of the centre-left coalition and the subsequent shorter phase of National Solidarity saw a massive increase of unemployment protection for workers in big industrial firms, most significantly through the introduction of the CIGS and its subsequent expansion. At the same time, UI, the only unemployment benefit that was open to the majority of the workforce, remained at a very low level and no minimum income scheme was introduced.

In principle, the centre-left coalition agreed on extending state intervention in the economy and DC and PSI were, for political reasons, inclined to expand social policy based on universal principles:

> [Welfare universalism] could be presented to the voters as a 'structural reform' of both progressive *and* Western character that would satisfy the demands of the labour movement for renewal and would at the same time reassure the capitalist establishment.
>
> (Ferrera 1993: 264, emphasis in the original)

In other words, reform projects, such as significantly expanding UI, would have had sufficient 'redistributive' appeal to the left-wing voters of PSI and would not have conflicted seriously with the centrist DC voters. Rather, for the centrist perspective of defending liberal democracy and capitalism this policy strategy promised to integrate workers and voters on the left into the system. However, just on these grounds the project was strictly rejected by the PCI. Instead, the PCI fought for benefits that were defined on a class basis. This would bring material benefits to its supporters and, at the same time, ensure that they remain in a distinct organizational realm that was dominated by the PCI and its affiliated organizations. The CIGS conformed to this conception. The scheme was limited to the core labour class (workers in big industrial firms) and unions had an important role in activating payments. In this way, the CGIL could work as an organizational link between the PCI and workers benefitting from CGIS.

However, the 'workerist' approach of the PCI was only one aspect that motivated its support for CIG. In addition, the CIG was a complementary policy to strong dismissal protection, which was a primary goal for the left. Remember that the CIG was effectively turned into an unemployment benefit but officially its recipients remain employed. Hence, by supporting this benefit programme the policy position of the PCI did not change from demanding employment to demanding financial support for the unemployed, but it shifted from employment creation to employment protection. In fact, dismissal protection was pressed for successfully by the PCI and, more generally, the worker movement in the same period in which CIG was expanded.

The very flexible and generous *Cassa Integrazione* gave firms the possibility to survive economic crises or to conduct internal restructuring without laying off workers. Therefore, once that dismissal protection was pushed through by the left, the firms subjected to this regulation developed an interest in CIG themselves because it provided them with a degree of numerical labour force flexibility at collective costs. For this reason, up to today, CIG is appreciated and supported by the employers who can make use of it. Regarding the left, by contrast, support for the *Cassa Integrazione* is strictly related to the left's policy objective of employment protection. In this sense, the CIG can be seen as the market-obstructing alternative to market-making UI (Kreile 1985: Ch. 6).

The policy emphasis on employment protection reflected that the period of the centre-left had a completely different institutional and economic background than the 1950s. Economic and political institutions were consolidated and Italy had experienced rapid economic growth and socio-structural change. Indeed, in 1963 unemployment reached its all-time low (3.9 per cent) and the Italian labour market came as close to full employment as it would ever get. In addition, in 1951 agriculture had still been the most important sector, compared to industry and services, comprising 40 per cent of the labour force. Only ten years later, this leading role was occupied by industry (39.4 per cent of labour force) and even services had started to overtake agriculture (29.5 per cent, Flora *et al.* 1987: 551). Therefore, politics had to respond to a totally different socio-economic situation. The main political task for the PCI was not to combat mass unemployment in a strongly agrarian economy but to promote and secure the social and economic standards of a prevalently industrial working class.

In fact, the industrial working class started a long wave of mobilizations in the early 1960s. It began in 1962 with the renewal of the national contract of the metalworkers that was accompanied by strikes and violent clashes, particularly in Turin. It subsequently reached its peak in the years 1968–73 with widespread wildcat strikes and political mobilization in the factories (in particular the so-called 'Hot Autumn' in 1969). The wave of mobilizations came to a symbolic end when in 1980 40,000 people, including many FIAT employees and workers, demonstrated in Turin *against* a strike that had blocked the FIAT factories (Ginsborg 1990: Ch. 9; Musso 2002: 229–44). This wave of mobilizations coincided with the lopsided expansion of unemployment benefits and other reforms in favour of industrial workers. However, a traditional left power argument is insufficient to explain these reforms. After all, the left was not in power. The only left-wing party that participated in government, the PSI, was relatively small and much less connected to the mobilizations than the PCI.

Moreover, even the PCI did not directly represent the protesting workers. On the contrary, the outburst of these mobilizations in 1968 and 1969 was rather the expression of a lack of political representation. The protests were led by factory committees and small political groups. They explicitly criticized the major union confederations as well as the PCI for being too moderate. The established trade unions soon adapted to the outbreak of activism and managed to get on top of it. However, in this process the unions liberated themselves from their close partnership with parties. Hence, also the PCI lost some of its close connection with the CGIL. Furthermore, small revolutionary groups had popped up that aspired to politically organize social unrest and to replace the PCI as the leading left-wing organization. Although these aspirations were out of proportion in terms of real organizational strength they proved, in addition to the radicalization of the CGIL, that the PCI risked being outflanked on the left. In short, rather than being the natural representative of working class demands, the PCI had to struggle in order to respond to these demands after first having failed to do so.

I argue that two mechanisms helped to translate the strength of the radical left into policy output. Both are related to polarized competition but one worked at the electoral level, the other at parliamentary level. First, the PSI was continuously losing votes to the PCI in this period. Consequently, it had to adjust to the demands of the radical left in order to contain this haemorrhage of electoral support. To counter the rising strength of the PCI was, of course, also in the interest of the DC because the PCI was still seen as a threat to the system. Therefore, the government coalition had incentives to accommodate the demands from radical workers and PCI. On the other hand the PCI, if anything, had to radicalize its position in order to maintain its electoral support from the worker movement. The DC's worries about the strength of the PCI culminated in a dramatic election campaign in 1976 when it seemed possible that the PCI would take over the DC's place as strongest party in parliament. In the end, the so-called *sorpasso* (overtaking) by the Communists failed. However, in the following legislative period they entered the National Solidarity pact with the DC and, hence, gained a more direct influence on government policy. So, if one of the DC's motivations for forming the centre-left coalition in the first place, was to divide the left and weaken the PCI, it tragically failed. The centre-left coalition did divide the left but to the benefit of the PCI and to the detriment of the DC's coalition partner PSI (Tamburrano 1990: 203–20).[13]

A second mechanism that enabled the PCI to push through its policy objectives was its influence on the decision-making processes in parliament. Although the public positions of parties were at loggerheads, in parliament and away from public attention the PCI cooperated. In fact, most legislative provisions either explicitly or tacitly obtained the approval of the PCI (Cazzola 1972). This collaboration was partly a consequence of the veto points in the parliamentary process that the Communists could exploit (Pasquino 2002) and partly it resulted from the necessity to maintain elite-level collaboration in an otherwise polarized system (Bartolini 1999; 2000). This collaboration was kept in the realm that Sartori called 'invisible politics' – invisible to some extent because it is escapes public attention, and to some extent because it is actively hidden. It does not contradict the polarized competition between parties that is part of 'visible politics' (Sartori 1982: 199–210). All parties put forth their own specific interests in this elite-level bargaining. Lacking the possibility to adopt comprehensive reforms, this bargaining led to small-scale adjustments that were often targeted on particular social groups (Cotta 1996). It explains the impressive fragmentation of the Italian system of unemployment benefits along occupational distinctions.

Recapitulating these years of welfare expansion with respect to the politics of unemployment benefits, first, unemployment benefits remained underdeveloped because PCI and PSI called for creating employment rather than paying transfers to the unemployed. Then, generous unemployment benefits were introduced, but only for industrial workers because the PCI promoted policies that were defined on a class basis and matched the emphasis on securing employment. In both cases, the government parties (first, mainly DC; later, DC and PSI) were forced to adjust to the demands of the PCI. The electoral strength of the PCI was rooted in its radical social base that, if anything, threatened to defect more to left. As the PCI was continuously gaining votes, the DC, and later the PSI, were forced to react to this trend.

In a nutshell, we might say that the strength of the radical left prevented the introduction of a comprehensive unemployment compensation. This conclusion is at odds with traditional partisan theory, which associates the strength of the left with universal social protection. However, two points have to be underlined. First, it was the *radical* left with a communist party as its main actor that had this influence on policy development. This has to be clearly distinguished from social democratic parties. Too often partisan approaches to explaining policy-making refer generically to 'the Left'. Second, the conclusion above is only partly correct. The strength of the radical left by itself has no linear relation to the segmentation of unemployment benefits. Rather, it is important to consider its role within the party system. In the Italian case the Communist Party was strong enough to induce a centrifugal dynamic of competition, but it was too weak to come to power. Ultimately, the highly fragmented benefit system with wide generosity differences corresponded neither to the Communist nor to the Christian democratic (nor probably to anyone else's) policy ideal. It was the result of a blocked party system where particular actors could push through their interests in small-scale policy changes but no compromise on a more general reform could be found. This contrasts to the German party system where only three parties and, in particular, two moderate catch-all parties competed over satisfying the social needs of the core sections of society, thus establishing comprehensive benefits without extreme generosity differences.

8   Germany
Two political logics of segmenting reforms

The previous chapter has analysed how different dynamics of party competition have driven the emergence of very diverse systems of unemployment compensation in Italy and Germany. Putting it simply, centripetal competition in Germany has contributed to the rise of a benefit system with a low degree of segmentation, while centrifugal competition in Italy has brought about a strongly segmented system of unemployment compensation. When the economic conditions changed in the middle of the 1970s, the role of party competition in social policy-making also changed. After all, the political task was not to 'hand out' any more public benefits to the electorate, but to restrict and redesign existing entitlements. The new policy changes were no longer something that political parties wanted to claim the credit for but something they wanted to avoid being blamed for (Pierson 1996).

For our comparative purposes, it is convenient that in the first 10–20 years of this phase of austerity the party systems in both countries remained basically the same as during the phase of expansion. This allows us to study the effect of the same logic of competition under different economic conditions. Later on in this phase of austerity, the dynamics of party competition changed in both countries. In Italy, the party system changed entirely in the early 1990s. In the new party system two pre-electoral coalitions competed against each other. This created centripetal competition between the coalitions, but competition between parties within those coalitions continued to show centrifugal tendencies. In Germany, the change of party competition was more moderate. It was triggered by a limited electoral demand shift in favour of more liberal socio-economic reforms. This demand shift led to moderately more centrifugal competition in two stages. First, competition shifted to the right due to the lack of a left-wing counterweight in the party system. This, however, led to an exacerbated policy reaction with respect to the only limited shift in policy demand, thus enabling the rise of a relevant left-wing competitor left of the Social Democrats. Certainly, these were moderately centrifugal tendencies while German party competition remained prevailingly centripetal.

In Chapter 5 we observed how efforts to reform unemployment benefits were more limited in the beginning and became more decisive only during the 1990s (Italy) and early 2000s (Germany). In the present and following chapter, I argue that these changes in pace, but also in the content of reforms, are related to the transformations of party competition that both countries experienced. This chapter analyses the German case and the next chapter the Italian case. For each country the respective chapter contains two sub-sections: the first examines the effect that the old party systems had on unemployment benefit reforms after the economic conditions had changed; the second analyses how the changing configurations of party competition have altered the reform paths while the economic conditions remained similarly restrictive.

In Chapter 7 we saw that in Germany competition between two catch-all-parties, on the centre-left and centre-right of the political spectrum, created incentives to pursue comprehensive unemployment benefits that appealed to large groups of voters. At the same time, policies were stratified: the core labour market groups (blue- and white-collar employees with standard contracts) were covered by a more generous scheme (UI) and gained first from expansions. However, this stratification was gradually reduced as benefit access for marginal labour market groups was improved and the less generous benefit schemes were enhanced over time. Under economic conditions that no longer allowed the distribution of goods but necessitated restrictions, this policy trajectory of decreasing segmentation was reversed. Centripetal competition had the effect that retrenchment started with the more marginal groups and remained more limited with respect to the core labour market groups. Hence, segmentation increased.

Later, the emerging centrifugal tendencies in German party competition in the 2000s again had the effect of increasing benefit segmentation, but in a different way. First, centrifugal competition towards the right encouraged a more fundamental reform. For the first time, this reform also affected the core labour market groups more clearly. Yet, the thrust of the reform was a dualization of the benefit system with a comprehensive but basic benefit for those excluded from UI. When centrifugal competition extended to the left, this did not lead to an improvement of the basic scheme but to repealing some of the cuts that affected the core workers, thus, again augmenting segmentation.

Incremental retrenchments: centripetal competition and welfare consensus

After 1975, during the first years of welfare state restructuring, the stable three-party system with centripetal competition, as described in Chapter 7, persisted for some years more. However, starting from the early 1980s, this party system was gradually pluralized. In 1980, the Green Party (*Die Grünen*) participated for the first time in a national parliamentary election but failed to pass the 5 per cent threshold. They managed to enter parliament on their second try in 1983. Partly as a consequence of the rise of the Green Party, but also due to more general socio-structural change, the two big parties gradually lost electoral ground over the 1980s. During the 1970s, the three established parties (SPD, CDU, FDP) had reached an extraordinary degree of electoral mobilization. In the elections of 1972 and 1976, turnout was at an all-time high of 91 per cent and the three parties taken together obtained 99 per cent of the votes (see Table 7.1). This level of mobilization was not maintained. After its landslide victory in 1983, the CDU saw its vote shares declining and since 1972 the SPD have continued loosing votes. In addition, electoral turnout went down and the vote share of non-parliamentary ('other') parties slowly started to increase in the middle of the 1980s. Therefore, the two big parties increasingly came under electoral pressure.

The Green Party was politically located on the left of the established parties. However, its presence did not have a significant effect on competition around welfare state or labour market issues because it mobilized mostly on 'post-materialist' topics such as environmental protection, civil rights, and pacifism. In the expert survey on party competition conducted by Laver and Hunt (1992) in 1990 experts were asked to rate the importance of various dimensions of competition for each party. The dimension that comes closest to welfare state issues concerns the political choice between either increasing public services or cutting taxes. Experts at the time assessed that the only party for which this dimension was relatively unimportant were the Greens. For the Greens, the importance of this dimension was below the average importance of all eight dimensions taken together. On the other hand, for German party competition as a whole, the issue 'more public services versus less taxes' proved to be very salient. When taking the mean across all parties, weighted by the vote share of each party, this was the third most important dimension (after environmental policy and social liberalism).

Figure 8.1 illustrates the German party system along the socio-economic political dimension at the end of the 1980s. Party positions are based on the mentioned dimension 'more services versus less taxes' in the Laver and Hunt (1992) survey, conducted in 1990. The strength of each party is indicated by its vote share in the 1987 federal election. Since the Greens do not play a relevant role in competition around welfare issues, they are omitted from the graph. We can see how the two dominant parties are placed neatly on the centre-left and centre-right of the political spectrum. The greater electoral strength of the CDU and the presence of the FDP just to the right of the CDU may add a certain bias to the right. But, overall, competition in this party system is clearly over the centre of the political space.

On the demand side, during the 1980s there was a continuously strong consensus in favour of maintaining social protection. This can be seen from responses to the German General Social Survey (ALLBUS, see Table 8.1).[1] Thus, in 1984, 64 per cent of the population wanted to sustain current levels of social protection and 26 per cent were in favour of expanding it. This adds up to an imposing majority of 90 per cent welfare state defenders. Moreover, in the same year, 91 per cent agreed either somewhat or fully with the statement that the state must ensure that people have a decent living in situations of need such as unemployment. Conversely, 29 per cent fully disagreed and 36 per cent somewhat disagreed with the statement that generous social benefits (including unemployment benefits) reduce the willingness to work.

The sheer size of the group of voters who support current welfare state structures made it indispensable for the two big contending parties. Moreover, this is

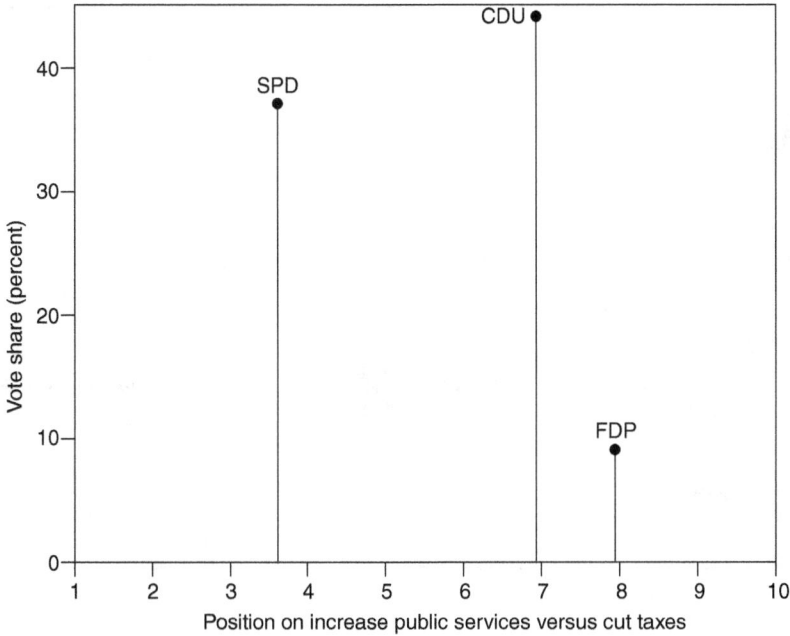

Figure 8.1 German party system on economic left–right dimension at the end of the
1980s (sources: Laver and Hunt (1992), www.bundestag.de).

Notes
Party positions are from the Laver and Hunt (1992) expert survey conducted in 1990 (originally, on a
1–20 scale). Vote shares are the election results of 1987. The Greens are excluded from the graph
because they do not compete on this political dimension.

the most important group in the centre of the political space. This is shown by
Table 8.2, which reports the proportion of social policy preferences differentiated
by the various sections of the political space (on a general left–right dimension),
on which respondents could place themselves.[2] In addition, the table shows the
distribution of left–right self-placements as such. Evidently, the concentration of
voters in the centre of the left–right dimension reinforces the importance of the
centre for party competition in addition to the spatial effect of bipolar competition.
In just these central sections of the political space (sections 5 and 6 on the 1–10
scale) the prevailing opinion was that current levels of social provision should be
maintained. The second-biggest preference was in favour of welfare state expansion. Therefore, a party that proposed to cut back social protection risked losing
voters in the centre of the political space. An important topic such as this could
easily make the difference between winning and losing an election for SPD and
CDU. The FDP, however, competed on the right of the CDU and, being a small
party, could target more limited groups of voters. Accordingly, it could try to
attract the voters in favour of reducing social provisions that were most numerous
(even if not the majority) towards the right end of the political spectrum.

Table 8.1 Social policy preferences in German public opinion, 1984–2004

	1984 (%)	1991 (%)	1994 (%)	2000 (%)	2004 (%)
Should social provisions (*Sozialleistungen*) be reduced, sustained, or expanded?					
reduce	10.3	n/a	9.8	20.2	23.2
sustain	64.0	n/a	53.4	53.7	55.1
expand	25.7	n/a	36.7	26.1	21.7
The State must ensure that people have a decent living even if they are sick, destitute, unemployed, or old.					
fully agree	55.8	56.7	52.4	42.5	43.5
somewhat agree	35.1	35.5	36.6	44.1	41.0
somewhat disagree	7.2	6.5	9.0	11.6	13.7
fully disagree	1.9	1.3	2.1	1.7	1.8
If social security benefits such as wage continuation in case of illness, unemployment benefits, and early retirement pensions are as high as they are now, this only leads to people being less willing to work.					
fully agree	11.1	n/a	11.1	n/a	17.1
somewhat agree	24.1	n/a	25.3	n/a	32.3
somewhat disagree	35.9	n/a	34.5	n/a	32.4
fully disagree	29.0	n/a	29.1	n/a	18.2

Source: ALLBUS (German General Social Survey), own calculations.

Table 8.2 Distribution of social policy preferences on left–right political dimension in Germany 1994 and 2004

Should social provisions be reduced, sustained, or expanded?

	Left	2	3	4	5	6	7	8	9	Right	Mean
1994 (%)											
expand	70.2	57.7	45.5	37.4	40.6	28.3	26.9	20.1	25.7	18.5	36.7
sustain	27.7	37.5	47.4	55.8	52.9	58.4	55.3	62.7	51.4	51.9	53.5
reduce	2.1	4.8	7.2	6.8	6.4	13.3	17.8	17.2	22.9	29.6	9.8
Overall left–right self-placement of respondents (%)											
	2.1	3.7	11.2	13.8	32.2	20.8	7.6	6.1	1.3	1.2	5.1
2004 (%)											
expand	39.3	32.4	21.8	21.6	21.2	20.9	16.0	17.2	17.9	21.9	20.9
sustain	60.7	53.5	61.8	61.0	59.0	50.7	47.7	51.0	25.0	53.1	55.2
reduce	0.0	14.1	16.4	17.5	19.8	28.4	36.2	31.8	57.1	25.0	23.9
Overall left–right self-placement of respondents (%)											
	1.2	3.1	12.0	12.9	26.6	22.9	11.3	7.2	1.2	1.7	5.3

Source: German General Social Survey (ALLBUS), own calculations.

Note
Percentages in the first three rows (of each year) are the proportion of respondents in favour of expanding, sustaining, or reducing levels of social provision within each section of the left–right scale.

However, while parties were confronted with a large consensus in favour of the welfare state, problem pressures in the labour market arose in terms of high unemployment and associated cost pressures, in particular after German reunification. Thus, starting from the middle of the 1990s, employer associations increasingly mobilized against high non-wage labour costs in the form of social insurance contributions (Paster 2010). Parties had to react to labour market problems and interest group pressures, but they were blocked by the welfare consensus in central sections of the electorate. In the field of unemployment compensation, this consensus especially regarded UI as this scheme is relevant not only for its direct recipients but for all workers and employees in standard employment who are concerned about the risk of becoming unemployed (cf. Rehm 2009). Consequently, restructuring had to leave the core of the unemployment benefit system intact. Instead, reform efforts targeted less salient policy features (such as eligibility, conditions of receipt, and sanctions) on the one hand, and the subordinate benefits (UA and SA) on the other. In both cases, it primarily affected more marginal beneficiary groups.

These reform measures were accompanied by frequent public interventions from leading politicians complaining about the supposed unwillingness of long-term unemployed to work and about abuse of unemployment benefits. These debates mostly occurred in phases of rising unemployment and approaching elections (Oschmiansky *et al.* 2003). That this blaming of the long-term unemployed was, from the point of view of electoral competition, a sensible strategy can be seen from the fact that, in spite of generally high support for social benefits, a relatively large share of the electorate was sceptical about the effect of benefits on willingness to work (Table 8.1).

At the same time, the groups affected by retrenchment measures were electorally less important. As we have seen, the incremental cutbacks negatively affected mainly the recipients of UA and SA as well as labour market entrants. Initially, UA and SA claimants made up only a small part of the electorate. In the election year 1976, at the beginning of welfare state restructuring, they constituted only 2.5 per cent of those entitled to vote.[3] By 2002, their numbers had generally risen: UA recipients accounted for 2.8 per cent and SA beneficiaries for 4.5 per cent of the electorate. These numbers were not necessarily negligible for electoral competition, especially as large parties had, in principle, incentives to address broad sections of the electorate. However, for electoral purposes we have to take into account that the group of SA recipients was very heterogeneous and that socially marginalized persons, such as assistance recipients, tended to participate less in elections.[4] However, the main point here is that, on the one hand, parties were under intense pressure to reform and, on the other, to preserve the core benefit scheme, UI. After all, UI was potentially relevant for vast numbers of politically active core groups of the labour market that were essential for electoral competition between CDU and SPD. This shows how centripetal competition benefits marginal groups only under sustained favourable economic conditions (see the introduction of social assistance, Chapter 7). As the economic tide turned, those groups were the first to be affected by retrenchment.[5]

Fundamental reforms: centrifugal tendencies and a limited shift in demand

After German reunification in 1990, a fifth party entered the scene: the Party of Democratic Socialism (PDS), the successor party of the Socialist Unity Party of Germany (SED), which had ruled the German Democratic Republic. This party was situated further to the left than the Greens but, as opposed to the Greens, socio-economic issues did play a relevant role on its agenda. Nevertheless, until recently the PDS had a limited impact on national level competition. Its electoral success was mainly based on a centre-periphery cleavage that was created by the difficult reunification process. Thus, the PDS mobilized mainly East German voters who strongly identified with their shared experience under state socialism and felt disadvantaged or alienated by the way reunification had transformed East German society. Moreover, being the successor party of the SED, the PDS was strongly stigmatized in West Germany, where it never received much more than 1 per cent of the vote (Neugebauer and Stöss 1996).

Since the middle of the 1990s, public attitudes towards the welfare state shifted somewhat in favour of restructuring. The share of people preferring an expansion of social provisions declined from 37 per cent in 1994 to 22 per cent in 2004. At the same time, the share of respondents who support cuts in social benefits increased from 10 per cent in 1994 to 23 per cent in 2004. Yet, during the same period, those preferring to sustain current levels remained an absolute majority, with shares between 53 and 55 per cent (Table 8.1). Similarly, those who somewhat disagree with the proposition that the state should ensure a decent living in case of unemployment rose from 7 per cent in 1991 to 14 per cent in 2004. On the other hand, the share of people overall agreeing with the statement remained overwhelmingly high, but less people continued to fully agree, and more people just somewhat agreed. Finally, both those who somewhat agree and those who fully agree that generous benefits reduce the willingness to work increased between 1994 and 2004. The share of people somewhat disagreeing remained more or less stable and high, but the percentage of people who fully disagree declined. As a result, in 2004, for the first time the two groups were almost even, i.e. 49 per cent agreeing and 51 per cent disagreeing that benefits reduce work willingness. Therefore, a public opinion shift in favour of restructuring was clearly recognizable at the beginning of the 2000s, even though support for maintaining (and even for expanding) social protection levels remained substantial.

This limited shift in policy demand had uneven consequences for party competition. It disproportionately favoured the Christian Democrats as well as Liberals and disadvantaged the Social Democrats. This can be seen when analysing party preferences within groups of respondents who share the same social policy preferences. In order to see which party has an electoral advantage or disadvantage in each social policy preference group, we have to compare the share of party supporters in such a group with the share of party supporters in the overall electorate. Table 8.3 reports this comparison by subtracting the party preferences

Table 8.3 Electoral advantages – difference of party voters between social policy preference groups and total electorate (in per cent)

	CDU/CSU	SPD	FDP	Greens	PDS	Others	Abstention
Reduce							
1984	59.3	−52.1	46.8	−57.2		3.5	−27.5
1994	57.0	−35.9	29.4	−50.2	−100.0	68.6	−4.4
2000	33.3	−29.1	114.4	−33.8	−67.6	22.7	−25.4
2004	33.3	−22.7	82.6	−28.2	−51.8	−41.1	−47.4
Sustain							
1984	10.4	−4.2	29.3	−18.3		−14.1	−38.3
1994	10.0	−0.7	9.9	1.0	−63.1	−2.2	−17.8
2000	4.7	7.4	−19.3	15.1	−24.5	−35.0	−13.2
2004	−6.4	18.4	−20.3	23.7	−3.5	4.7	−11.6
Expand							
1984	−51.6	32.5	−31.6	103.3		−16.4	9.9
1994	−35.3	8.1	1.8	29.6	141.0	−5.6	−3.3
2000	−32.2	5.9	−23.5	0.3	98.4	81.8	21.8
2004	−24.5	−1.8	−9.5	−19.1	96.4	48.4	43.3

Source: ALLBUS (German General Social Survey), own calculations.

Notes
The party preference share in the whole electorate is subtracted from the party preference share
within a social policy preference group. The result is divided by the party preference share in the
whole electorate. Social policy preferences as in Table 8.1. Party preferences are based on: 'If next
Sunday there was a parliamentary election (*Bundestagswahl*), which party would you vote for with
your party list vote (*Zweitstimme*)?'

within the total electorate from the party shares within policy preference
groups and dividing the result again by the party share in the total electorate. The
resulting figures show (in per cent) how many more or fewer voters a party has
in groups with shared social policy preferences as compared to the total electorate. Positive numbers indicate that a party has an electoral advantage among
people with a given policy preference, negative numbers indicate electoral
disadvantages.

In 1984, the CDU had 59 per cent more prospective voters among those who
wanted to reduce social protection than among the total electorate (1994, 57 per
cent more). The FDP also had an advantage in this group. The SPD, in contrast,
had 52 per cent fewer prospective voters in this group than in the total electorate
(1994, 36 per cent less) although this was the group that increased since the
middle of the 1990s. By contrast, among the diminishing voters who favoured
welfare expansion, the picture was roughly the opposite. These were less relevant for the CDU with 52 per cent fewer voters in this group compared to the
total electorate (minus 35 per cent in 1994) and they were more important for the
SPD, which had an electoral advantage of 33 per cent in this group (8 per cent in
1994). These patterns are confirmed by an analysis (not reported here) of other
social policy preference items (see Table 8.1). Thus, in the 1990s, precisely the
group in which Christian Democrats had an advantage was rising in numbers

and the group in which Social Democrats had the upper hand was declining. It is clear that if the SPD wanted to return to power, it had to do something about this imbalance.

In the central group of people who favour maintaining the welfare state, the picture is less clear-cut and electoral advantages or disadvantages are on a lower scale. It is interesting to note, however, that the CDU had a relative advantage in this important group while it was in power (see years 1984 and 1994, Table 8.3). The same was true for the SPD during its period in power (see 2000 and 2004). This reinforces the point that this section of the electorate plays an important role in party competition.

Two aspects should be underlined here in order to highlight the difference between this analysis and a traditional partisan politics approach. First, Table 8.3 is based on the percentage of party supporters among people with the same social policy preferences (and the total electorate). The table does not analyse the relative importance of social policy preference groups for a given party, as a partisan politics study would do. For that purpose, we would have to look at percentages of people with different welfare state preferences among the supporters of a given party. Second, the crucial point for my argument is not the indicated change in preferences itself but how parties react strategically to this change and how this reaction is conditioned by the party system (see below). Again, this contrasts with a partisan approach, where the political position of a party would be a function of the relative importance of social preference groups in its electoral constituency.

Up to this point, we have registered a limited shift of public opinion and have identified the electoral implications that this shift would have had without any strategic response from parties: CDU and FDP had an electoral advantage in the opinion group that was increasing while the opposite was true for the SPD. Now, how did parties react to the opinion shift in favour of restructuring? The FDP was the first to grab the opportunity. During the 1990s the party accentuated its market liberal position in order to benefit from the rise of people that were inclined in its direction. This accentuation found expression in 1994 in a much discussed phrase of the party secretary when calling the FDP the 'party of the well-to-do people' (*Partei der Besserverdienenden*).[6] Moreover, the FDP's stance for economic liberalization was encouraged by increasing demands from employer and business associations to reduce non-wage labour costs (Kinderman 2005). The move of the FDP put the CDU under pressure to act. If it wanted to maintain its own strong position in the increasingly relevant pro-reform section of the electorate it had to follow the FDP in stressing more market liberal positions.

Figure 8.2 reports the relative emphasis on economically left- versus right-wing policies in party manifestos. It illustrates how the FDP had sharpened its market liberal profile over the 1980s and 1990s and was competing with the CDU on this side of the political spectrum. The CDU had starkly emphasized economically liberal policies when it came to power in 1982/3 after a long spell of social-liberal coalitions. Yet, it quickly pulled back this emphasis in the next

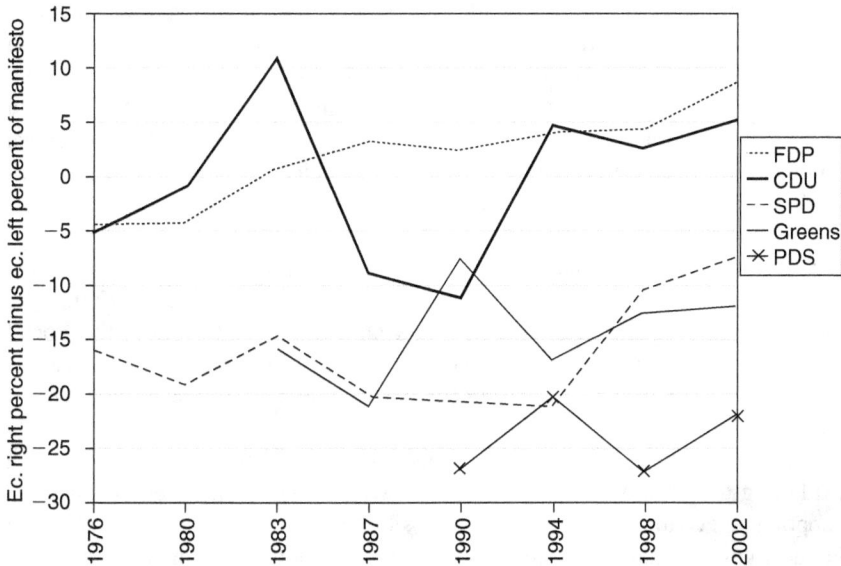

Figure 8.2 Relative emphasis on economically left- and right-wing positions in party manifestos, Germany 1976–2002 (sources: Klingemann *et al.* (2006), Budge *et al.* (2001), own calculations).

Notes
The indicator adds up the proportion of each manifesto containing right-wing positions on social and economic policy and subtracts the proportion containing left-wing positions. Items that are counted as right-wing are: Free Enterprise (Positive), Incentives (Positive), Economic Orthodoxy (Positive), Welfare State Limitation (Positive), Labour Groups (Negative). Items counted as left-wing are: Economic Planning (Positive), Corporatism (Positive), Keynesian Demand Management (Positive), Controlled Economy (Positive), Nationalisation (Positive), Marxist Analysis (Positive), Social Justice (Positive), Welfare State Expansion (Positive), Labour Groups (Positive).
   The results cannot easily be interpreted in terms of left–right *positioning*. Rather, they indicate relative *emphasis* on different kinds of positions. Moreover, the value zero cannot be interpreted as the centre of the scale because there are more left- than right-wing items.

election. Only in 1994, when the opinion shift set in, the CDU again stressed economically right-wing policies. This time it stayed on course for the next two elections. The SPD, in turn, followed the Christian democratic shift away from economic leftism just one election later, in 1998.[7] This was its clearest move towards emphasizing more liberal social and economic policies since the 1960s. It can also be recognized by the party's claim, in 1998, to forming the 'New Centre' (*Neue Mitte*) and the campaign slogan that in government it will 'not do everything differently [from the previous government] but many things better'. In fact, the Social Democrats gained 4.5 percentage points in party list votes during the 1998 election and, together with the Greens, re-took control of government from CDU and FDP.

   Looking at Figure 8.2, one may find it surprising that the CDU–FDP government did not adopt more radical labour market reforms after the right-turn of the

CDU in 1994, although the data in the figure is based on party programmes and actually adopting reforms is a different matter. The black–yellow coalition, during its last term in office, did in fact intensify reform efforts, but in pushing through these reforms, it was strongly constrained by left-wing competition from the SPD. Had the CDU adopted decisive cuts in unemployment benefits it would have incurred high vote losses in favour of the SPD. After all, the pro-reform opinion shift was only limited and many of its voters still subscribed to maintaining high social protection. In fact, the increased reform efforts and the more market-liberal party programme of the CDU did already play into the hands of the SPD in terms of popular support. Consequently, the election campaign of the Social Democrats attacked this weak spot of the CDU, further weakened by rising unemployment (up to 1997). Right after their 1998 victory, the Social Democrats made good on election promises by repealing some of the restrictive reforms that the previous government had introduced (Blancke and Schmid 2003).

Therefore, in 1998, the SPD managed to strike a difficult balance between exploiting the negative image of the CDU with respect to the welfare state and adopting an economically more liberal position itself. This strategy was reflected in the main campaign slogan 'innovation and justice' and in the two front-runners Gerhard Schröder and Oskar Lafontaine: the first was considered a 'modernizer' and the second a 'traditionalist'. However, this strategy could succeed precisely because of the spatial logic of Germany's party system at the time. The right-turn of the CDU was decisive enough to leave space for the SPD to move to the centre without fearing to be leapfrogged by its main competitor. Still, CDU voters unhappy with the new liberal agenda of their party could not but turn to the SPD as their next best option. At the same time, the Social Democrats did not have to worry about losing voters to the left because there was no relevant competitor on that side. As argued above, the Greens did not compete sufficiently on socio-economic issues and the PDS was regionally confined.

However, by the beginning of 2002, towards the end of its first term in office, the SPD-Green coalition government had made no real dent in the problem of unemployment. Chancellor and SPD Chair Schröder had presented a joint essay with Tony Blair in 1999 that proposed far-reaching reforms in the labour market, based on the idea of moving people from welfare to work (Schröder and Blair 1999). However, in the years following this legislative period these ideas were not put into practice in Germany (Schmid and Picot 2001). The unemployment rate had declined since 1997, mainly due to favourable economic development, but the official rate remained above the symbolically important threshold of 10 per cent.[8] However, in 2001, the economic slump that was triggered by the bursting of the dotcom stock market bubble and by the 9/11 attacks sent unemployment up again and shook economic confidence. Unemployment had been a crucial political issue ever since reunification and in the upcoming elections of 2002 it was sure to play an important role in the public's evaluation of the SPD's first term back in government since 1982. Accordingly, the CDU tried to exploit this situation by presenting itself as the party of economic competence in the

2002 election campaign. 'Just this issue [of unemployment] became a dominant topic in the first half of the election year and led to an increasing advantage of CDU/CSU' (Oskar Niedermayer 2006: 122).

In this situation of competitive pressure, the uncovering of irregularities in the BA gave Chancellor Schröder an opportunity to demonstrate the reform-willingness of his party, by setting up the Hartz commission (see Chapter 5). The official task of the commission was to elaborate proposals for modernizing labour market administration. However, the commission took a comprehensive approach to the issue and included reform proposals for unemployment benefits. The commission report was published in August 2002, and the red–green government immediately pledged full implementation of its recommendations in case of winning the elections. A month later, they won. It is likely that the Hartz reform project of the red–green coalition helped to make up some of the electoral disadvantage of the SPD among those voters who prefer to reduce social protection. Thus, this disadvantage declined from minus 29 per cent voters in this group regarding the general electorate in 2000 down to minus 23 per cent in 2004 (Table 8.3, the table also shows that this was part of a process that had already begun before). At the same time, as mentioned, the risk of losing voters was small because there was no credible left-wing competitor. In fact, the PDS did not even manage to enter parliament in the 2002 election (apart from two directly elected seats).[9]

The structure of the party system shortly after the 2002 election is depicted in Figure 8.3. It shows the party system on an economic left-right dimension. The spatial positioning of parties is based on the expert survey by Benoit and Laver (2006) that was conducted in 2003. For the reasons mentioned above, the Greens and the PDS are excluded from the graph. In fact, regarding the Greens, the survey confirms that, as in 1990, they were the only party for which the issue 'more public services versus less taxes' was less important than most other political dimensions. By contrast, when we consider the average importance of each dimension across all parties (weighted by vote shares) the socio-economic one was the most important dimension of party competition in 2003.

Comparing Figure 8.3 to the party system at the end of the 1980s (Figure 8.1, above) we can see that, in fact, the whole party system had shifted to the right. The FDP was situated almost at the extreme right of this political dimension. This widened the space between FDP and CDU although the CDU itself moved moderately to the right. On the other side the SPD took up almost a centre position in 2003 rather than a centre-left position as at the end of the 1980s. The main competition in this party system was still between SPD and CDU but the terrain over which they compete had shifted to the right. Seen from the point of view of spatial competition, the fact that the SPD was situated so close to the centre was a clear advantage for the party because on socio-economic issues the voters on its left had no alternative to vote for (considering that Greens and PDS were not relevant on this dimension). However, in the context of German multi-party competition the ample space on the left created incentives for a new competitor to occupy this terrain. This is of course what happened in 2005 with the

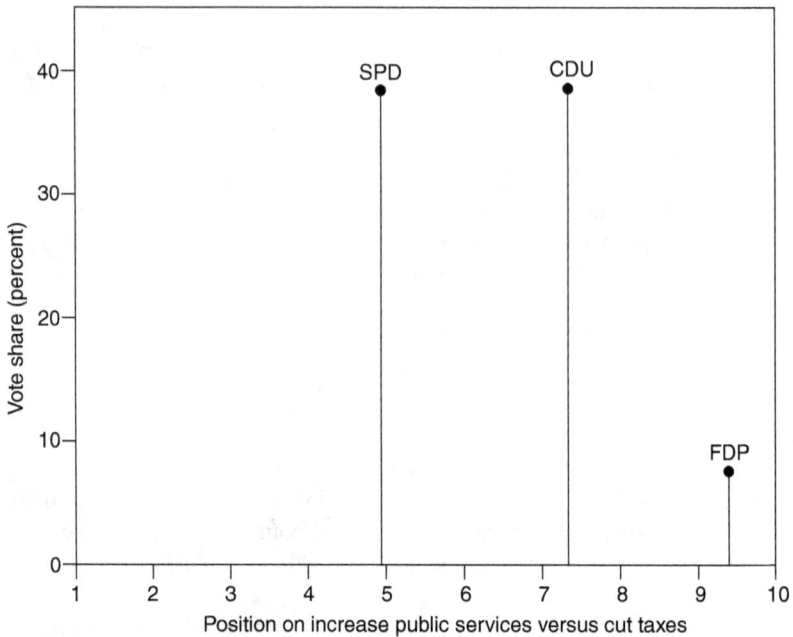

Figure 8.3 German party system on economic left–right dimension at the beginning of the 2000s (sources: Benoit and Laver (2006), www.bundestag.de, own calculations).

Notes
Party positions are from the Benoit and Laver (2006) expert survey conducted in 2003 (originally on a 1–20 scale). Vote shares are the election results of 2002. Greens and PDS are excluded from the graph because they are not relevant for national competition on this political dimension.

emergence of the '*Die Linke*' (The Left). However, up to that point, essentially the constellation depicted in Figure 8.3 persisted. In combination with continuing electoral pressure on the SPD, it helps to explain why the only limited shift in public opinion had such a big effect on labour market reforms.

The policy demand in this period (for 2004) is shown in Table 8.2. In those sections of the political space (on a general left–right dimension) where competition was concentrated (sections 6 and 7) the respondents who preferred to maintain current welfare state levels were still the majority. However, as opposed to the situation in 1994, the second largest group in 2004 was made up by those who favoured reductions of social provision. Moreover, we can see how the supporters of welfare state cutbacks increased towards the right of the political spectrum. This was the direction in which political competition moved during the beginning of the 2000s and which the SPD had to emphasize in order to win voters.

At the same time the overall electorate was still concentrated in the centre and more or less symmetrically distributed on both sides (if not somewhat biased to the left, see Table 8.2). Hence, a lot of voters regarded themselves as left of centre. This distribution of voters was based on a general left–right dimension, while the party system in Figure 8.3 is depicted on an economic left–right dimension. However, considering that the economic dimension was the most important one for party competition in this period, the spatial incongruence between the distribution of voters and the party system is conspicuous. In the short-term, party competition could be shaped more strongly by the party system than by the distribution of voters, but in the mid- or long-term and in a multi-party context, this incongruence constituted a clear opportunity for a new left-wing competitor.

Right after the 2002 election, the SPD came again under competitive pressure from CDU and FDP. The election had been won only by a close margin. A few months later, the red–green coalition was severely attacked on financial policy and supposedly having deceived the voters on deficits in the state budget.[10] Furthermore, the SPD suffered heavy defeats in regional elections in Lower Saxony and Hesse at the beginning of 2003 that were both won by the CDU. It was against this backdrop that in March 2003 (one month after the lost regional elections) Schröder gave a government declaration in parliament, in which he announced a range of social and economic reforms under the title 'Agenda 2010', including the Hartz reforms. Already in the introduction to his speech he declared: 'We will have to cut public benefits, promote individual responsibility, and demand more self-reliance from everyone.'[11] Moreover, he announced for the first time that the new UA scheme, which the Hartz commission had proposed, was to be on the level of SA and that the maximum durations of UI were to be clearly reduced. These two cuts in generosity had not been specified in detail by the Hartz report itself. The competitive pressure pushed the SPD further down the path of modernizing the labour market, scaling down benefit levels, and reducing non-wage labour costs.

In the legislative process for adopting the Hartz IV reform concerns were raised from the left wing of the SPD, which, however, had little impact on the reform. On the other side, the CDU, through the upper chamber of parliament (*Bundesrat*) objected to the implications that the fusion of UA and SA had in administrative terms for local government. Yet, the crucial elements of the reform, as far as the differentiation of social rights is concerned, were maintained.

To abolish status-related UA and to cut UI durations were significant retrenchments in social protection against the risk of unemployment. Analogously to the general incongruence between party system and voter self-placement, noted above, these reductions constituted a misfit between policy supply and demand. After all, in 2004, 22 per cent of the population still favoured an expansion of the welfare state, 44 per cent fully agreed that the state should ensure a decent living for the unemployed, and 18 per cent completely disagreed that high social benefits reduce individuals' willingness to work (see Table 8.1). Even leaving aside the large group of more moderate welfare state supporters, the 'welfare expanders' constituted a high proportion of the electorate that was likely to be repelled by the Hartz reforms and Agenda 2010. Moreover, the specific content of Hartz IV contributed to widespread rejection of the reform. The reduction of UI maximum duration, and the abolition of status-related UA, made a rapid decline of social status of the unemployed more likely and, hence, more threatening – even to those who had jobs but were worried about losing them.

As mentioned, the strong welfare supporters were not taken into account by the SPD because it reacted to the competitive incentives in the party system that pulled it to the right. In this move it was not constrained by a relevant left-wing competitor. After 2002, the still significant proportion of staunch welfare state supporters in the German electorate was not represented by any parliamentary party. In West Germany, this group did not even have a relevant party to vote for in order to express its concerns because the PDS was not an option for most West Germans due to its SED-past. Accordingly, Table 8.3 shows that by 2004 the SPD had completely lost the electoral advantage that it once had among those who support welfare expansion. The only party that had an advantage among these voters in 2004 was the PDS. But even more clearly, the percentage of people not intending to vote had grown markedly among supporters of welfare expansion and exceeded the share of abstainers in the total electorate by 43 per cent in 2004. In absolute terms, 26 per cent of those who favoured an increase in social benefits said they would abstain from voting, as opposed to 18 per cent of the total electorate. This lack of political representation threatened to become a problem of political integration. Accordingly, public discontent about the Hartz IV reform voiced itself in a wave of large demonstrations in 2003 and 2004 that were often organized independently of established parties or interest organizations.

The Hartz IV reform came into force in January 2005. In the meantime, also within the SPD, the Agenda 2010 and Hartz IV in particular caused heated conflicts. Still in January 2005, several left-wing party officials and trade unionists defected and founded the social democratic splinter group Electoral Alternative: Labour and Social Justice (WASG). In the following months the SPD lost the regional elections in its traditional strongholds Schleswig-Holstein and North Rhine Westphalia. After the latter defeat (in May 2005), the party leadership announced that it would seek anticipated national elections. The prospect of these elections encouraged WASG and PDS to join forces under the new name, *Die Linke*. This critically changed the strategic position of the PDS – it was no longer a predominantly East German party and, therefore, could profit from disaffection with the SPD among West German welfare state supporters. Consequently, the party went from receiving 4 per cent to an unprecedented 8.7 per cent of the vote in the 2005 parliamentary election, including 4.9 per cent in West Germany. High-scoring results in regional elections since then have confirmed this new strength.

Therefore, the programmatic shift of the SPD and, not least of all, its fundamental and controversial reform of the unemployment benefit system, enabled the transformation of the PDS into a relevant left-wing competitor (Nachtwey and Spier 2007). In other words, the reform of social protection that had been enabled by a right-shift in the party system had a feedback effect on the party system itself, rebalancing it to the left. The new structure of the party system again changed the dynamic of competition. While previously a bias towards the right had prevailed on social and economic issues, the *Linke* now added a left-wing tendency to party competition. Hence, the new party system generates two contradictory tendencies of political competition. First, the old competition over the political centre between the two biggest parties, CDU and SPD, continues. But, second, both of these two parties face competition from the margins of the political space regarding social and economic policies: the Christian Democrats on their right through the FDP and the Social Democrats on their left through the *Linke*. To be sure, the centripetal tendency prevails because the party system is still bipolar and the two more 'extreme' actors are not anti-system parties (even if minority factions within the PDS and now *Linke* can be considered 'anti-system'). Nevertheless, the centrifugal trend complicates party competition.

Much depends on coalition formation. Under a grand coalition of SPD and CDU the centrifugal pulls from both sides, i.e. from *Linke* and Greens and from FDP, are strong. An alternative would be the formation of two alternative blocks: CDU and FDP on one side and SPD, Greens, and *Linke* on the other side. In the latter case, bipolarity would be restored and centripetal competition could prevail, even if political distances are greater than before. At the national level the problem for SPD and Green Party in the latter half of the 2000s was that without the *Linke* they could not obtain a parliamentary majority. But for pro-grammatic, historical, and even personal reasons SPD and Greens refuse to form a coalition with the *Linke*.

Under these conditions, the Grand Coalition that was formed in 2005 had a precarious status from the start. The temporary limitation of competition between the two big centre-left and centre-right parties strengthens competition from the more extreme parties. But also within the coalition conflicts broke out frequently and the logic of competition was not fully suspended. The strengthening of the extreme parties is confirmed by the success of the *Linke* and of the FDP in regional elections after the formation of the Grand Coalition and in the 2009 federal election. Moreover, we can observe in several areas of economic policy how this centrifugal competition affected the programmatic positions and policy-making of SPD and CDU.[12]

With respect to the segmentation of unemployment benefits, the consequences of the *Linke* entering the scene are so far ambiguous. There are two main points that this new party criticized about the Hartz IV reform: the reduction of maximum durations of UI, which concerned labour market insiders, and the low level of the new UA scheme, which is relevant for labour market outsiders. The SPD has reacted ambiguously to these challenges. It could not ignore the criticism because it threatened to win over many left-wing SPD voters. However, the party also wanted to defend the reform it had adopted and claim its success in reducing unemployment. As it turned out, at least initially, mainly the labour market insiders profited from the new left-wing competition. In autumn 2007, on the initiative of the SPD, longer UI terms for older unemployed were re-introduced. This partly reversed the cuts by the Hartz IV reform and confirms, once more, the relevance of party competition for policy development. Assistance recipients, on the other hand, so far have not significantly benefited from the new left-wing competition. The main push for improving the assistance scheme came from the Constitutional Court in 2010. In the negotiations over the necessary adjustments, the SPD advocated a higher benefit level, but in the end the restrictive approach of the CDU-FDP government prevailed. Therefore, it still has to be seen whether the emergence of a left-wing competitor to the SPD will reduce benefit segmentation or whether it only helped to repeal reductions for labour market insiders.

I argued above that the SPD adopted the Hartz reforms at least in part for reasons of electoral competition. Concerning the reform proposal before the 2002 election, this seems clear enough and even successful. However, after adoption and implementation of the reforms, the SPD continuously performed poorly in elections and polls, falling to a historic low of 23 per cent vote share in the parliamentary election of 2009. Does this not put into question my argument? First of all, I have to point out that my argument focuses on electoral considerations in the policy decisions of parties and not on explaining the outcome of elections. Hence, it is well possible that electoral considerations have played a role in a policy decision but then prove ineffective or even go wrong. I maintain that this was the case of the SPD and its Agenda 2010. So, what was the mistake that the SPD made in its electoral considerations? Two points are relevant here.

First, under intense competitive pressure the Social Democrats chose their strategy based on the current party system. They underestimated the possibility of a party splinter and rise of a new competitor. Within the party system at the time, the Agenda 2010 was a sensible strategy. It was mainly the emergence of the *Linke* that created lasting problems for the SPD. The possibility that a new competitor could enter the scene was outside the party's frame of reference at the moment of the reform decision.[13]

Second, the SPD had hoped that the reforms would produce positive effect in terms of declining unemployment and a more flexible labour market in time for the forthcoming elections.[14] The plan was to implement the reforms in due time before the important state elections in Schleswig-Holstein and North Rhine Westphalia. By the time of the next federal election, scheduled for 2006, the reform was expected to pay off in terms of diminishing unemployment and, consequently, in terms of election results. This time frame was disrupted by the CDU that temporarily blocked the reform in the *Bundesrat* on behalf of *Länder* and municipality interests. Consequently, the troublesome implementation of the reform took place only few months before the elections in Schleswig-Holstein and North Rhine Westphalia. Technical problems in the BA, public protests, and, not least, the fact that the integration of SA recipients into UA statistically increased the number of unemployed – all these implementation problems under-mined all attempts to present the – anyhow controversial – reform as a success at the time of the mentioned two regional elections.

In sum, the limited rise in public demand for welfare state reforms enabled the fundamental Hartz reforms, but it had this strong effect only because of the spatial structure of the party system. It favoured the economically right-wing parties, consequently the SPD had to move towards centre in order to return to power and stay in power. The Hartz reforms were an important part of underlining its credibility as a welfare-reforming party. It was able to pursue this course because it faced no relevant left-wing competitor on socio-economic issues. Nevertheless, the strategy backfired because this new left-wing competitor emerged as a feedback effect of the unemployment benefit reforms.[15]

Therefore, in Germany we find two competitive configurations that have increased benefit segmentation – even if in different ways. First, the same party system as during welfare expansion now had the opposite effect. During welfare expansion centripetal competition meant that the core voters were taken care of first and less important voters later. Under conditions of austerity, the less important voters were the first target of retrenchment. However, as over the 1990s the pro-welfare consensus was weakened, the CDU and FDP moved to the right and 'pulled' the Social Democrats along because they were not held back by a relevant left-wing competitor. This brought about more fundamental reforms that dualized the benefit system.

9 Italy

Party system change facilitating de-segmentation

As was the case in Germany, Italy also entered the phase of economic constraints with the same party system that had structured the politics of welfare expansion. Reform efforts started in the 1980s, but in the field of unemployment benefits any significant restructuring was blocked by persisting polarized pluralism. Party system change in the beginning of the 1990s subsequently opened the opportunity for more notable reforms. However, continuing centrifugal tendencies in the new party system prevented the structural reforms of unemployment compensation that most policy experts called for.

The impediments of continued polarization

Over the course of the 1970s the economic situation had deteriorated in Italy. As a consequence of the first oil crisis, the national economy experienced a slump of –3.6 per cent of its GDP in 1975. Inflation was high and was fuelled by currency devaluation and wage indexation. Public deficits also started to rise during this decade, which remained substantial over the 1980s so that by 1990 the total public debt corresponded to 105 per cent of GDP. However, given the polarized and intense political competition in the 1970s, and worrying levels of political violence, restrictive welfare reforms did not even enter the agenda.

In 1978, government decided to join the European Monetary System. This implied that a more rigorous financial policy had to be adopted. The PCI opposed the step and revoked the pact of National Solidarity that it had entered in 1976. In the elections of 1979, the PCI could not repeat its success in 1976. Instead, it lost 4 percentage points of its vote share. Therefore, the threat of overtaking the DC that had been so vivid in 1976 was clearly averted and the PCI was again removed from government influence.[1] From 1979–92 the government coalition consisted almost continuously of the same five parties (DC, PSI, PSDI, PRI, and PLI) and was consequently dubbed *Pentapartito*. The political weakening of the PCI as well as the economic constraints of the European Monetary System made it possible that economic and social reform entered the political agenda (Ferrera and Gualmini 2004).

However, we have seen that no clear changes took place in the field of unemployment benefits during the 1980s. On the one hand, maximum levels for CIGS benefits were introduced that gradually became more restrictive. On the other hand, new passive measures, such as early retirement, were adopted. Only towards the end of the 1980s, two rulings of the Constitutional Court brought up the issue of adjusting UI and reforming SA. In fact, despite some political shifts, up to 1989 the party system was still characterized by polarized pluralism and impeded decisive reforms of unemployment benefits – just as in many other sectors.

In the 1980s, the PSI moved yet more towards centre, thus intensifying competition with the DC. Paradoxically, the Socialists now benefited from their institutionally and culturally somewhat less entrenched relationship with the electorate, compared to DC and PCI. This helped them to find more flexible responses to the changed socio-structural context of the 1980s. By contrast, the DC suffered a painful electoral blow when in the run-up to the 1983 elections it campaigned on a platform of party renewal and public sector reform. This did not go down well with its electorate (Ginsborg 2001: Ch. 5). The PCI in this period held on to its core electorate but lost votes in every election, descending from the previous 34.4 per cent in 1976 (see Table 7.2) to 26.6 per cent in 1987 (see Table 9.1).

Judging from the electoral results, it seems that this time round the inclusion of PSI and not PCI in the government coalition did create the effect that the DC had hoped for in the 1960s: the divide of the left isolated and weakened the PCI. The reason behind these different consequences lay presumably in the tension between a changing social structure and new social problems, on the one hand, and the entrenched and inflexible mass party organization of the PCI, on the other. In terms of party positions, it may be argued that the degree of polarization in the party system had diminished by the 1980s. The PCI was less perceived as an anti-system party due to years of elite-level cooperation. However, it stayed faithful to its communist identity and remained rooted in its traditional

Table 9.1 Italian parliamentary election results, 1979–92

	DP/ PRC	PCI/ PDS	PSI	PSDI	PR/ Verdi	PRI	DC	PLI	Lega	MSI	Others	Turnout
1979	1.4	30.4	9.8	3.8	3.5	3.0	38.3	1.9		5.3	2.7	90.6
1983	1.5	29.9	11.4	4.1	2.2	5.1	32.9	2.9		6.8	3.2	88.0
1987	1.7	26.6	14.3	3.0	2.6	3.7	34.3	2.1		5.9	6.0	88.8
1992	5.6	16.1	13.6	2.7	2.8	4.4	29.7	2.9	8.7	5.4	8.3	87.3

Source: *Ministero Dell'Interno.*

Notes
Party results are per cent of party list votes for the Lower House (*Camera dei Deputati*). Turnout is per cent of those entitled to vote.
1979: DP/PRC column reports result of PdUP (thereafter: DP), PR/*Verdi* column reports result of PR.
1987: among others is *Lista Verde* 2.51 per cent.
1992: PCI is now PDS, PR/*Verdi* column reports result of *Verdi* (PR: 1.24 per cent), DP/PRC column reports result of PRC.

cultural-ideological constituency. On the other side of the political spectrum, the blackmail power of the MSI had diminished (Sartori 1982: Ch. 11). Yet, Figure 9.1 shows that the essential characteristics of the party system were still very much the same as in the beginning of the 1970s (compare Figure 7.2).[2] The basic tripolar structure was still in place and, more specifically, the PCI continues to hold its position as a strong opposition party on the radical left.

Between 1980 and 1987 unemployment continued to rise steeply (see Figure 4.1). Data from the International Social Survey Program (own calculations) shows that 57 per cent of the Italians wanted to see 'more' or 'much more' government spending on unemployment benefits and 85 per cent said a decent living standard for the unemployed should be 'definitely' or 'probably' a government responsibility. Given that the formulation of the question was most probably understood as referring to ordinary UI, this demand is not surprising. After all, we have seen that the benefit system that was still in place in the middle of the 1980s provided extremely little financial help to the officially unemployed. Nevertheless, government did not respond to these demands by increasing UI.

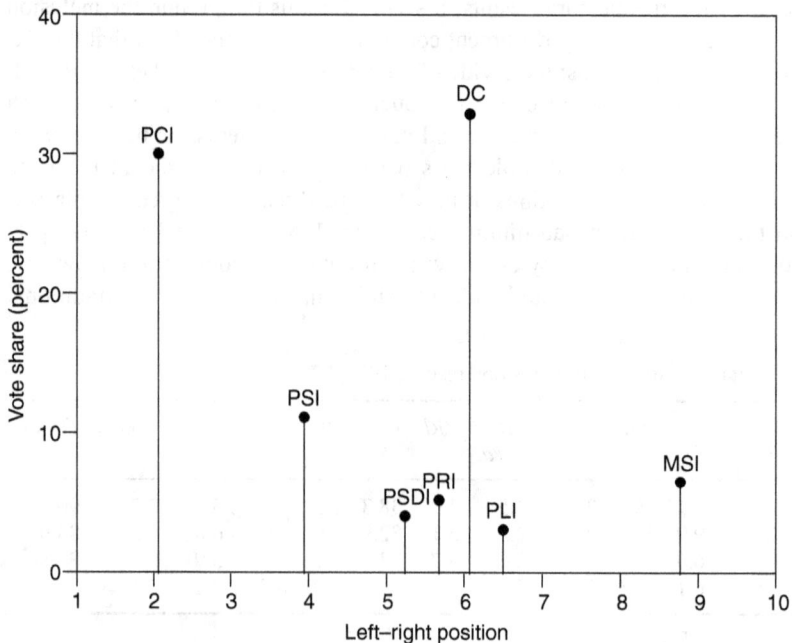

Figure 9.1 Italian party system at the beginning of the 1980s (sources: ITANES 1985, *Ministero Dell'Interno*).

Notes
Left–right positions are based on voters' average placement of parties on a general left–right dimension. Vote shares are the election results of 1983. DP and PR are excluded from the graph because they were not relevant parties, following Sartori's (1976) criteria. The left–right value of PSDI is inter-polated.

Instead, it introduced new passive measures. Two of these essentially benefited the insiders of the labour market: early retirement and solidarity contracts
were meant to redistribute work opportunities while safeguarding the economic
situation of the workers who retired early or reduced their working hours. But
even the redistribution of work opportunities was originally opposed by the
CGIL and PCI. When the more moderate union federation CISL proposed to
reduce the weekly working hours in order to create new jobs for the unemployed,
this was rejected by their more radical unionist colleagues from the CGIL who
considered the initiative as being motivated by a poor relief mentality and
lacking ambitions for structural reforms (Kreile 1985: 186–9). The other measure
that government introduced in this period was the *Lavori Socialmente Utili*,
which was formally a public work programme but essentially had the effect of
transfer payments and functioned on a discretionary basis.

Hence, policy-making generally followed the pattern of the previous policy
phases. The radical left demanded employment protection and employment creation rather than unemployment subsidies, but it went along with measures that
benefited the core industrial workers. At the same time, the fragmentation of the
benefit system was further increased as the DC set up new measures that could
be used on a discretionary basis in order to secure electoral support.

More of a puzzle is the introduction of benefit ceilings for CIGS. How was it
possible to introduce this reform that over time proved to have incisive effects
on the generosity of CIGS? After all, that scheme was one of the principal measures for protecting the core industrial workers and it was backed by PCI and
trade unions. The reform has received extremely scarce attention in the politological as well as historical literature and did not receive a lot of media attention
at the time either. Therefore, it is hard to find evidence on its political background. However, three aspects may help to explain this reform, although each
taken on its own is probably insufficient.

First, the respective law 427 was passed in 1980, being a year in which
the labour movement lost force and had to start defending its achievements
rather than making further progress. When the PCI quitted the National
Solidarity pact it had to pay the price for government cooperation in the
following election in 1979 because of the credits it had lost among anti-system
voters. The Communists had traded office-seeking for a loss of votes and now
lacked a convincing new strategy. At the same time, the employers started to
challenge union power when in October 1979 FIAT sacked 61 militants that the
management accused of acts of violence. Also the dire economic situation and
rising unemployment forced the unions onto the defensive starting from 1980
(Musso 2002: 245–8; Reyneri 1987: 168–73). However, the decisive blow that
made the worker movement lose confidence was the large demonstration in
Turin protesting against a strike at FIAT. This manifestation and the related
labour conflict at FIAT took place only in September and October 1980 while
law 427 was passed in the middle of August. However, it further underlines that
in this period unions were losing the broad popular consensus they previously
enjoyed.

Second, Reyneri indicates that law 427 converted 'the instable equilibria that unions and employers had reached in the collective bargaining process of 1979' (Reyneri 1987: 169). It is not entirely clear which collective agreement he refers to; yet, this was probably part of the aftermath of the so-called EUR union accord.[3] In February 1978, in the face of the ongoing economic crisis, the three major union confederations agreed on wage restraint in return for government efforts to fight unemployment. However, this accord had been inspired by neo-corporatist logic, and a crucial condition that had encouraged especially the CGIL to make this concession was the PCI's indirect participation in the National Solidarity governments. In 1980 National Solidarity had ended. Consequently, the political conditions for PCI and CGIL to endorse a significant cut in workers' entitlements no longer held.

Third, it is possible that in this reform the government successfully applied a strategy of obfuscation (cf. Pierson 1994). In fact, the negative effects of this reform could be felt immediately only by those recipients of CIGS whose previous gross wage exceeded the average production worker's wage by more than 11 per cent.[4] Only in the following years, as it rose at 80 per cent of the indexed wage rises, did the benefit ceiling slowly become more restrictive.[5] In addition to these relatively hidden effects, the date that the law was adopted – 13 August 1980 – raises suspicion. The whole of August is a holiday month in Italy and Assumption Day (15 August) is its apex. This summer break largely applies to party politics as well. Therefore, it is well possible that government chose a moment with extraordinarily low public and opposition attention to adopt this potentially controversial measure.

Bipolarism and reduced benefit disparity

In 1992 the Italian party system entered a crisis with dramatic consequences for the established parties. As will be explained below, this transformation began, in fact, with the demise of state communism in Eastern Europe. Starting from 1994, then, we can identify a new configuration of party competition that is bipolar but still relatively polarized. Due to the fundamental changes in Italian politics, the time since 1992 is commonly called the 'Second Republic'. The concept is controversial because usually different republican orders are distinguished by constitutional change. However, in the Italian case, the transition between 1992 and 1994 principally concerned the party system and the electoral system (which, formally, is not part of the Italian constitution; Fabbrini 2000). Nevertheless, today the term 'Second Republic' is widely used in public discourse. Moreover, as a consequence of party system change the effective relation between political institutions has altered to some extent and some constitutional reforms have actually been introduced (Guarnieri 2006: 98–106).

Other commentators have argued that the transition of the Italian political system actually continues (e.g. Pasquino 2002; Lepre 2004). It is true that the party system is still in flux and that several institutional reforms are still being discussed (e.g. the electoral system and federalism). However, I will argue below that some common characteristics of the party system can be identified for the years 1994–2008 (see also Vassallo 2005). It is undeniable, that the Italian party system changed in that period and is still changing. But, against the extraordinary stability of the previous party system (1948–89) there is also a certain risk of overrating the instability that followed.

Transition

Before analysing the post-1994 configuration of party competition, let us consider the transition of the party system that had itself already affected reforms of unemployment compensation. As mentioned, the crisis of the Italian party system was triggered by the collapse of East European state communism. Certainly, even before that there were first signs of rising pressures for party system change (Cotta and Isernia 1996). Over the 1980s several new small parties entered the scene: the Radical Party (PR), the Greens (*Verdi*), and the new-leftist Democrazia Proletaria (DP). These parties gained representation in parliament, but generally remained small and insignificant to party competition. However, their emergence, together with the increasing vote for 'other' parties (see Table 9.1), showed that the old party system no longer adequately represented all political interests and preferences. More influential than the other new parties became the *Lega Nord* that was founded in 1991 when several Northern regionalist movements merged. The *Lega Nord* built its support on the Northern middle classes' discontent with the tax burden that was imposed by the central state while, at the same time, many public services remained of poor quality. More in particular, the *Lega* profited from disappointment with the DC. In 1992, the first election in which it stood as a united party, it shot up to 8.7 per cent of the vote.

By the end of the 1980s, there were signs of programmatic change among the established parties. The public debt of the Italian state became an ever more pressing issue and the ideas of economic liberalism started to challenge the traditional social democratic and social Catholic views that had sustained a strong welfare state and public intervention in the economy (Ginsborg 2001: 166). Also in public opinion, support for the welfare state declined between 1985 and 1990. The share of people who responded that reducing income differences 'definitely should be' a government responsibility dropped by ten percentage points (from 48 per cent to 38 per cent; ISSP, own calculations). About half of this drop was compensated by a rise of people saying it 'probably should be', but also the share of respondents stating reducing income differences 'probably should not be' a government responsibility rose by five percentage points.

The first parties to respond to these changes in electoral demand were the small PLI and PRI that started to emphasize much more economically liberal policies in their election manifestos of 1987 (see Figure 9.2). In spite of the moderate size of these parties, they still constituted relevant competition to the right of the DC on socio-economic issues. Accordingly, the figure shows that the DC followed this right-shift. These moves to highlight market liberal policies met, however, the opposition of the PCI, which, on the contrary, accentuated economic left-wing policies in 1987. Thus, positions on socio-economic issues diverged over the 1980s, but two points should be noted in this respect. First, a look at the whole post-war period (not shown here) reveals that in 1979 the range of positions had been particularly constrained, presumably due to National Solidarity that had only just ended and the terrorist threat that had gripped politics. Second, the divergence in policy emphasis, as in Figure 9.2, is not equivalent to polarization. After all, this data should not be interpreted directly in terms of spatial positions but rather in terms of programmatic emphasis. Hence, the divergence suggests the rising importance of this dimension of political competition.[6]

The expert survey conducted by Laver and Hunt (1992) provides us with data for the party positions on the socio-economic dimension (phrased in terms of 'more public services versus less taxes') at the end of the 1980s. Figure 9.3 illustrates the Italian party system in 1987 on the socio-economic left–right axis. Note that the MSI is less right-wing here than it would be on a general left–right dimension because it stood in the tradition of 'social fascism'. Vice versa, the PLI and PRI turn out more right-wing than they would be on a general left–right

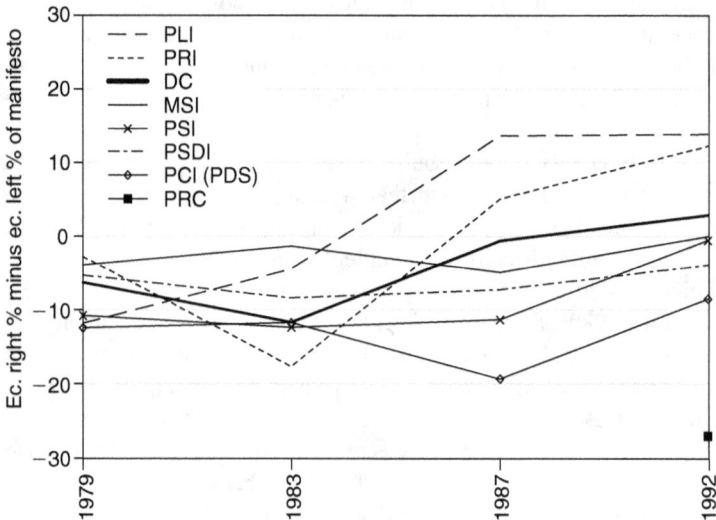

Figure 9.2 Relative emphasis on economic left- and right-wing positions in party manifestos, Italy 1979–92 (sources: Klingemann *et al.* (2006), Budge *et al.* (2001), own calculations).

Notes
The indicator adds up the proportion of each manifesto containing right-wing positions on social and economic policy and subtracts the proportion containing left-wing positions. Items that are counted as right-wing are: Free Enterprise (Positive), Incentives (Positive), Economic Orthodoxy (Positive), Welfare State Limitation (Positive), Labour Groups (Negative). Items counted as left-wing are: Economic Planning (Positive), Corporatism (Positive), Keynesian Demand Management (Positive), Controlled Economy (Positive), Nationalisation (Positive), Marxist Analysis (Positive), Social Justice (Positive), Welfare State Expansion (Positive), Labour Groups (Positive).
   The results cannot easily be interpreted in terms of left–right *positioning*. Rather, they indicate relative *emphasis* on different kinds of positions. Moreover, the value zero cannot be interpreted as the centre of the scale because there are more left- than right-wing items.

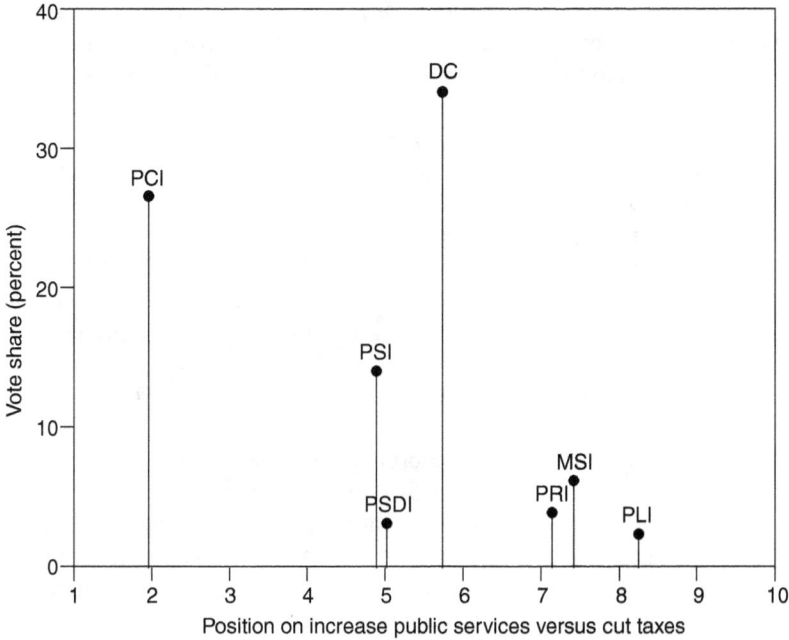

Figure 9.3 Italian party system on an economic left–right dimension in 1987 (sources: Laver and Hunt (1992), *Ministero Dell'Interno*).

Notes
Party positions are from the Laver and Hunt (1992) expert survey conducted in 1990 (originally a 1–20 scale). Vote shares are the election results of 1987. DP, PR, and *Verdi* are excluded from the graph because they were not relevant parties, following Sartori's (1976) criteria.

dimension because their stance on civil rights issues was more libertarian than authoritarian. More interestingly, the PSI is very close to the centre and hence in competition with the DC and leaves a wide gap between itself and the PCI on the left margin. In terms of spatial competition this gap creates a strong incentive for the PCI to move more towards centre. In this way, it could have hoped to gain some of the PSI votes while the voters on its left would have had nowhere else to go, except for the risk that a new party or a splinter party emerges. The continued far-left position of the PCI indicates its persisting (even if by that time somewhat formal and empty) anti-system status. However, it was continuously losing votes since 1979 (see Table 9.1). Therefore, a change of strategy must have had some appeal. In fact, this move to the left and the splitting off of the party's left wing is what happened after 1989.

Overall, the party system was already under considerable strain, when on 9 November 1989 the Berlin Wall fell. This event had almost immediate effect on the PCI. Only three days later, the party secretary announced that the party would change its name – without indicating yet the new name. After a long internal debate, in January 1991, the party adopted the name 'Democratic Party of the Left' (*Partito Democratico della Sinistra*, PDS). Of course, this was not only a nominal change but was understood as turning away from communist ideology *tout court* and towards a more reformist stance. This did not go down well with the party's left wing that, consequently, founded a new party – the Communist Refoundation Party (*Partito della Rifondazione Comunista*, PRC).

Keeping in mind the caveat that the manifesto data cannot be interpreted directly in terms of spatial positioning, Figure 9.2 nevertheless nicely shows the effect of this party split. In the run-up to the 1992 election the PDS moderated its emphasis on left-wing economic issues and moved closer to PSDI and PSI, just as the spatial reasoning based on Figure 9.3 suggested. However, this move was contrasted by the PRC that emphasized even more left-wing economic policies than the PCI had done in the previous election. In the medium-term, this left-wing competition by *Rifondazione* was bound to keep in check the centre-tendency of the PDS.

Against the background of the transformation of the PCI we have to understand the important unemployment benefit reform that was adopted in 1991. To recall, the main change that this law introduced was to limit the duration of CIGS payments and to introduce the mobility benefit for workers who were laid off from firms eligible for CIGS. This was a significant step towards correcting the distorted role that the CIGS had assumed in practice (even though the reform was not forcefully implemented). In the same year, the nominal replacement rate of UI was raised to 20 per cent. Reforming the rules of CIGS had actually been on the agenda for several years. In 1986 the trade unions had already basically agreed to a government reform project but the PCI continued to contest the contents of the proposal and put forward a less restrictive alternative.[7] In 1991, however, the new PDS could not afford to put into question the more reformist approach that it stood for, by blocking the reform of CIGS in the same way as the PCI had done. This gave government more leeway to adapt the proposal also to the requests of the Italian employers' federation, *Confindustria*, which had in the end raised serious concerns about administrative costs of the reform.[8]

The breakdown of international communism and the transformation of the PCI into a more reformist party had further consequences on the whole party system. For the entire First Republic the DC and the smaller centrist party had found their principal legitimation in saving the system against the double threat of communism on one side and fascism on the other. This legitimation had insulated them against many demands, expectations, and discontent with their government performance. To some extent it had even protected them against unconditional scrutiny and control from other branches of government, in particular, the judiciary. The neo-fascist threat had diminished by itself since the end of the 1970s. Now, the vanishing of communism deprived the centrist parties of anti-communist arguments for securing electoral support and for their institutional legitimation.

In February 1992, the first politician was arrested in the judicial enquiry that became known under the name *Mani Pulite* (Clean Hands). This enquiry uncovered a huge system of corruption and illegal party financing that soon was named *Tangentopoli* (Bribesville). Although the full scandal only became public after the elections of 1992 these were already affected by the new development. Especially the DC lost votes, although the vote loss of the PDS was mainly caused by the party transition and split from its left wing. The *Lega* won 8.7 per cent of the vote. In addition, the category of 'other' parties rose considerably and turnout declined – all of which were signs of public discontent. As the vast extent of corruption became public and many leading politicians and parliamentarians (especially from DC and PSI) were prosecuted, all bar two established parties collapsed. Only the former anti-system parties survived, but both profoundly reorganized themselves. The PCI, as mentioned, became the more moderate PDS. The MSI changed its name into National Alliance (*Alleanza Nazionale*, AN) and turned from neo-fascist to post-fascist or national-conservative.

The collapse of the old party system and the corresponding loss of credibility and authority by political parties created a political void. The gap was filled in two ways: by so-called 'technical governments' and by the cooperation of trade unions and business associations (Ferrera and Gualmini 2004). The governments that were called 'technical' consisted, at least partly, of ministers without party affiliation. The Amato I government, which took office after the 1992 elections, was originally an ordinary party government led by Giuliano Amato (PSI) and stayed in office until April 1993. Due to the crisis of the governing parties it increasingly liberated itself from party control and some of the ministers who had to resign because of the judicial enquiry were replaced by independent candidates (Guarnieri 2006: 70). There followed a government headed by Carlo Azeglio Ciampi, former director of the Bank of Italy. This was the first republican government led by someone who was not a member of parliament and had no party membership. It was replaced after the elections in 1994 by the first Berlusconi government, but this first party government, based on the emerging new party system, did not last long and was replaced again by a technical government in January 1995. The government under Lamberto Dini as Prime Minister was the first and only government fully composed of independent ministers. It remained in office until the next election in April 1996, which brought the centre-left into power for a few years (Prodi I, D'Alema I, and D'Alema II governments). Only at the end of the legislative period were these centre-left governments replaced by, for the time being, the last technical government, again led by Amato who by now was without party affiliation himself. In short, the main phase of technical governments was between 1992 and 1996, and was interrupted only by the Berlusconi I government. Only somewhat later, in 2000–1, did the Amato II technical government follow.

The technical governments also took the initiative and looked for partners beyond the political parties in order to support their reform projects. This led to the greater involvement of trade unions and business associations, particularly in the Amato agreement of 1992 (abolition of *scala mobile*), Ciampi agreement of 1993 (reform of collective bargaining and income policy), and the agreement between Dini and the unions on pension reform in 1995. After the 1996 election, the centre-left governments continued on the path of concerted action. However, as political parties returned to government they assumed a stronger role in the social agreements. Moreover, the focus shifted from principally restrictive measures to more 'recalibrating' policies (Ferrera and Gualmini 2004: 139–47). The centre-right, on the other hand, quite bluntly disrupted social concertation in 1994. When it returned to power in 2001 it clearly once more reduced the extent of consultation and negotiation with industrial organizations (Baglioni *et al.* 2008). Therefore, to the extent that the new party system established itself, the role of social agreements declined, although centre-left governing coalitions were more willing to involve unions and employer associations than centre-right coalitions.

The time of party system crisis and technical governments (1992–6) brought about several important reforms that were meant to recalibrate the Italian political economy and, in particular, to rein in public deficits in order to put Italy on track to fulfilling the Maastricht criteria (Ferrera and Gualmini 2004). However, in the field of unemployment benefits no major reform took place in those years. Unemployment benefits did not constitute a major item of public spending and, probably for this reason, did not enter the short-list of urgent reforms. From this perspective, it is interesting that the only two significant policy changes between 1992 and 1996 were two increases of the nominal replacement rate of UI (in 1993 from 20 to 25 per cent and in 1994 to 30 per cent); the first adopted under a technical government, the second under the first Berlusconi government. This indicates that even in a time of cutting costs the need to improve UI was recognized. In addition, some of the restrictions on CIG payments were repealed in this period. Overall, as opposed to other policy sectors, the crisis of the party system (1992–6) did not have many consequences for unemployment compensation. However, the beginning of party system change, with the transformation of the PCI into PDS, had enabled a significant reform (the 1991 reform of CIGS) before the old party system broke down.

Polarized bipolarism

After the election in 1994 none of the parties that had constituted the First Republic party system was to be found in parliament.[9] Both PCI and MSI had survived but each with a new name and more moderate policy outlook. The new party system has remained unstable up to the time of writing (March 2011). Nevertheless, I argue that across the period 1996–2008 we can identify some continuous features of the structure and mechanics of the party system. This period is framed, on the one hand, by the end of the technical governments (except for the Amato II government in 2000–1). Actually most of the new characteristics already played a role in the 1994 election, but due to the sheer novelty of the situation, the stormy nature of the Berlusconi I government, and its rapid replacement by another technical government, we cannot speak of a new pattern of party competition at that point yet. On the other hand, the period is delimited by the 2008 election that broke again with some of the party system characteristics of the preceding years.

The main attribute of the 1996–2008 party system was that two broad elect-oral coalitions of parties confronted each other that were both internally very diverse (Cotta and Verzichelli 2007: Ch. 2). This party system created, in Sar-tori's terms, centripetal competition between the two coalitions but produced also centrifugal tendencies between the parties that made up each coalition.[10] To some extent, these new features were shaped by the new electoral rules that were introduced in 1993 and again reformed in 2005. At the time of the party crisis, popular disaffection with the entrenched party system had, in fact, been expressed by two referenda (in 1991 and 1993) that changed the electoral system from a proportional to a more majoritarian system. Parliament was forced by these referenda to adopt a new electoral law in 1993, which parties used as an opportunity to retain some influence on the electoral system. The 1993 law arranged for three-quarters of the seats in each house to be assigned on a majori-tarian basis and the remaining seats by a proportional formula that penalized the parties that had already obtained 'majoritarian seats'. However, the proportional element was subjected to a 4 per cent threshold for the lower house (*Camera dei Deputati*) and was limited by the low number of 'proportional seats' in each multi-member constituency for the upper house (Senate).

The majoritarian thrust of this electoral system should have induced a process of concentration in the Italian party system – in the first place, by forming pre-electoral coalitions, but in the long-term by reducing the number of parties. The pre-electoral coalitions were built immediately and, indeed, constituted a major novelty in Italian politics. However, the overall fragmentation of the party system persisted and even increased in terms of parties represented in parlia-ment. Bartolini *et al.* (2004) have shown that this fragmentation was not caused by the proportional component of the new electoral system but by party efforts to build encompassing coalitions that safeguarded the interests of small parties. Thus, various parties, including small ones, were included in one electoral list and in pre-electoral negotiations each party was assigned a certain number of safe seats. It is not entirely clear why the larger parties committed to including even sometimes tiny parties in these coalitions but overall, it is evident that the breadth of a coalition increased the chance to win 'majoritarian seats' and, hence, had an important effect on winning elections. The importance of the coa-litions can be seen from the history of the three elections that were fought under the 1993 electoral law.

Thus, in 1994, the centre-right coalition won because *Forza Italia*, the party founded by Silvio Berlusconi only some months before the election, was able to form a coalition with AN and *Lega Nord* even though to this end two regionally separate alliances had to be formed. On the centre-left, by contrast, the PDS had only *Rifondazione* as a relatively strong coalition partner while the PPI, one of various successor formations of the DC, had not yet entered the centre-left coali-tion. In 1996, by contrast, the PPI (itself part of an electoral list called '*Popolari per Prodi*') did join the centre-left block with the PDS and several smaller centrist or moderate left parties. The PRC, on the other side, abandoned the electoral coalition but agreed to an electoral pact that avoided competition with the centre-left coalition. On the centre-right, the *Lega* pulled out of the coalition. Consequently, in 1996 the centre-left had the more comprehensive alliance and won the election. The whole game turned around again in 2001. The *Lega* joined the centre-right coalition and *Rifondazione* did not renew its electoral pact. Hence, the centre-right won (Vassallo 2005). Obviously, this coalitional algebra provided even small parties with considerable intra-coalitional power. For coalition-building, the problem was accentuated by extreme parties that had an electoral incentive to defect from coalitions in order to satisfy the voters who were unhappy with coalitional compromises. This was particularly true for the PRC on the left and the *Lega Nord* on the right.

In 2005, the electoral law was again reformed. While under the 1993 rules internally fragmented coalitions were mainly the result of parties' strategic choices rather than legislative incentives; the new electoral system induced the building of fragmented coalitions more directly. The new and still current electoral system is essentially proportional but assigns a majority bonus to the most successful electoral coalition of parties. The bonus is assigned on a national basis for the House of Representatives and on a regional basis for the Senate. Moreover, parties that stand for election independently, face a 4 per cent hurdle for entering parliament while coalition parties only have to exceed 2 per cent. Therefore, the coalition leaders have an incentive to gather the widest coalition possible in order to win the majority bonus. At the same time, the smaller parties have incentives to join coalitions and, once within a coalition, have no reason to renounce their party autonomy to the benefit of the coalition (Guarnieri 2006: 107–10).

In the 2006 election, both the centre-left and the centre-right managed to hold together their respective coalitions without significant defections. The consequence was an extremely tight race. However, in the House of Representatives the minuscule advantage of the centre-left in terms of votes was amplified by the majority bonus in terms of seats, but in the Senate the regional bonuses for both camps neutralized each other. As a consequence, the centre-left government that took office faced the task of governing with a negligible majority in the Senate and of holding together an extremely broad and diverse government coalition. All in all, the effect of the 2005 electoral system on party competition was similar to the effect of the 1993 system, although in 2005 this resulted from institutional incentives whereas in 1992 it result from the party strategies of dealing with the electoral system. In both cases, parties formed broad and internally diverse coalitions. This pattern was broken in 2008 in spite of the 2005 rules still being in place, which essentially testifies to the autonomy of party strategies, but an analysis of this issue is beyond the scope of this study (for the election results from 1994–2008 see Table 9.2).

Corbetta and Segatti (2004) have shown that there was much more movement of voters between parties of one coalition than between the two coalitions. That is to say, an important part of party competition was played within each

Table 9.2 Italian parliamentary election results, 1994–2008

	PRC	PdCI	Verdi	PDS/DS	PPI/Margh.	PR	Segni-Dini/IdV	CCD/UDC	FI	AN	LN	Others	Turnout
1994	6.1		2.7	20.4	11.1	3.5	4.7		21.0	13.5	8.4	8.8	86.1
1996	8.6		2.5	21.1	6.8	1.9	4.3	5.8	20.6	15.7	10.1	2.7	82.9
2001	5.0	1.7	2.2	16.6	14.5	2.2	3.9	3.2	29.4	12.0	3.9	5.3	81.4
2006	5.8	2.3	2.1	31.3		2.6	2.3	6.8	23.7	12.3	4.6	6.2	83.6
2008	3.1			33.2			4.4	5.6		37.4	8.3	8.1	80.5

Source: *Ministero Dell'Interno*.

Notes

Party results are per cent of party list votes for the Lower House (*Camera dei Deputati*). Turnout is per cent of those entitled to vote.
1994: *Segni-Dini/IdV* column reports result of *Patto Segni*, CCD candidates were included in the FI list, others include PSI (2.19 per cent, dissolved at end of 1994);
1996: PPI/Margh. column reports result of '*Popolari per Prodi*', *Segni-Dini/IdV* column reports result of *Rinnovamento Italiano–Dini*;
2001: *Segni-Dini/IdV* column reports result of IdV (under the name *Lista di Pietro*), others include *Democrazia Europea* (2.39 per cent, two senators);
2006: DS and *Margherita* present a joint electoral list called *Ulivo*, PR is *Rosa nel Pugno*, others include UDEUR (1.4 per cent, three senators);
2008: PRC column reports result of *Sinistra Arcobaleno* (no seats), DS and *Margherita* have merged into PD, FI and AN present the joint electoral list PdL, others include *Movimento per l'Autonomia* (1.13 per cent, two senators) and *Destra* (splinter of AN, 2.43 per cent, no seats).

coalition. However, this does not imply that competition between the two coalitions was irrelevant. After all, between two almost equally strong coalitions even small voter shifts can be crucial. But the difficulties of the internally diverse coalitions were largely created by that internal competition: first, the more radical parties of a coalition had electoral incentives to defect; second, coalition parties competed for votes against each other.

The party system as of 1996 is illustrated by Figure 9.4. We can distinguish easily the two electoral coalitions on the centre-left and centre-right respectively.[11] Competition between the two coalitions was bipolar and, hence, the centre of the political space was important for winning elections. The picture within each coalition is very different. Here we have one dominant party roughly in the centre of the coalition that is flanked by smaller parties on each side. In terms of competition between coalition members this means that competition was centrifugal. Yet, for the dominant party the intra-coalitional competition of more centrist parties only reinforced the centripetal tendency of the inter-coalitional dynamic. Therefore, the real challenge was posed by the more

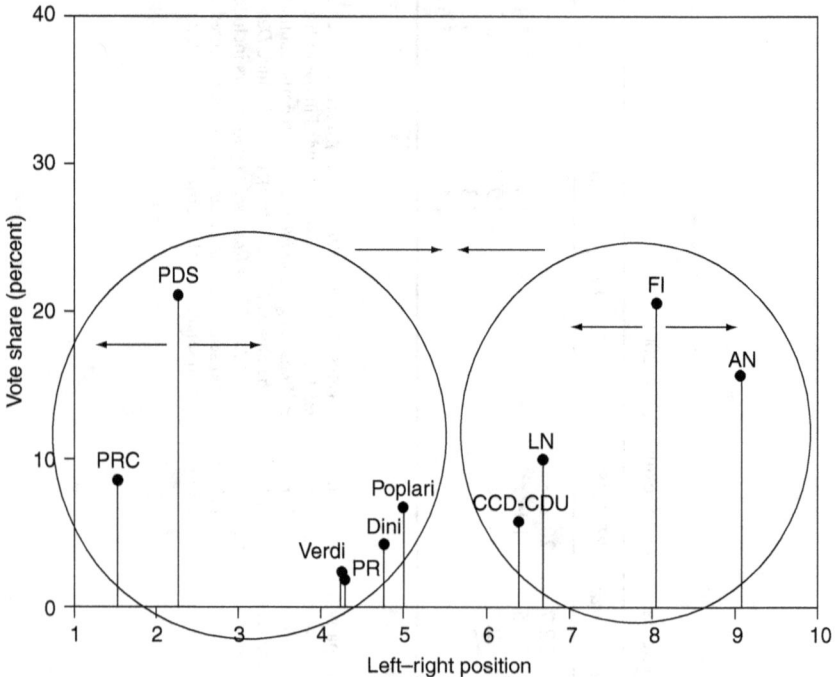

Figure 9.4 Italian party system in 1996 (sources: ITANES 1996, *Ministero Dell'Interno*).

Notes
Left–right positions are based on voters' average placement of parties on a general left–right dimension. Vote shares are the election results of 1996.

Encircled parties indicate party coalitions (however, LN was formally not a member of the centre-right coalition in 1996). Arrows indicate directions of competition (between coalitions and within coalitions).

extreme parties. Taking the far-left competition in the centre-left coalition and the far-right competition in the centre-right coalition together, they even create a centrifugal effect also on the system level.[12]

Although the precise composition of the party system changed and the vote shares fluctuated, the general picture of party competition in 1996 can also be confirmed for the following years up to 2008. However, the configuration changes somewhat when we analyse the party system on the socio-economic policy dimension instead of the general left–right dimension (see Figure 9.5). Here, I use again the item 'more public services versus less taxes' from the Benoit and Laver (2006) expert survey. In addition, I include only those parties for which the survey indicates that this dimension is relevant.[13] Consequently, on the centre-left *Verdi* and IdV are dropped, having moderately more left and right positions compared to DS respectively (after a further party reform in 1998 the

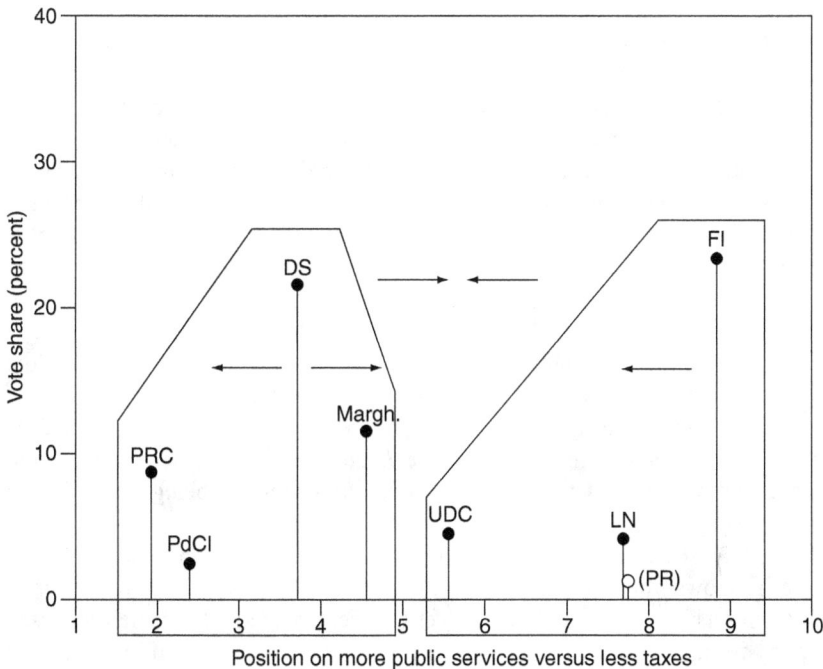

Figure 9.5 Italian party system on economic left–right dimension in 2004 (sources: Benoit and Laver (2006), ITANES (2004)).

Notes
Party positions from the Benoit and Laver (2006) expert survey conducted in 2003 (originally a 1–20 scale). Vote shares are vote intentions from the ITANES survey 2004.

Figure includes only parties for which this policy dimension is relevant. PR is bracketed because evidence on the relevance of this policy dimension is ambiguous.

Demarcated groups of parties indicate party coalitions (however, PR is in fact part of the centre-left coalition). Arrows indicate directions of competition (between coalitions and within coalitions).

The impact of LN on competition within its coalition is not adequately reflected because of its regionalism.

PDS had been renamed into the Left-wing Democrats: *Democratici di Sinistra,* DS). On the centre-right, AN is dropped, which has a centrist position on this axis, i.e. much more to the left than its 'general' position. However, if we take for each dimension the weighted average of the importance across all parties we find that in 2004 the 'taxes versus services' dimension was estimated to be the most important dimension in Italian party competition.

Figure 9.5 shows that on socio-economic issues only the DS faced competition from both sides of the coalition in 2004. As mentioned, competition on its right side only reinforces the centripetal tendency of inter-coalitional competition so that opposition from PRC and PdCI was the real strategic problem. By contrast, FI had only competitors towards the centre as it was itself the most liberalist party in the centre-right coalition. Moreover, FI is actually the only party that gives most importance among all issues to the 'more services versus less taxes' dimension. This facilitates exchange deals with the other coalition members. The centrist direction of competition for the FI is confirmed by the fact that in the 2001 election the party had adopted a strongly pro-market stance that was slowly moderated in successive years.

So, compared to the DS, FI is clearly in a more comfortable position on the dimension of social and economic policy. In terms of competition it had incentives to introduce a reform of unemployment benefits that would expand UI or SA. This would have appealed to more centrist voters while FI had no competitor to the right which would restrain such a move. If anything its own market liberal starting point impeded this kind of reform, or made it likely to proceed only gradually and to combine expansion with a tightening of conditionality. However, one aspect is not adequately reflected in the graph: the specific role of LN. As mentioned, LN mainly woos Northern voters where it attracts middle class voters and recently ever more industrial workers. It strongly opposes to increases in social security contributions or taxes that are not confined to public spending in the North. In particular, the *Lega* rejected schemes of minimum income that would inevitably lead to a lot of resources being spent in the Mezzogiorno.

Table 9.3 provides data on the distribution of policy preferences in the Italian public. It shows voters' agreement with a statement on reducing taxes even if this implies a reduction of public services (hence, essentially the same issue used for party positions in Figure 9.5). These policy preferences are differentiated by respondents' self-placement on a general left–right axis. The figure, therefore, takes the percentages of responses to the policy question within each spatial segment. For the sake of completeness I also report the distribution of voters across the left–right axis. However, bear in mind that parties cannot choose any point in political space by numbers of voters, rather they make their move depending on the presence of other parties.

Towards the left voters tend to fully disagree with tax reduction at the expense of public services while right-wing voters somewhat agree with it, and the highest percentage of people fully agreeing with this policy approach can be found on the extreme right. Hence, if FI and the centre-right coalition compete

Table 9.3 Distribution of social policy preferences on left–right political dimension in Italy 2001 (%)

Agreement with statement: Taxes should be cut even if this leads to a reduction of public services

	Left	2	3	4	5	6	7	8	9	Right	Mean
Fully agree	14.3	6.8	10.8	10.0	12.3	12.0	13.6	18.6	18.3	20.1	13.3
Somewhat agree	19.5	25.3	23.8	26.1	35.4	36.4	44.5	42.3	45.0	43.9	34.3
Somewhat disagree	25.3	27.2	30.0	36.1	29.5	36.4	28.6	21.8	28.3	19.5	29.0
Fully disagree	40.9	40.7	35.3	27.9	22.9	15.2	13.3	17.3	8.3	16.5	23.3
Overall left–right self-placement of respondents											
	6.1	6.4	12.7	11.0	16.0	12.4	12.1	12.1	4.7	6.5	5.4

Source: ITANES (2001), own calculations.

Note
Percentages in first four rows are the proportion of respondents agreeing or disagreeing with the statement within each section of the left–right scale.

for more voters in the centre they have to de-emphasize tax reduction and offer more public services. But, as mentioned, FI had to take account of the regionalist position of the *Lega* that is critical of public spending by the central state. The DS and the centre-left coalition, on the other side, had to de-emphasize public spending for competing with the opposite coalition, However, for competing with the radical left and for keeping it in the coalition, the DS had to promote more public provisions. It was caught in a double bind.

Centripetal competition between the electoral coalitions was the main factor that facilitated reforms of unemployment benefits, but, at the same time, a structural reform of the benefit system was prevented by centrifugal tendencies. For centre-left governments the main obstacle was posed by the radical left (PRC, PdCI, and CGIL). From this side of the political space, much of the game was still played around protecting employment rather than increasing unemployment compensation. Even in 2007 a high official of the CGIL described the union's position in a journal article, saying: '[T]he objective must not be to simply alleviate the effects of unemployment, but, within the limits mentioned below, to avoid unemployment' (Treves 2007: 202). The article goes on to propose extending the CIG regime, with some modifications, to all sections of the labour force. At the level of party politics these demands were supported by the PRC whereas the DS started to promote the concept of 'flexicurity', i.e. combining a flexible labour market with appropriate social security.[14] In addition, the radical left was sceptical of SA reform, which was regarded as poor relief rather than effective social security. But the main obstacle to a structural reform of unemployment compensation was the political support for the CIG regime.

The centre-right also had to take into consideration the potentially fierce opposition by CGIL and the radical left parties to any serious cutbacks of CIG and other important entitlements of the core industrial working force. This was a lesson it learned when it attempted to push through a pension reform in 1994. At the same time, within the centre-right coalition, mainly the position of the *Lega Nord* and its rejection of spending that goes disproportionately to the South impeded a comprehensive reform of unemployment benefits. This applied especially to the introduction of a minimum income scheme.

The double requirements of centripetal and centrifugal competition explain why in this period the disparity of unemployment benefits has been reduced while at the same time it was impossible to adopt a more structural reform of unemployment compensation. The improvement of UI was a measure that each coalition, for its own reasons, was able to agree to. For the centre-left, this constituted part of a modernization of the existing system and made good for cuts in other parts of the welfare state with extremely generous social protection, especially pensions. Unemployment insurance is the central pillar of most modern systems of unemployment protection and it allows for more flexible markets than CIG. At the same time, increasing the replacement rate of UI meant increasing social protection. The radical left found it more and more difficult to strictly oppose this in spite of its continuing preference for employment creation and employment protection. From the perspective of the centre-right, enhancing the generosity of UI was an opportunity to avoid the image of caring only about free enterprise. At the same time, expanding UI did not involve dramatic redistribution from North to South. In fact, it benefited workers from small firms in the North (Jessoula *et al.* 2010) and, therefore, a constituency of *Lega Nord*. In addition, it was acceptable for liberalist voters because it is a more liberal policy than CIG. Indeed, after the crisis of the party system the successive increases of UI were adopted to more or less equal parts by centre-left and centre-right majorities: 1994 by the centre-right, 2000 by the centre-left (but formally under a technical government), 2005 by the centre-right, and 2007 by the centre-left.

The SA reform and the attempted introduction of a minimum income scheme (RMI) have played a similar role in the politics of the centre-left. Again, this could be presented as a way to modernize the Italian welfare state as (basically) all advanced industrial states have a scheme of this kind. Furthermore, it was acceptable to centrist voters because it was not a highly generous transfer scheme but required recipients to put some effort into finding work or socially integrating themselves in other ways. PRC and CGIL actually opposed the introduction of RMI for similar reasons for which it was acceptable for centrist voters. However, the reform was set to increase social protection for the poorest sections of society. Hence, left-wing critics were in a weak position. However, the RMI experiment was abandoned by the following centre-right government, and it was mainly the opposition of the *Lega* that prevented a continuation of the scheme. This opposition was facilitated by the fact that the Minister of Labour and Social Policies came from the *Lega*. Accordingly, he publicly judged RMI to be expensive and ineffective, even though the costs were estimated around 0.2 per cent of GDP (Sacchi 2007: 428).

In two other important examples of labour market reforms, even if not directly related to unemployment benefits, the mentioned dynamics of competition can be found as well. In 1997 parliament adopted the so-called Treu-package (named after the Labour Minister Tiziano Treu), which deregulated atypical work contracts. In the parliamentary process that Gualmini describes (1998: 253–62), actors' positions were expressed in wider terms so that the reform can serve more generally as an example of labour market policy in this period. First of all, the law was adopted under a centre-left government and, being a deregulatory provision, it conformed to centripetal competition. In the Senate it was strongly contested by *Rifondazione,* precisely because of deregulation. This reflected the centrifugal counter-tendency that the party system created. This intra-coalitional opposition brought about a compromise that included a more moderate deregulation and extra funding for public work programmes in the South. Also the parties of the centre-right reacted in ways that correspond to the political positions on economic issues, already discussed. The post-DC party CCD–CDU was available for cooperation with the centre-left, *Forza Italia* criticized the measure for not deregulating sufficiently, and the *Lega* appreciated the deregulation as helpful for Northern enterprises but criticized the extra funding for public work in the South. Gualmini (1998: 259) notes that the two Labour Commissions of the Senate and the Camera respectively functioned as arenas of political confrontation rather than technical problem solving. More-over, she observes how the dimension 'flexibility versus rigidity' that structured the debate coincides with the right–left political dimension. Therefore, in this example, policy-making was clearly structured by the configuration of the party system and contained the expected centripetal and centrifugal tendencies.

The relevance of continuing polarization can also be observed in the attempt of the centre-right government to reduce dismissal protection. In autumn 2001 it presented a draft bill that included the proposal to exempt companies under spe-cific conditions from article 18 of the *Statuto dei Lavoratori*, which strictly regu-lates dismissals. The unions, especially the CGIL, immediately mobilized against the plan. They saw article 18 not only as a crucial protection of workers,[15] but also as a symbolic achievement of working class struggles. In spring 2002 the CGIL organized a general strike against the reform plan. About three million workers participated. The other unions, CISL and UIL (*Unione Italiana del Lavoro*), eventually participated in negotiations with the government and signed a 'Pact for Italy' in summer 2002. The agreement included a reduced proposal to reforming article 18. At the same time, it pledged to increase the level of UI and to intervene in favour of low income workers and economic development in the Mezzogiorno. However, the biggest union federation, the CGIL, did not sign the pact and maintained its strict opposition to modifications of article 18 (Ferrera and Gualmini 2004: 156–61; Vesan 2008: 17–19). Moreover, a number of left-wing parties and unions, including parts of the CGIL, initiated a referendum that would, on the contrary, extend the field of application of dismissal protection also to firms with less than 15 employees. In the end, the referendum failed to reach the necessary quorum, but, furthermore, the reform of article 18 was not adopted. Agreed, the example does not correspond well to the centripetal logic of competition between electoral coalitions. Shortly after winning the election and returning to government office the major government party (*Forza Italia*) tried to implement some of its market liberal agenda. However, the example nicely illustrates the remaining elements of polarization and the continuing pref-erence for employment protection by the radical left, which made labour market reforms difficult for both the centre-left and the centre-right.

Summing up, the lack of decisive reforms of unemployment compensation during the 1980s can be explained by persisting polarized pluralism. Although polarization was moderated by many years of elite-level cooperation it was still entrenched in the structure of the party system and impeded programmatic com-petition. Since the beginning of the 1990s, more significant reforms became pos-sible due to the transformation of the party system. Initially, this was driven by a moderation of the left, following the collapse of state communism in Eastern Europe. After the uprooting of the old party system in 1992–4, centripetal dynam-ics of competition emerged as a centre-left, and a centre-right pre-electoral party coalition competed against each other. This enabled the gradual but recognizable reduction of benefit disparity. However, within each coalition the competition between parties continued to generate centrifugal tendencies, which impeded the introduction of more fundamental reforms of unemployment compensation.

The election of 2008 and subsequent developments have again transformed the Italian party system. *Democratici di Sinistra* and *Margherita* (one of the post-DC parties) fused into the Democratic Party (*Partito Democratico*, PD), which decided early on to stand for the 2008 election on its own and not as part of a large electoral coalition – even if in the end it did form a coalition with 'Italy of Values' (*Italia dei Valori*, IdV, a peculiar party of anti-Berlusconi, anti-corruption, and pro criminal-justice positions). As the PD declined to extend this coalition, the radical left formed a joint electoral list of its own but did not manage to enter parliament. Also in response to the PD fusion, FI and AN formed the 'People of Freedom' party (*Popolo della Libertà*, PdL). Therefore, the election of 2008 notably simplified the party system where, at first only four relevant parties (PdL, LN, PD, and IdV) and no anti-system parties (except for, possibly, the secessionist LN) remained.[16]

However, since then the political scene has changed again. On the left, the 'Left, Ecology, and Freedom' party (*Sinistra-Ecologia-Libertà*, SEL) headed by the charismatic president of a South-Italian region has gained some political clout. More importantly, the former AN-leader Gianfranco Fini became increasingly critical of Berlusconi. In consequence, a group of former AN parliamentarians split off from PdL and formed the 'Future and Freedom' party (*Futuro e Libertà*, FLi). This jeopardized the government majority. Nevertheless, Berlusconi managed to rebuild his majority by a close margin. This has increased the relevance of even small groups of parliamentarians and generated a new tendency of fragmentation. In addition, party politics is ever more concentrated on the person of Berlusconi and his judicial trials and affairs, dividing parties into pro- and anti-Berlusconi camps. This almost suspends competition on other issues and raises highly uncertain prospects about party system development once Berlusconi leaves government.[17]

In the short period since 2008, there is no clear evidence on the effect that the new and still volatile configuration of the party system had on unemployment benefits. The Italian reaction to the economic crisis consisted mainly in boosting CIG spending. In itself, this emphasis on wage supplementation for short-time workers could be observed in many countries. What was more specific of the Italian crisis response was that much of the CIG spending went into discretionary exemptions from the normal application of CIG (*CIG in deroga*, cf. Sacchi *et al.* forthcoming). Partly, these ad hoc extensions of CIG coverage were of course a consequence of the need to act quickly and, in particular, to take care of small firms and their employees that are an important electoral basis of *Lega* and PdL. In addition, the continuing fragmentation of the party system has contributed to this trend. As we have seen the simplification of the party system after 2008 did not last. The diminishing of the government majority has strengthened the bargaining power of small parties, which remains anyway substantial due to the electoral law that encourages large and heterogeneous coalitions. Therefore, the logic of party system fragmentation persists, which favours narrow interests and discretionary policy-making such as in the extension of CIG.

10 Party competition and benefit segmentation across advanced welfare states

The analysis so far was a historical comparison between Italy and Germany. We traced the influence that the two very different party systems in these countries had on the segmentation of unemployment benefits since the Second World War. We focused on the number of parties as well as their positioning in political space. In the post-war decades of welfare expansion the unemployment benefit systems in both states took very different paths. We have shown in Chapter 7 that this divergence can be explained to a large extent by the different party systems. Also for the phase of welfare restructuring we have seen that reforms were affected by party competition and the configuration of party systems.

It was possible to isolate the impact of party systems due to a careful case selection that controls for many other causal variables. The partisan composition of government, the political institutions, the policy traditions, and the economic models – all these aspects were relatively similar in post-war Italy and Germany with respect to the wider set of advanced capitalist democracies. The fact that we find an influence of the two different party systems while controlling for other variables suggests that party systems also have an effect on the segmentation on social protection in other cases. In this chapter I will provide evidence that this is indeed the case.

In order to show that party systems shaped the segmentation of unemployment benefits in other advanced welfare states, beyond Germany and Italy, I will proceed in two steps. First, I will show how the benefit systems at the end of the formative phase of welfare expansion correspond to different types of party systems that prevailed during that phase of expansion. Analysing that period should be the most important basis for explaining the patterns of segmentation as they are today. Obviously, the benefit systems subsequently were reformed in many ways that may have modified the segmentation of social protection. Unfortunately, it is impossible in the context of this chapter to trace all those reforms. Rather, and this will be the second step, I will pick out a time span of eight years for which good data is available and will analyse the reforms that took place in that period. Note, therefore, that the analysis in this chapter should be seen against the background of the systematic historical comparison of Italy and Germany and as a preliminary step towards testing the argument on more cases.

Party system types and the formation of benefit systems

This section confronts the party systems that prevailed in 15 advanced welfare states during post-war expansion and the unemployment benefit systems at the end of that phase. For this purpose we, first, have to take stock of what the segmentation of unemployment compensation was like at that point. I choose for this purpose the early 1980s. This is already some years into the phase of welfare state reform, but in this way I can profit, as one of my sources, from the 'Growth to Limits' project, headed by Peter Flora, that reported detailed country descriptions as of the early 1980s (Flora 1986b). Most countries had not introduced structural labour market reforms at that point yet.

As in Chapter 3, we have to account for two dimensions of benefit segmentation: (1) the dimension of division, which regards how many benefit schemes there are and how inclusive or exclusive they are; (2) the dimension of generosity differences between the various benefit schemes. The first dimension is measured by considering the benefit schemes that were in place in each country and their respective beneficiary rates. The second dimension, unfortunately, cannot be accounted for very well regarding this early period because we lack data on the generosity of the secondary benefit schemes. In order to have at least a rough estimate I assume that low replacement rates of UI imply low differences of generosity if a secondary scheme – SA or UA – exists. A summary of the descriptive data can be found in Table 10.1, while the categorization based on this descriptive data follows below. In addition, Table 10.1 reports when SA was introduced in each country, which indicates how early in the phase of welfare expansion the interests of the socially excluded were taken into account by the political system.

Based on the information from Table 10.1, we can identify the pattern of benefit segmentation in each country. As in Chapter 3, I distinguish between four categories on the dimension of division: 'inclusive, assistance-based', 'inclusive, insurance-based', 'stratified, three-tier', and 'exclusive, insurance-based'. The inclusiveness of each benefit system is judged by considering the accessibility of the more generous schemes. Hence, benefit systems can be inclusive because the main benefit provides income support to everyone in need (inclusive, assistance-based). Or they can be inclusive because eligibility criteria for UI are easy to fulfil so that the scheme has a high beneficiary rate (inclusive, insurance-based). Among the less inclusive system we can distinguish two types, by looking at the lower levels of the benefit system. Some states have a middle tier, which is designated to the long-term unemployed. Therefore, the prevailing characteristic in these states is the stratification into more than two tiers (stratified, three-tier). In other states with low beneficiary rates of UI there is only one level of income support for the rest of the unemployed (exclusive, insurance-based).

The dimension of generosity differences is populated by three groups of states that I label 'equal but low', 'pro-insider', and 'outsider-gap'. Therefore, some states have only minuscule differences between benefit schemes or even no differences at all. However, these states usually provide low benefit levels overall

Table 10.1 Unemployment compensation in 15 advanced welfare states in the early 1980s

Country	Benefit schemes (a)	(b)	(c)	Beneficiary rate UI	Beneficiary rate UA	NRR UI	Introduction SA
Australia	UA	UA	UA	–	79	48 (UA)	n.av.
New Zealand	UA	UA	UA	–	78	54 (UA)	n.av.
United Kingdom	UI (flat)	SA	SA	44	–	36	1949
Belgium	UI	UI	SA	116	–	68	1974
Denmark	UI	SA	SA	105	–	82	1961
Norway	UI	SA	SA	118	–	70	1964
Sweden	UI	SA/UA	SA/UA	50	58	88	1956
Austria	UI	UA/SA	SA	62	n.av.	65	1971–8
Germany	UI	UA	SA/UA	60	19	69	1961
Netherlands	UI	UA/SA	SA	30	41	54	1963
Finland	UI	UA	UA	35	35	44	1956
Ireland	UI	UA	UA	53	50	50	1975
Switzerland	UI	(SA)	(SA)	n.av.	n.av.	n.av.	(1977)
Italy	UI	–	–	(66)	–	8	–
United States	UI	(SA)	(SA)	38	–	68	(1964)

Sources: Flora (1986b), Scruggs (2004), OECD (2010b)

Notes

- Beneficiary and net replacement rates are in per cent.
- Countries are ordered by similarity of their benefit systems (cf. Table 10.2).
- '–' means measure does not apply, 'n.av.' means data is not available.
- The coding of benefit schemes indicates the benefits for the following sequence of qualification statuses: (a) main benefit, (b) main benefit exhausted, (c) not eligible for main benefit.
- Beneficiary rates are averages for years 1979–83. They are based on beneficiary numbers by Scruggs (2004) and harmonized unemployment levels by OECD (2010b). The use of harmonized unemployment numbers explains why the beneficiary rate can be above 100%. The rate for Italy is a rough estimate and probably too high.
- For more information on the concept of benefit segmentation and the measures used, see Chapter 3.

('equal but low'). Others have a level of support for the more marginalized unemployed that is similar to the 'equal but low' benefit systems, but they pay higher benefits in the UI scheme ('pro-insider'). The third group of states has average or above-average levels of compensation for insiders becoming unemployed, but lacks adequate social protection for those excluded from the more generous benefit ('outsider-gap'). Table 10.2 reports where on both dimensions the 15 welfare states considered here can be located.

Out of the 15 advanced welfare states three can be categorized as inclusive on the dimension of division and as having small differences in generosity, if only at a low level, at the beginning of the 1980s. Australia and New Zealand already had just UA at the time. UK is a more ambiguous case; in 1981 the earnings-related benefit supplement, which had been introduced in 1966, had been abolished as one of the first retrenchment measures. Apart from this temporary top-up, UI was always flat-rate in UK. This fact also qualifies the relatively low beneficiary rate of UI. Being a flat-rate benefit amounting to 36 per cent of the wage of an average production worker, the difference to the secondary scheme (SA) was considerably lower than in countries with earnings-related UI benefits.

Four of the countries analysed here – Denmark, Norway, Sweden, and Belgium – had very inclusive and generous UI and are, therefore, categorized as inclusive on the dimension of division and 'pro-insider' in terms of generosity differences. Assigning Sweden to the inclusive group is less clear because its beneficiary rate of UI was clearly lower than in the other three countries. However, the context of full employment in Sweden is relevant here as well as the fact that UI was voluntary and union-administered while UA was designed as the state-administered backup that still had insurance characteristics such as contributory requirements. Therefore, when adding up the beneficiary rates of UI and UA (together 108 per cent) and keeping in mind the implications of full employment for voluntary insurance and take-up rates, it becomes clear that Sweden was anyhow closer to the group of inclusive benefit systems than to the stratified or exclusive benefit systems.

Table 10.2 Patterns of segmentation in 15 advanced welfare states, early 1980s

Division: generosity differences:	Inclusive (assistance-based)	Inclusive (insurance-based)	Stratified (three-tier)	Exclusive (insurance-based)
Equal but low	AU, NZ, (UK)			
Pro-insider		BE, NO, DK, (SE)	NL, AT, DE	(IE), (FI)
Outsider gap				US, IT, (CH)

Notes
The arrows indicate increasing segmentation, but the two dimensions are not linear. Ambiguous cases are in brackets. Patterns of segmentation are based on: benefit schemes and beneficiary rates for dimension of division, UI NRR and existence of SA or UA for dimension of generosity differences.

Welfare states with three benefit schemes, where UA takes care especially of those who exhaust UI, are classified as stratified. These states have also relatively generous UI and are, consequently, counted as pro-insider on the dimension of generosity differences – falling into this category are Austria, Germany, and the Netherlands. Finland and Ireland were hard to classify – both had two benefit schemes (UI and UA) and rather low beneficiary rates of UI; hence, they are labelled as 'insurance-based and exclusive'. Their replacement rates of UI were not very high. However, both had earnings-related insurance schemes which distinguish them from the equal but low benefit schemes in terms of generosity differences. Consequently, they are categorized as 'exclusive/pro-insider' but remain somewhat ambiguous. In the following analysis they will be considered jointly with the group of stratified/pro-insider systems because their overall level of segmentation is similar, the main difference being that they contain two instead of three strata.

Clearly more segmented, however, are those countries that lack sufficient social protection for the unemployed who cannot receive UI. In addition, beneficiary rates of UI in these countries are low. Such is the case in the US where no full-fledged SA programme exists but only food stamps. Regarding the Italian case, we know from Chapter 4 that there were more benefit schemes besides UI, which were much more generous and exclusive. There was not much data on Switzerland in the sources used here. Switzerland introduced national regulation for SA in 1977, but without specifying national standards for benefit levels. Moreover, it only introduced compulsory unemployment at the national level in 1982. The administration of UI was fragmented into many funds in the early 1980s even if subject to federal supervision and regulation. The lack of a social right to minimum assistance levels and the high fragmentation of UI add up to including Switzerland in the category of 'exclusive and outsider-gap' benefit systems. It has to be added though that full employment attenuated the issue of benefit segmentation.

Most advanced welfare states introduced their first unemployment benefits before the Second World War (Alber 1981). However, as with other social security schemes, they were massively expanded only after the Second World War. Therefore, the phase between 1945 and the 1970s can be regarded as the formative phase of unemployment benefit systems, in which political conditions, such as the party system, left their imprint. For the party systems that prevailed in that period I rely on Sartori's (2005) typology as well as his empirical analysis. As explained in Chapter 1, his typology is suitable for our purpose because it combines the number of parties with the question of ideological polarization. Empirically, his analysis is appropriate because it focuses on the early post-war decades (his book was first published in 1976).

Among the 15 advanced welfare states analysed here, five had two-party systems between the Second World War and the 1970s: UK, Australia, New Zealand, the US, and Austria. Sartori looks not only formally at the number of parties and polarization but is concerned with the 'mechanics' of how party systems function. In two-party systems each party constitutes an alternative government so that their competition gives rise to alternating governments. Up to

1966 this was not the case in Austria where both parties governed in a grand coalition. Therefore, Austria is an ambiguous case (Sartori 2005: 164–5). Following our hypotheses (see Chapter 1) having only two big parties in a party system should give rise to encompassing benefit schemes, such as assistance benefits, that are very inclusive but are neither very costly nor make big differences in generosity.

The second type in Sartori's typology consists of party systems where one party dominates but elections remain competitive. Usually these predominant party systems contain more than two parties. Due to the predominant party, again our argument applies that large parties have incentives to construct comprehensive benefits rather than focusing on narrow interests. In our sample Norway and Sweden had party systems where the Social Democratic Party was predominant. Denmark also had a very strong Social Democratic Party but, in contrast to Sweden and Norway, it mostly ruled in coalition.

Party systems of moderate pluralism are characterized by many parties (between three and five) and the absence of ideological polarization. Related is segmented pluralism that consists of more parties but also lacks ideological polarization and, hence, has similar political dynamics and is included by Sartori among the moderate pluralist systems. States that fall into this group are Denmark, Belgium, Germany, Ireland, and, as segmented pluralism, the Netherlands and Switzerland. In these party systems we would expect a greater differentiation in unemployment compensation, but no extreme segmentation due to the centripetal tendency of competition that prevails.

In the sample of 15 states the only clear case of polarized pluralism (more than five parties and ideological polarization) is Italy. Finland is an ambiguous case according to Sartori (2005: 144–6). Its six parties and the presence of a strong Communist Party are reasons for including it in this category. However, there was no relevant anti-system party on the extreme right. Moreover, the Communist Party did participate in government for a few years and did not manage to pose a continuous electoral threat as its vote share did not increase significantly over time. For the states with polarized and fragmented party systems I hypothesize marked segmentation of unemployment benefits.

Table 10.3 confronts party system types and patterns of unemployment benefit segmentation. The general tendency in the table is clear: more dispersed party systems during welfare state expansion have generated more segmented systems of unemployment compensation.[1] Two-party systems were closely associated with inclusive benefit systems that had equal but low benefit levels. In fact, these benefit systems emerged only in states where two large parties compete for power. Both states with predominant party systems brought about benefit systems that were built around highly inclusive and generous UI. For sure, the predominant parties in both of these states were social democratic. Therefore the result conforms to traditional partisan theory as well as to my prediction on the effect of large parties and low polarization.

The benefit systems that emerged under moderate pluralism are more diverse, but they are mostly at a moderate level of segmentation. An exception is

Table 10.3 Cross-tabulation of party systems and unemployment benefit segmentation for the phase of welfare state expansion

	Two parties	Predominance	Moderate pluralism	Polarized pluralism
Inclusive, equal but low	UK, AU, NZ			
Inclusive, pro-insider		NO, SE	DK, BE	
Stratified, pro-insider	(AT)		DE, NL*, IE	(FI)
Exclusive, outsider gap	US		CH*	IT

Notes
Columns more to the right are more dispersed party systems (by number of parties and polarization). Rows towards the bottom are more segmented unemployment benefit systems. Cases in brackets are ambiguous with respect to the party system. Cases with an asterisk belong to the sub-type 'segmented pluralism' with a high number of parties.

Switzerland with a more segmented benefit system. However, the argument of this book suggests that this is related to the higher number of parties in the culturally fragmented country. Apart from Switzerland, moderate pluralism only has brought about benefit systems with generosity differences that favour insiders while still providing basic protection for outsiders. Austria is the only country with a clearly stratified benefit system where moderate pluralism did not prevail. Yet, as mentioned, Austria was not a typical case of two-partyism either. Finally, the single unambiguous case of polarized pluralism (Italy) introduced a strongly segmented benefit system.

The only real exception from the association of dispersion in party systems and segmentation in unemployment compensation is the US, which had a two-party system but institutionalized a highly segmented benefit system. However, parties are particularly weak in the US (Katz and Kolodny 1994). Presidentialism weakens party discipline and candidate selection, through primaries, further strengthens the individual member of Congress vis-à-vis the party. Therefore, it is not surprising that two-party competition does not have the same effect on US policies as, for example, in British parliamentarism with strong parties.

The identified link between party systems and systems of unemployment compensation might be spurious insofar as it might be driven by a third variable. In the context of this chapter it is not possible to control systematically for other variables. However, I briefly want to discuss two rival political factors: electoral system and left government. There seems to be an association between those states that have highly inclusive but meagre unemployment benefits and majoritarian electoral systems. Among the three states with equal but low benefit levels New Zealand and UK have majoritarian electoral laws. Australia's system is not purely majoritarian because the upper house is elected proportionally. Yet, the lower house is elected in single-member districts, which generates a majoritarian logic even if, more precisely, the system is based on instant runoff voting. The only state with clearly majoritarian elections that does not have low benefit segmentation is the US. As is well known, majoritarian electoral systems tend to bring about two-party systems (for a critical discussion see Nohlen 2009, Ch. 10.3). Therefore, the association of low benefit segmentation and majoritarian electoral law does not disprove my argument. Rather, it points out a cause behind party systems. However, other authors have argued that electoral systems themselves generate incentives for parties and politicians to focus on broader or narrower social interests (Estévez-Abe 2008). In theory, these incentives can also work independently of the party system. I argue that in most cases they will be reflected in the number of parties (see the discussion in Chapter 1). Nevertheless, the policy incentives that result from electoral rules and their interaction with party system structures would merit further research.[2]

Figure 10.1 compares the average cabinet share of left parties during welfare expansion (data only available from 1960) and patterns of segmentation. It shows that the explanatory power of traditional partisan politics theory for explaining benefit segmentation is low. To some extent, it indicates that dominance of left parties in government produces inclusive benefit systems with generosity differences in favour of insiders as in Norway, Denmark, and Sweden. However, two of these are also predominant party systems so that in these cases the dominance of left parties is coupled with the party system argument. On the other hand, Austria had a similarly high share of left partisanship but produced a stratified system of unemployment compensation. For all other levels of left-partisan

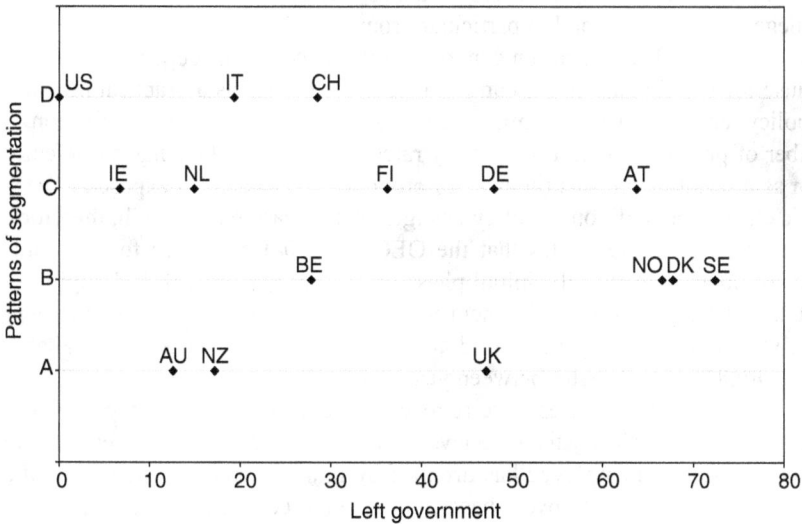

Figure 10.1 Left government and segmentation of unemployment benefits (sources: Armingeon *et al.* (2010) and Table 10.2 above).

Notes
Left government is the average cabinet share of left parties between 1960 and 1982. Patterns of segmentation are A=inclusive/equal-but-low, B=inclusive/pro-insider, C=stratified/pro-insider, D=exclusive/outsider-gap.

government the effect on segmentation of unemployment compensation is even less clear. UK and Germany had both a left-partisan share of 47–8 per cent between 1960 and 1982 but developed markedly different benefit systems. Similarly, New Zealand and Italy had very similar partisan shares of 17 and 19 per cent respectively; but the difference in benefit segmentation could not be greater.

Number of parties and reforms of unemployment benefits

So far, the evidence suggests that the dispersion of power in party systems (in terms of the number of parties and of polarization) can help to explain the segmentation of unemployment compensation that emerged over the phase of welfare expansion. As a next step, I will test the party system argument for the phase of welfare state reform that began in the 1970s. For this purpose, I will focus only on the part of the argument that refers to the number of parties. A categorization of party systems into Sartori's types was not available and requires detailed knowledge of each party system. Instead, I will measure here the number of parties with the commonly used Laakso-Taagepera formula for the 'effective number of electoral parties' (see Chapter 2). As argued in Chapter 1, a high number of parties can be expected to increase unemployment benefit segmentation on both dimensions. Benefit fragmentation increases because small parties focus on narrow interests. And generosity differences widen because only large parties have incentives to comprise the interests of assistance recipients and tax-payers in a comprehensive benefit system, whereas small parties may privilege the policy demand of particular groups.

In this section I will focus on generosity differences as the dependent variable because for this dimension we can use replacement rates as a practical measure of policy changes. The potential measures for the dimension of division – number of programmes and beneficiary rates – either do not change sufficiently often as a result of reforms (number of programmes) or are too exposed to economic changes in addition to policy changes (beneficiary rates). I will, therefore, use the net replacement rates that the OECD (2010a) calculates for two situations of unemployment: the initial phase of unemployment with full eligibility for UI, and long-term unemployment when UI has expired. These replacement rates, which have already been used and discussed in Chapter 3,[3] are available for 28 OECD member states between years 2001 and 2008.

In that period many states have retrenched the benefit level for the 'outsider unemployed' more clearly than the level of UI. On average the replacement rate for the long-term unemployed has dropped by four percentage points while the rate for the 'insider unemployed' has actually increased on average by one point. Hence, some states have also raised the benefit level of UI. In that case they often have raised it more than the benefit level of the assistance benefit (e.g. Hungary) or they have even cut back the assistance benefit at the same time as expanding the more generous benefit (e.g. Iceland). Therefore, overall segmentation of unemployment benefits has increased in most states over the 2000s because generosity differences have widened.

Of the 28 OECD states, I have filtered out those countries where a significant change (larger than standard deviation) in either or both of the two replacement rates has taken place. My objective is not to explain *whether* countries reformed unemployment benefits but *how* they reformed them. As the time period 2001–8 is quite narrow, the fact that a country has not changed its benefit system during the spell is not meaningful. This is also the reason why I do not conduct a pooled time series analysis, but just a cross-sectional analysis of the reform cases. The selection leaves 15 cases in my dataset ('reform countries').[4] The dependent variable, therefore, is the change in replacement rates in each country between 2001 and 2008. I use the proportional change of each replacement rate with respect to its value in 2001 as well as the difference between these two change rates. The latter is a summary measure for the change in generosity differences.[5] By subtracting the change of the outsider benefit level from the change of the insider benefit level, negative values indicate an increase in generosity differences – or a decrease of benefit equality. Assuming no change on the dimension of division, a drop in benefit equality implies a more segmented benefit system.

Inspecting the times series of annual replacement rates, I identified the crucial reform year for each of the 15 'reform countries', by singling out the year previous to the clearest change of the replacement rate. In three states no abrupt change took place: Australia, Czech Republic, and Finland. However, the continuous benefit decline in these countries can still be based on deliberate political choices, such as the choice of an unfavourable or even lacking indexation mechanism. Even if this is not the case it is still a political issue why the decline of benefit generosity that accumulates over time is tolerated (Streeck and Thelen 2005; Hall and Thelen 2009). At some point such a decline begs the question why the interests of those adversely affected are not taken up by political parties. Independent and control variables are coded at their value in the reform year or their average value for the previous years. In cases without reform year the average of 2001–8 was taken. As mentioned, the main independent variable used here is the effective number of electoral parties. As control variables I use the cabinet share of left-wing parties, institutional veto points, unemployment, and the initial replacement rate of either benefit scheme.

If we plot the difference between changes of both replacement rates against the number of parties, a clear and significant negative trend emerges (coefficient –0.065, p-value 0.03; see Figure 10.2). States with more fragmented party systems have reduced the replacement rate for 'outsider unemployed' more strongly than for 'insider unemployed'. As we deal with only 15 cases, this analysis is of course sensitive to single data points. The countries with the greatest deterioration of benefit equality are the Slovak Republic and Iceland. The former has a highly fragmented party system, the latter less so. Consequently, excluding the Slovak Republic weakens the correlation (coefficient –0.016, p-value 0.69). In addition, excluding Iceland restores a clear negative trend but not its significance (coefficient –0.031, p-value 0.33).

When we add the control variables to the regression (for all 15 reform cases), party system fragmentation has again a significantly negative effect on benefit

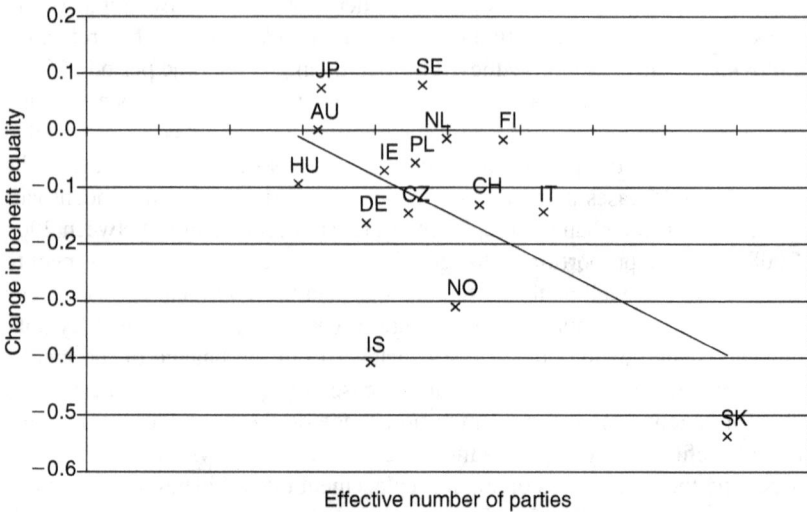

Figure 10.2 Correlation of number of parties and change in unemployment benefit equality
in 15 advanced welfare states with significant reforms between 2001 and 2008
(sources: OECD (2010a), Gallagher and Mitchell (2008), own calculations).

equality. A higher number of parties leads to stronger differences between insider-oriented and outsider-oriented benefit schemes. If a reform takes place, the rise in generosity difference is 12 per cent greater for each additional effective party in the party system. Among the control variables, surprisingly, only the previous levels of both unemployment benefit schemes are significant. Left government, veto points, and unemployment rate make no significant difference for overall changes in benefit equality (see Table 10.4).

The summary measure for change in generosity differences of course obscures which of both replacement rates has actually been adjusted by governments. As mentioned above, the descriptive data shows that generally there have been more incisive reforms of the secondary benefit scheme, which, for convenience, here is called UA although it can also be SA. These secondary schemes have on average been cut back more often, while UI has been reformed less and expansions slightly prevail over reductions. Therefore, overall, the increase of generosity differences is mainly caused by retrenchment of the benefit for the weaker section of the unemployed.

When we run the regression model separately for change in each type of benefit it reveals how the explanatory variables affect each side – the upper and the lower level – of the overall changes in generosity differences (see Table 10.4). The number of parties has a significant effect in both of the differentiated models. Interestingly, a higher number of parties is associated with retrenchment of the replacement rate for outsiders, and with expansion of the replacement rate for insiders. This conforms to our argument that assistance schemes are more

Table 10.4 Determinants of changes in benefit equality between 2001 and 2008

	Change in benefit equality	*%-change replacement rate UI*	*%-change replacement rate UA*
Dependent variable:			
Effective number of parties	−0.1248** (0.0394)	0.0646* (0.0319)	−0.0630** (0.0244)
Left government	−0.0022 (0.0013)	0.0015 (0.0010)	−0.0007 (0.0008)
Veto points	−0.0368 (0.0329)	0.0076 (0.0266)	−0.0283 (0.0234)
UA level in 2001	−0.0051* (0.0027)	–	−0.0067*** (0.0019)
UI level in 2001	0.0093* (0.0046)	−0.0112** (0.0037)	–
Unemployment	0.0120 (0.0105)	−0.0188* (0.0085)	−0.0061 (0.0069)
Constant	0.2107 (0.3077)	0.5319** (0.2376)	0.7055*** (0.1667)
	$R^2 = 0.6784$	$R^2 = 0.5379$	$R^2 = 0.7833$
	Adj. $R^2 = 0.4373$	Adj. $R^2 = 0.2811$	Adj. $R^2 = 0.6629$
	N = 15	N = 15	N = 15

Sources: OECD (2010a, 2010b), Gallagher and Mitchell (2008), Armingeon *et al.* (2010).

Notes
*p < 0.1, **p < 0.05, ***p < 0.01, standard errors in brackets.

comprehensive and more likely to be supported by large parties. If, by contrast, the representation of social interests is fragmented, those benefit schemes fare better that are by definition more selective (notwithstanding, of course, wide variation in the strictness of eligibility criteria).

Regarding the control variables, higher previous replacement rates make it more likely that the respective benefit scheme is cut back. High unemployment has only a significantly negative impact on the replacement rate of UI but not on the replacement rate of the assistance schemes. Left government and veto points are not relevant in any of the models. This does not exclude of course that across time within each country the alternation of left- and right-wing governments makes a difference. But cross-sectionally, in this sample, left government does not explain why some states introduce reforms that widen the differences between benefit levels for different groups of unemployed. The fragmentation of party systems, by contrast, does contribute to explaining increases in benefit segmentation.

To be sure, this empirical test is based on a small number of cases and a relatively short reform period. More extensive tests should be conducted in order to confirm these results. Nevertheless, the evidence suggests that party systems have had an impact, not only on the emergence of different patterns of segmentation, but also on the changes of benefit segmentation during welfare state reforms. Party systems with few parties are less likely to increase generosity differences than party systems with many parties. More specifically, a high number of parties makes it more likely that insider-oriented benefit schemes profit, and that broad-based assistance schemes are cut back.

11 Conclusions and future research

The starting point for this book was that policy decisions of parties are influenced by the context of party competition. Certainly, the ideological 'family' a party belongs to and the social basis from where the party originates matter as well; but in order to understand the actions of parties we have to take account of the party system in which they act. Accordingly, the present study has demonstrated that the number of parties and the positioning of parties in political space shape social policy development, in particular the segmentation of unemployment benefits. This was shown by comparing in depth two welfare states with very different party systems but otherwise similar structures. Moreover, I have provided evidence that party systems also influence the segmentation of social protection in other advanced welfare states.

In this concluding chapter I will first review the findings of this book; next, I will relate these findings to a more general concept of 'politics of segmentation', and finally, I will propose some avenues for future research.

Findings of the book

The basic argument put forward in this book is that party competition has its own logic and, for this reason, has an independent effect on policy-making. This is still not sufficiently recognized in welfare state research. The analysis of the partisan effect typically focuses on parties' core constituencies and long-standing ideological affiliations, while it disregards the competitive context that parties face. Party competition is shaped by the structure of party systems. The number of parties, as well as their positioning in political space, matter. More specifically, I have proposed three arguments on how party systems shape social protection. First, a higher number of parties implies smaller parties and, in turn, a focus on narrower interests. Second, in ideologically polarized party systems, anti-system parties can easily block the policy-making process. This leads to more particularistic policies and to a considerable policy influence of anti-system parties. Third, if the party system is not polarized its spatial configuration determines which groups of voters electoral competition focuses on.

Before exploring these causal arguments, I introduced the concept of unemployment benefit segmentation and examined how segmentation varies across advanced welfare states. Then, I traced how the benefit systems in Italy and Germany evolved and how their segmentation changed over time. This descriptive analysis constituted the explanandum, which was tackled in Part III of the book where I analysed the impact of party competition on the policy development in Italy and Germany, and on benefit segmentation in advanced welfare states more generally. Regarding the case studies of Italy and Germany this analysis consisted of basically three comparisons.

A first comparison between Italy and Germany in the post-war phase of welfare expansion demonstrated how the polarized and fragmented party system in Italy brought about a system of unemployment benefits that was highly fragmented itself and contained wide differences between benefit levels. In the German three-party system two catch-all parties competed in a centripetal logic. This has led to a benefit system, which was stratified into three tiers but featured a relatively inclusive UI scheme and only moderate differences in generosity with respect to the lower benefits. As important other political, institutional, and economic conditions were relatively similar at the outset and during this phase of welfare expansion, a clear comparative case can be made that the policy divergence was driven by the different party systems.

The second comparison analysed how the essentially same party systems affected policy developments in both countries as the economic context changed and required a restrictive approach to unemployment policy. In Italy there was little room for decisive reforms as long as the party system remained blocked by ideological polarization. In Germany, centripetal competition created incentives to spare core sections of the labour market from incisive retrenchment. Rather, tightened eligibility criteria and incremental generosity cuts affected more marginal sections of the labour force, who were less relevant as voters.

Third, in both countries we could examine how changes in party competition in the 1990s and 2000s altered reform efforts while economic conditions remained broadly similar. In Italy the dramatic transformation of the party system introduced centripetal competition between pre-electoral coalitions. This enabled a series of gradual reform, which, taken together, amounted to a significant reduction of generosity differences. However, the centrifugal tendencies within each party coalition prevented any fundamental reform of the benefit system. In Germany, a limited change in policy demand led to a blown-up policy response because the spatial configuration of the party system encouraged the Social Democrats to focus on more liberal voters. However, the fundamental reforms had a feedback effect on the party system as a new left-wing competitor emerged.

Following the comparative historical analysis of Italy and Germany, I applied the party competition argument to a wider set of advanced welfare states. The results indicate that the dispersion of party systems – in terms of number of parties and polarization – during welfare expansion has led to the introduction of more segmented social protection. For the phase of welfare state reform, I found evidence that a higher number of parties makes it more likely that reforms increase generosity differences – even when partisan composition of government, political institutions, unemployment, and path dependency are controlled for.

The careful comparison of Italy and Germany and the cross-sectional analysis of advanced welfare states have provided sufficient evidence to conclude that party competition matters for policy development, in particular for the segmentation of social rights. More dispersed party systems lead to more segmented social protection. Moreover, the case studies have indicated that the spatial configuration of the party system determines on which voters parties focus their attention in electoral competition so that the preferences of these voters are reflected in policy decisions. Given the various analytical perspectives applied in this study, it is fair to conclude that the findings are quite robust. The results should nevertheless be tested in further case studies and with more systematic statistical analyses on the wider set of advanced capitalist democracies.

The theoretical implications of this research are best understood in contrast to the traditional approach to political parties and social policy. The traditional approach has argued and shown in many empirical studies that the 'political colour' of the parties in government makes a difference for policy output. While this remains true for many cases, it is not sufficient because it misses out on other party-based mechanisms (see also Häusermann *et al.* 2010). The traditional approach reduces the role of parties to transmitting interests from a social base to government. However, what parties do is not only determined by their electoral constituency – it is also influenced by the competition they face. Most clearly this could be seen in the post-war phase when governments in Italy and Germany were dominated by Christian democrats. However, both Christian democratic parties had to come to terms with extremely different party systems, which largely explains the differences in policy output.

Therefore, this book contributes to our understanding of welfare state development by highlighting the impact of party competition. This was made possible by drawing on literature on party systems and, hence, bridging the gap between welfare state studies and research on political parties. Another contribution lies in the new way of analysing the differentiation of social rights in the field of unemployment compensation and by applying this segmentation framework to today's advanced welfare states, as well as to the development of unemployment benefits across time in Italy and Germany.

Three other observations are worth noting although they were not at the centre of this research. First, in the German case we have seen that the party system not only affects policy development but that the causal path can also run in the opposite direction. The controversial Hartz reforms, which the Social Democrats adopted as part of their wider 'Agenda 2010', have triggered the splitting off of a group of left-wing Social Democrats who subsequently merged with the post-socialist PDS. This way, the labour market reform has led to the creation of a new party (*Die Linke*) that became a serious competitor to the SPD in the following years. This kind of feedback effect of social policy on the party system has rarely been studied so far. Obviously, Pierson (2001b) as well as Esping-Andersen (1990) have drawn our attention to the feedback effects of welfare states, but they focused on policy preferences and the social structure rather than the party system.

Second, the present study raised some questions about the effect of a divided left (cf. also Watson 2008). In the Italian case (up to the 1990s), the division of the left was one aspect of the polarized party system where the Communists maintained their far-left position, while the Socialists moved gradually towards centre. The moderation of PSI and fundamental opposition of PCI were incompatible and contributed to the deadlock of programmatic competition. In Germany, by contrast, I showed that the SPD could introduce the radical Hartz reforms because it did not face a relevant left-wing competitor on social and economic issues (given the regional confinement of the PDS and the focus on sociocultural issues by the Greens). The emergence of the *Linke*, however, divided the left. Although this new competitor clearly influences the policy decisions of the SPD, so far the effect of this new configuration on the segmentation of social protection is not entirely clear because the *Linke* advocates insider interests (such as duration of UI) as well as outsider interests (such as the benefit level of UA). The only notable consequence so far is the re-extension of maximum durations of UI.

All this suggests two preliminary conclusions on the impact of a divided left. (1) If one of the left-wing parties is in fundamental opposition this inhibits programmatic competition, strengthens particular interests, and increases policy segmentation. (2) If none of the left-wing parties is an anti-system party, programmatic competition between them will bring policy attention back to the preferences of social constituencies that are neglected in purely centrist competition.[1] However, in this case the party fragmentation within the left apparently still impedes a truly encompassing approach that would also include marginalized sections of the labour force. Put differently, in a programmatic context, a division of the left may help to raise awareness of neglected interests – but its downside is increasing party fragmentation.

The third observation, aside from the core focus of this work, is that the weakness or strength of party organizations matters. Where parties are weak we cannot assume the same party system logics to be at work because politics is not structured by parties but by individual politicians or groups of politicians. As I suggested in the cross-sectional comparison of party systems and patterns of segmentation during welfare expansion (Chapter 10), this is the main reason explaining the outlier position of the US with a two-party system but highly segmented unemployment compensation. The point also relates to Estévez-Abe's (2008) argument on the role of electoral systems in shaping parties' incentives to pursue particularistic or universal policies. If voters cast their vote in the first place for candidates, as is the case in the US, this leads to more particularistic policies than in electoral systems with a strong party vote.

Politics of segmentation

At this point, I would like to take a step back in order to discuss how the findings of the book contribute to a more general concept of politics of segmentation.

In modern democracies the puzzle of policy segmentation lies in the fact that equal political rights do not give rise to equal social rights. This is what the politics of segmentation is about: the translation of equal political rights into unequal policy output. Marshall (1950) had projected the opposite. The core principle of citizenship, in his account, is equality. The development of citizenship started with equal civil rights, which were later supplemented by political rights. Those political rights, in turn, gave weaker sections of society the power to demand social rights, which would improve their position in the social order and reduce inequality.

For sure, social rights can abate class differences also by being focused on the lower classes. That is to say, they do not necessarily have to be equal for all in order to increase equality. However, the whole thrust of Marshall's argument implies, rather plausibly, that equal political rights should lead to equal social rights. Moreover, if we allow for social rights being limited to the worse off it is not obvious where this line should be drawn and, in fact, comparative welfare state research has shown that we find many different patterns in which social rights are differentiated (see Chapter 3). This gives rise to the mentioned question: why do equal political rights not lead to equal social rights?

The basic reply that I propose is that formal political rights do not secure political inclusion. Marshall's chain of argument can be reformulated in the following way: political in-/exclusion determines policy in-/exclusion, which, in turn, contributes to social in-/exclusion. However, the problem is that political rights are not a sufficient condition of political inclusion. Instead, several intervening factors determine the degree of political inclusion and differentiate the leverage that each citizen enjoys with his or her political rights.

A first important factor is mobilization and organization. Those groups that mobilize more successfully have a greater clout in determining policy output. This is, in a nutshell, what power resource theory and traditional partisan politics theory emphasize. At the origins of the welfare state, trade unions and socialist parties provided an effective political voice to working class demands. However, the working class was not an electoral majority (Przeworski and Sprague 1986). Therefore, socialist parties had to come to terms with enlarging their electoral basis, with finding coalition partners, and with competing over working class votes with other left-wing parties or with Christian democratic parties. In short, the political strategy of a labour party was far from clear and depended strongly on the party system.

As Rueda (2007) has pointed out for the more recent decades, a narrow scope of mobilization can have a negative effect on political inclusion and, consequently, on policy inclusion. He argued that left parties today represent mainly labour market insiders and, consequently, defend their interests, such as employment protection. Meanwhile, labour market outsiders are left in the cold. From the perspective of the present book, this is too bold a claim as the precise constituency of left-wing parties and the representation of labour market outsiders is conditioned by the party system. However, it is true that a narrow electoral focus of parties is an important determinant of political exclusion. Quite in contrast to

Rueda, but following a similar logic, Häusermann (2010) points out that, at least in some countries, left parties increasingly give a voice to new social interests, such as service employees and workers in atypical contracts.

We see, therefore, that the degree to which social interests are represented by parties is an important factor of political inclusion. To some extent, this reflects the genuine capacity for collective action of certain groups (cf. Olson 1971), but, in the perspective put forward in this book, the representation of interests depends largely on the party system. All three sub-arguments of the book apply to how party systems structure political inclusion. (1) A fragmented party system leads to a fragmented representation of social interests. A multitude of parties provides a voice to many different interests, but it also generates a struggle between these interests. By contrast, if the number of parties is low each party integrates a wider range of interests. (2) Ideological polarization generates deep divisions between different interests and impedes common solutions. (3) The spatial configuration of a party system determines which voters are decisive for winning elections. Therefore, not all citizens have equal political weight.

Note that in this view it is somewhat less surprising why Marshall (1950) was so optimistic about political rights leading to political inclusion. After all, his analysis was based on the British experience and Britain was most of the time characterized by a two-party system. The dominant cleavage between labour and capital was not crossed by any other significant cleavages and the low number of parties was reinforced by the first-past-the-post electoral system. It is reasonable to expect a greater inclusion of different social interests if only two parties compete for power and have to gather support from people of many different backgrounds.

Hence, the argument of this book is at odds with Lijphart (1999) who saw consensus democracy, based on proportional representation, as the more inclusive political system than majoritarian democracy. His view is of course based on the capacity of political institutions to integrate the conflicting interests pronounced by many different actors. By contrast, my argument stresses how large political actors (here, political parties) incorporate many different interests in the first place, thus generating less need for integration through institutions. Ultimately, these are two alternative ways of integrating political interests. Once a society is highly fragmented, for example by numerous cleavages, integration through inclusive institutions may be the only feasible way. Certainly, it does lead to an integration of many different interests. But I maintain that the resulting policies are on average more fragmented than in the case of integration through inclusive actors.

The distinction between majoritarian and proportional electoral systems matters for Lijphart's (1999) typology on a macro level, but also on a micro level electoral laws play a role in translating political rights into political inclusion. They determine how much a certain vote counts towards the distribution of power in representative institutions (Nohlen 2009). In addition, they generate incentives for parties and politicians in terms of the social interests they should focus on (Cox 1990; Estévez-Abe 2008). In this sense, the policy impact of electoral systems works in a way similar to the impact of party systems, because party systems also guide the attention of political actors towards specific groups of voters.

Finally, on a more sociological level, social in-/exclusion feeds back into political in-/exclusion. As is well known, political participation is differentiated by socio-economic status. Citizens with low income and low education tend to be less politically active (Gallego 2007, Brady *et al.* 1995). This creates, of course, the risk of a vicious circle. If certain groups of voters are not effectively included in the political process their interests will be neglected in policy-making. This neglect can lead to social exclusion, which, in turn, depresses political participation and, hence, inclusion.

Therefore, the politics of segmentation consists of many elements that are well known in political science. That equal political rights do not bring about equal social rights is determined by patterns of mobilization, party systems, political institutions, electoral systems, and levels of participation. However, the relevance of party systems for political inclusion has received less attention in political science so far. Moreover, the mentioned elements are not always discussed regarding their effect on policy output.

Future research

The results of this book suggest mainly three avenues for further research. The first departs from the more general concept of politics of segmentation proposed above. How are equal political rights translated into unequal political inclusion and unequal policy inclusion (i.e. policy segmentation)? As mentioned, a lot of research is concerned with various aspects of this question. However, it would be desirable to analyse how the different elements interact or reinforce each other in order to get to a more complete understanding of the politics of segmentation. For example, under what conditions are the votes of even socially marginalized citizens important? My argument suggests that this is the case in two-party systems, provided that electoral races are sufficiently tight. The point is, of course, related to the electoral system. Not only the two-party system but also the logic of first-past-the-post electoral laws bolsters the relevance of dispersed and unorganized voters (Estévez-Abe 2008). At the same time, low participation of certain groups of voters withdraws them from the perception of politicians and parties, which can reinforce the effect of electoral rules and of the spatial configuration of the party system. Hence, the inequality of political participation, the capacity of party systems to focus political attention on different groups of voters, and the incentives of electoral systems should in future be studied in a common framework.

Second, my study has focused strongly on electoral competition. One of the main mechanisms I have explored is how parties try to attract new voters through the policies they advocate. This logic of competition is at odds with the logic of representation that is behind traditional partisan theory. In the standard approach, the actions of a party are determined by its social constituency. By contrast, I argue that parties often focus on swing voters, who might vote for a different party. The logic of representation can be also found in exciting new research arguing that the constituencies of parties have changed and that this explains why the parties take a different political position than they used to (for an overview see Häusermann *et al.* 2010). Rueda (2007), for example, argues that social democratic parties today represent labour market insiders but not outsiders, which is why they promote less universal policies. And Häusermann (2010) shows that certain sections of the middle class have become important constituencies of the left. This has opened up new reform perspectives focusing less on traditional social insurance and more on education, equal opportunities, and minimum income guarantees. My question to these arguments on changing constituencies is: how do the constituencies change? My own reply would be: a party attracts new constituencies by promoting policies that are attractive to this group of voters. Therefore, policy change is not a consequence of acquiring a new constituency but it helps in acquiring it. However, without any doubt parties often devise policies for their present constituency and not only with an eye to new voters. In the best of all worlds party leaders in fact find strategies that appeal to voters old and new. Still, it is an open question when policy decisions are driven mainly by representational logic, or rather by the logic of competition. This issue certainly merits more research (see e.g. Ezrow *et al.* 2011).

Third, party organizations have not yet been studied sufficiently concerning their consequences for policy strategies. In particular, different types of party organization can have important consequences for the issue discussed above: whether a party regards mostly the interest of its traditional constituency or the interests of wide sections of the electorate. A mass-integration party has much closer ties to its constituencies and is more likely to act as a representative of this group. In catch-all parties or the professionalized parties of today the links to the social basis are much weaker (cf. Katz and Mair 1994). Hence, they are more flexible in terms of the groups of voters they try to address. The relevance of party organizations for policy decisions has already been pointed out by Kitschelt (2001) and some new research is emerging on this topic (Blyth *et al.* 2010, Schumacher 2011).

Economic crisis and party systems

European welfare states face daunting challenges in the forthcoming years. Increasing numbers of people work in unstable and low-paid jobs. They often have inadequate access to social protection or, rather, the social protection they receive is flat-rate, subject to means tests, and conditional on various behavioural conditions (actively searching jobs, accepting job offers, participating in training measures etc.). Moreover, long-term unemployment persists and, generally, unemployment has surged after the financial and economic crisis of 2008–9. Germany has weathered the crisis exceptionally well by international comparison – but Italy has been badly affected.

At the same time as many people struggle to find gainful and stable employment, states are under intense pressure to balance their budgets – now, in the public debt crisis, even more than before. Hence, many governments have retrenched social protection and public employment in order to save costs. The young generation is particularly affected by unemployment and precarious jobs in most states. Considering the austerity measures of government, young people have little hope that their prospects will improve soon and have taken to the streets in Italy, Spain, Greece, France, and UK. Often these protesters blamed the established parties for not caring sufficiently about the precarious situation of the youth. Similar to the German situation when the Hartz reforms were adopted, the street protests reveal a lack of representation by the party system. In the German case political disaffection was later alleviated by the emergence of a new left-wing party. The new configuration of the party system has not made it easier to find encompassing solutions, but it has helped to give voice to some sections of the electorate that risked to become alienated from the political process.

The capacity of European political systems to respond to the double pressure of social needs and financial constraints will depend to a large extent on political parties. Currently, considerable sections of the population, at least in those states that are worst hit by the crisis, are becoming disaffected from established parties. It is doubtful whether the large parties will find innovative ways of reconciling their governmental responsibility for public budgets with effective solutions for those whose livelihoods are diminished by the crisis and austerity measures. In the absence of such an extraordinary achievement of political integration by the established parties, it is likely that smaller parties, in particular left- and right-wing populist parties, will profit at the polls. Depending on the extent that these smaller parties play by the democratic rules, this adaptation of party systems would still help to ease the political tensions created by the economic crisis.

Notes

1 Party competition and social protection

1 On cleavages and welfare state development see also Flora (1986a), Ferrera (2005a), and Manow (2009).

2 This is the most common way to conceptualize voter decisions (proximity voting). Other scholars have argued that voters decide based on whether a party supports their preferred direction of policy change and on how intensely voters and party favour this policy direction (directional voting, Rabinowitz and MacDonald 1989).

3 Empirically, however, parties are never as close to the centre as the Median Voter Theorem predicts. This empirical failure has spurred abundant theoretical modifications, such as the directional model (Rabinowitz and MacDonald 1989), taking policy preferences of parties seriously (Wittman 1973; Roemer 2001), the introduction of valence competition (Ansolabehere and Snyder 2000; Schofield 2003), and attention to characteristics of voters other than policy preferences (Adams and Merill 1999).

4 In the terms of economic theory we can say the political demand of anti-system voters is inelastic.

5 Lynch (2006) focuses directly on particularistic versus programmatic modes of competition and how they affect social policy development. I build on her work, but I take one step back. I argue that polarized party systems are one factor that can cause particularistic policy-making. On particularistic party-voter linkages and their effect on social policy see also Orloff and Skocpol (1984).

6 Of course, other factors play a role in determining the degree of programmatic versus particularistic competition. See *inter alia* Shefter (1977), Kitschelt and Wilkinson (2007), and Estévez-Abe (2008).

7 I leave aside here the question to what extent the policy preferences of voters may be endogenous, that is to say, that they are themselves influenced by political parties (see e.g. Padgett 2005). After all, the public interventions of parties may influence public opinion. I acknowledge that this endogeneity is possible. However, the time frame matters. In important distributive matters that are at stake here, I assume that voter preferences are not very elastic to the influence of parties. This may happen only in the medium- to long-term. Consequently, at a given point in time we can consider the policy preferences of voters as exogenous.

8 For an argument along these lines on relative polarization in the electorate and government spending see Lindqvist and Östling (2010). Also Haggard and Kaufman (1995: 166–74) have pointed out that fragmentation and polarization of party systems can hinder economic reform and lead to particularistic policy-making.

9 The number of five is not a precise threshold. Thus, in his discussion of spatial competition he includes the five-party systems in the group with centrifugal competition (Sartori 2005: 305–12).

10 As the main focus of this research is on party systems, parties are principally treated

as unitary actors. Some scholars have emphasized the role of intra-party factions in determining the policy positions of a party (see e.g. Zohlnhöfer 2001). Historically, party factions have been particularly salient in both the German and the Italian Christian Democratic Party (Sartori 1982: Ch. 6). However, I argue that the political strength of a party faction is reinforced or weakened by the competitive incentives that the party as a whole is subjected to. A left-leaning faction in a Christian Democratic Party, for example, is likely to prevail in inner-party conflicts if the party is in intense competition with a left-wing party. For this reason, I mostly pay no special attention to the dynamics within parties. However, these dynamics do become relevant, of course, if they have direct systemic consequences, that is, if they lead to a party split.

11 Some authors have argued that globalization leads actually to welfare expansion because exposure to international economic competition raises demands for social security. For an excellent summary of the debate see Swank (2010).

12 For an overview of recent research that moves further beyond the traditional partisan approach, some of which I cited above when outlining my own argument, see Häusermann *et al.* (2010).

13 On ideas and discourses see Heclo (1974), Hall (1993), Blyth (2002), V. Schmidt (2002a), Bleses and Seeleib-Kaiser (2004), Münnich (2010).

2 Comparing Italy and Germany

1 From 1949 to 1990 I look only at West Germany.

2 For an overview of the discussion on welfare state types see Arts and Gelissen (2002, 2010).

3 Although coming from a different angle, this argument is not in contradiction to van Kersbergen's (1995) findings. Van Kersbergen has stressed the specific policy impact of Christian democracy on continental welfare states. However, he has also acknowledged the variation between these welfare states and has pointed out how the historical conditions of party competition influenced the political strategies of Christian democratic parties.

4 An alternative is the effective number of parliamentary parties, based on seat shares. But due to our focus on electoral competition electoral parties are more relevant.

5 I do not use the data of the Comparative Manifesto Project (Budge *et al.* 2001; Klingemann *et al.* 2006) for measuring party positions because this data indicates, in the first place, the relative emphasis on different policy issues in party manifestos. Accordingly, I use this data in the analysis of political processes in Italy and Germany. For a discussion of different ways of measuring party positions, see Benoit and Laver (2006).

6 The mentioned two surveys contain estimates for several policy dimensions. The dimension that best applies to social policy is defined by the two opposing positions '[party] promotes raising taxes to increase public services' and 'promotes cutting public services to cut taxes' (Benoit and Laver 2006: 168).

3 Segmentation of unemployment benefits in advanced welfare states today

1 At the same time, some social rights, such as social assistance, go beyond the national population and include legal residents independently of their citizenship.

2 Neo-Marxist authors have, in fact, asserted the other extreme and claimed that the welfare state only stabilizes and reproduces the capitalist social order (O'Connor 1973).

3 Lynch (2006) discusses the effect of different systems of unemployment benefits on age groups. Katznelson (2005) contains an interesting analysis of racial segregation in US American UI of the 1930s.

4 Esping-Andersen 1999; Armingeon and Bonoli 2006; Rueda 2007; King and Rueda 2008; Palier and Thelen 2010; Emmenegger 2009; Häusermann and Schwander 2009. For an overview see Davidsson and Naszyk 2009.

5 But also Greece and the US have only insufficient protection for benefit outsiders. Moreover, as will become clear in the subsequent chapters Italy does have other unemployment benefits. But they tend to be even more focused on insiders than UI. Support for the poor in Italy is in the jurisdiction of regional government and varies widely.

6 One possibility to analyse the effect of low ceilings is demonstrated by Esping-Andersen (1990). His average benefit equality measure compares the benefit a standard worker can receive to the highest possible benefit in a given scheme. The non-flat-rate countries (as of 2008) that score highest in his results are Denmark (99 per cent), Sweden (82 per cent), Belgium (79 per cent), Finland (72 per cent), and Norway (69 per cent). However, these values are based on data from 1980 (Esping-Andersen 1990: 70).

7 The territorial governance of SA is complex. Most states administer SA on the local level. The real distinguishing criterion for our purposes is the existence of national standards. These are missing in Greece and Italy. In fact, they are also missing in Canada, Spain, Iceland, and Switzerland. However, the latter cases seem to have relatively effective protection in most regions, often because national legislation still fixes some requirements of providing assistance to the needy.

8 Regarding the high shares in Germany and Austria we have to assume that they refer not only to UI but also to UA, which is left open by the question. Moreover, note that this data was collected before the German Hartz reforms.

9 Arguably, Esping-Andersen's de-commodification measure is a comprehensive measure of benefit generosity. For unemployment benefits he includes information on NRR, qualifying period, waiting period, duration, means test, and coverage (Esping-Andersen 1990: 54). Another comprehensive measure can be found in Estevéz-Abe *et al.* (2001).

10 On the social safety nets in Spain and Portugal and the lack thereof in Italy and Greece, see Ferrera (2005b).

4 Italy and Germany: policy divergence after the Second World War

1 For overviews of these early policy developments in Germany, see Clasen (1994: Ch. 3); Schmid *et al.* (2001: 268–74); for more detailed descriptions see Frerich and Frey (1996); for a comprehensive historical study see Führer (1990); Münnich (2010) studies the impact of ideas on these developments.

2 Also Adolf Hitler was initially the head of a presidential cabinet. But, as this was only the starting point for his National Socialist dictatorship, he is usually not listed among the heads of presidential cabinets.

3 For overviews of these early policy developments see Ferrera *et al.* (forthcoming: Ch. 2) and Cherubini and Piva (1998: Ch. 2.2); for a comprehensive historical study of labour market administration see Musso (2004).

4 Over the decades the severance payment was then transformed into an end of contract payment (*trattamento di fine rapporto*), that is, into an old-age rather than an unemployment related measure.

5 Of course, the number of EOA beneficiaries may have been overstated for propagandistic reasons. At the same time, the number of registered unemployed probably underestimates unemployment levels. Agricultural and seasonal workers were excluded from UI and had no incentives to register as unemployed.

6 Where not indicated otherwise, this section is based on Schmid *et al.* (2001), Schmid *et al.* (2005), Schmid and Oschmiansky (2008a, 2006), Alber (1987), and Clasen (1994).

7 It is difficult to find the exact data for maximum benefits in these early years. In 1995, however, the maximum benefit for recipients without children was 99.7 per cent of the average production worker gross wage and for recipients with children 111.3 per cent (calculated from OECD 2010a: country-specific files).

8 This NRR for UI is taken from Scruggs (2004). The NRR for SA is calculated by me using data from Scruggs (2004), *Bundesministerium für Arbeit und Soziales* (2007), and MISSOC.

9 With respect to the comparison with the Italian unemployment benefit system, it should be added that Germany also introduced a wage supplementation fund for short-time work and a benefit for workers who are laid off due to bankruptcy. However, there are two important differences. First, these benefits were mostly applied according to their original purpose whereas the Italian wage supplementation fund was turned into a de facto unemployment benefit. Second, the fragmentation of these benefits along occupational lines was much lower in Germany (cf. Sacchi *et al.* forthcoming).

10 Where not indicated otherwise, this section is based on Ferrera (1987), Gualmini (1998), Vesan (2008), Ferrera *et al.* (forthcoming), Ferrera *et al.* (2006).

11 Years refer to the adoption of legislation not to its coming into force.

12 Also in 1948, the D'Aragona Commission, which had the task of proposing a comprehensive revision of the Italian welfare state, presented its report. Unemployment compensation played only a minor role in the report and the proposals were not very far-reaching, apart from the intention to extend coverage to agricultural workers (Ferrera *et al.* forthcoming: Ch. 2). In any case, the impact of the commission was low because it had been set up shortly before the break up of national unity and concluded its works only after this political turning point (cf. Ferrera 1993: Ch. 7).

13 This data is based on Scruggs (2004) and own calculations, see also Figure 5.1.

5 Italy and Germany: changing trends during welfare state restructuring

1 See, among others, Flora (1986a); Pierson (2001a); Iversen and Wren (1998); Esping-Andersen (1999); Bonoli (2006).

2 See, among others, Scharpf (2000); Genschel (2004); Huber and Stephens (2005); Rodrik (1997). Some scholars have argued that globalization contributed to expanding social policy, mainly because the social insecurity that it causes increases popular demand for social protection (e.g. Garrett 1998; Rodrik 1997; Swank 2002). A similar argument has, in fact, been made for post-industrialization (Iversen and Cusack 2000).

3 Where not indicated otherwise, this section draws on Schmid and Oschmiansky (2008b, 2005, 2007), Alber (1987), Clasen (2005), and SoVD (1997). For good overviews of recent German labour market policy see Ebbinghaus and Eichhorst (2006) and Eichhorst and Marx (2011).

4 All years refer to the adoption of legislation, not to its coming into force.

5 As acknowledged in Scruggs' (2004) data file, the effect of the 1981 reform that reduced the calculation base for UI benefits is not reflected in the data. However, the effect of this reform on the overall replacement rate is presumably small.

6 For a similar assessment see Clasen (2005: 64–7).

7 For a summary see Kemmerling and Bruttel (2006).

8 The basic benefit level was maintained. In addition, on the one hand, extra payments were reduced, on the other hand, the means test was loosened (for more details see Hassel and Schiller 2010: Ch. 2).

9 The change did not make all UA recipients worse off because of the modest replacement rate of the old scheme and the resulting benefit levels for people with low previous earnings. For this reason, some previous UA recipients had actually fallen below

the SA assistance level and not all of them had claimed SA to top-up their UA benefit. Unemployed in this group gained when they started receiving the new UA (for the situation before the reform, see also Alber 1989: 181–2).

10 Where not indicated otherwise, this section draws on Ferrera (1987), Gualmini (1998), Ferrera *et al.* (2006), Fargion (2001), Porcari (2004), CNEL (2003).

11 The NRRs for CIGS are relatively unique data. They are constructed on the basis of Scruggs' (2004) data set. But I collected and applied the maximum amounts of CIGS benefits from circulars of the government body administering the programme (INPS). I also corrected some other inaccuracies in Scruggs' data concerning both UI and CIGS.

12 For a good reconstruction of the various fates of this policy over time see Fargion (2001: 50–60).

13 First reference to this practice can be found in the circulars of the benefit administration (INPS) in 2001. Apparently, the practice evolved from governmental decrees to being a regular item in budget laws, starting from the 2007 budget. This way, *CIG in deroga* became institutionalized to the extent that from 2009 INPS lists it as one the standard benefits on its website (www.inps.it, last accessed 27 March 2011). However, the precise development of this practice is hard to determine.

14 Reoccurrence of this phrase was pointed out by Vesan (2008: 32).

6 Explaining labour market reforms in Italy and Germany

1 Moreover, high employment protection and the complementary institution of CIG protect the investment by firms and workers in firm-specific skills (Estevéz-Abe *et al.* 2001).

7 Italy and Germany: political driving forces behind different post-war paths

1 For general historical background, see Görtemaker (1999), Wolfrum (2007) and, regarding economic history, Abelshauser (2004).

2 The Bavarian CSU is formally independent of the CDU but they cooperate closely at the national level. Wherever there is no specific reason to distinguish between the two, I refer to 'CDU' for simplicity.

3 In 1949, it was sufficient if a party got more than five percent of the votes in only one region (*Bundesland*). In addition, parties in Germany can obtain seats in proportion to their vote share even without passing the 5 per cent threshold if they get direct candidates elected in three constituencies (*Grundmandatsklausel*). In the first two elections to the *Bundestag*, only one successful direct candidate was sufficient.

4 I thank Philipp Rehm for sharing his data on party positions (Rehm and Reilly 2010).

5 Minutes of the Cabinet Committee on Economic Affairs (*Kabinettsausschuss für Wirtschaft*), 15th meeting, 3 August 1954.

6 *Die Zeit*, 12 May 1961, '*Endspurt in Bonn*'.

7 Cited by *Der Spiegel*, 14 October 1974, '*"Die armen Schweine und die anderen"*'.

8 For general historical background, see Ginsborg (1990) and Lepre (2004).

9 Also in the trade union movement anti-fascist unity had ruled between 1944 and 1948 in the unitarian *Confederazione Generale Italiana del Lavoro* (CGIL). However, the split between the anti-fascist political parties projected itself on the trade unions. In 1948, first, a 'free' section split away from the CGIL. Later, in 1950, this section split in turn into the *Confederazione Italiana Sindacati Lavoratori* (CISL) and the *Unione Italiana del Lavoro* (UIL). Since then, Italian unions remained divided along political lines, the CGIL being communist–socialist, the CISL Christian democratic, and the UIL social democratic.

10 The figure is for 1973. But we know from the literature and other data that the basic structures of the party system remained stable from the early 1950s to the late 1980s.

11 *L'Unità*, 8 May 1946, '*Il Programma del PCI*'. This party manifesto was made available in electronic form through a joint effort between the *Zentralarchiv für Empirische Sozialforschung* (ZA), *Wissenschaftszentrum Berlin* (WZB), the *Vrije Universiteit Amsterdam* (VU), and the Party Manifestos Project.

12 PSI manifesto for the parliamentary election of 1953, provided by the Party Manifestos Project.

13 For an interesting discussion of the divided left in Spain and its effect on unemployment benefits see Watson (2008).

8 Germany: two political logics of segmenting reforms

1 *Allgemeine Bevölkerungsumfrage der Sozialwissenschaften (ALLBUS)* – German *General Social Survey 1980–2006*. From 1980–6 and in 1991, the ALLBUS programme was funded by the DFG (German Research Foundation). For all other surveys, state and federal funding has been made available through GESIS (German Social Science Infrastructure Services). ALLBUS is a joint project of GESIS-ZUMA (Mannheim) and GESIS-ZA (Cologne) and the ALLBUS scientific council. The aforementioned institutions and persons bear no responsibility for the use or interpretation of the data in this publication.

2 Unfortunately there is no data with self-placement of voters specifically on the socio-economic policy dimension. Comparing the party data on a socio-economic dimension (Figure 8.1) with voter data on a general left-right dimension is of course suboptimal. However, the German party system was bipolar, focusing attention on centre voters, also on the general left–right dimension. The main difference between the two dimensions concerns the position of the FDP.

3 The beneficiary data is from *Bundesministerium für Arbeit und Soziales* (2007), the data of those entitled to vote is from www.wahlen-in-deutschland.de/buBTW.htm (accessed 15 April 2008).

4 ALLBUS survey data shows that from the 1980s to the middle of the 2000s the proportion of unemployed intending to abstain from voting in federal elections was on average twice as high as among the total electorate (20.1 per cent of the unemployed as opposed to 9.3 per cent of the electorate). This includes, of course, recipients of UI and not only of assistance benefits. ALLBUS data does not contain an exact differentiation of beneficiaries. However, the correlation of social and political marginalization is well known (see e.g. Gallego 2007; Marx and Picot 2011).

5 Regarding the politics of SA, note that although it is administered by local governments the basic regulation is decided at the federal level. Since 1993 there is also a fiscal incentive for government to reduce the SA benefit level. Following a ruling of the Constitutional Court, the existence minimum, on which the benefit is based, became at the same time the point of reference for the basic tax exemption (*Grundfreibetrag*, see Manow and Seils (2000), *Die Zeit*, '*Rechnen, bis es passt: Die Bundesregierung manipuliert das Existenzminimum – zum Schaden aller Steuerzahler*', 28 December 2006).

6 In Lehmbruch's analysis the fact that the FDP reinforced its economic right-wing position was related to a more general policy shift of the party since the early 1980s. The rise of the Greens increasingly besieged the FDP on the left of the socio-cultural dimension. Consequently, the Liberals gradually abandoned this terrain. This weakened the social-liberal voices in the party and, hence, facilitated a radicalization on social and economic issues (Lehmbruch 2000: 49–52).

7 The main patterns in Figure 8.2 are confirmed also by looking just at the development of the more specific items 'Welfare State Expansion: Positive' and 'Welfare State Limitation: Positive'.

8 The official unemployment rate was higher than the standardized rate used in Figure 6.5.

9 It is, however, not decisive for my argument whether the red–green government won the election because of its stance on labour market and social policy. Obviously, other factors played a role as well, such as the opposition to the Iraq war and the handling of a flood crisis in East Germany. Rather, my argument maintains that the endorsement of the Hartz reforms was (at least in part) driven by an expectation that this would be electorally beneficial.

10 *Der Spiegel*, '*Koch und Kanzler*', Nr. 48, 28 November 2002.

11 Government Declaration by Chancellor Gerhard Schröder on the Agenda 2010, 14 March 2003.

12 See e.g. Spiegel-Online, '*SPD kupfert Wahlkampf-Idee bei Linkspartei ab*', www.spiegel.de/politik/deutschland/0,1518,607225,00.html, 12 February 2009; Spiegel-Online, '*Ministerpräsidenten verlangen Kurswechsel der CDU*', www.spiegel.de/politik/deutschland/0,1518,603299,00.html, 24 January 2009.

13 However, the problems of the SPD are, of course, not only 'external'. That the party leaders pushed through a drastic programmatic change also caused a lot of internal turmoil.

14 Interview with Prof. Werner Jann, former member of the Hartz commission and close observer of the reform process, 30 April 2008. See also Hassel and Schiller (2010: 161).

15 In a previous version, I made this argument in Picot (2009). The motivations of the SPD and the feedback effect on the party system are confirmed by the detailed account in Hassel and Schiller (2010).

9 Italy: party system change facilitating de-segmentation

1 During National Solidarity the PCI was not part of the cabinet but of the government majority in parliament.

2 According to the ITANES surveys, the distance between the two extreme party poles, PCI and MSI, actually increased from 5.93 in 1972 to 6.68 in 1985 and moderately declined to 6.36 in 1990 on the 1–10 scale.

3 The 'EUR accord' is named after the Rome neighbourhood where the meeting took place.

4 The benefit ceiling in 1980 was fixed at 600,000 lira and the nominal replacement rate of CIGS was 80 per cent. Therefore, the threshold of previous wages, above which the ceiling had an effect, was 750,000 lira. The monthly average production worker's wage in 1980 was 675,612 lira (Scruggs 2004; law 427/1980).

5 Besides, the benefit ceiling became officially more restrictive but that in practice ad hoc agreements may often have suspended the limits.

6 The expert survey by Laver and Hunt (1992) confirms that the question 'less taxes versus more services' was of particular importance to PLI and PRI at the end of the decade. Somewhat dubiously, the survey does not confirm the high relevance of this dimension for party competition overall. However, especially public debt – and, hence, also taxes and services – was undoubtedly a major political issue at the end of the 1980s. Possibly, the wording of the question in terms of public services and taxes did not fit to the Italian context. In 2004, however, this dimension was indicated to be the most important one for Italian party competition (see below).

7 *La Repubblica*, 20 June 1986, '*Cassa Integrazione: La riforma è vicina*'.

8 *La Repubblica*, 1 June 1991, '*La Cassa Integrazione cambia regole*'.

9 The PSI still entered parliament, but with only 2.2 per cent of the votes and was dissolved at the end of the year.

10 For a discussion emphasizing the centripetal trend, see Pappalardo (2001).

11 As mentioned, the *Lega* did not belong to the centre-right coalition in 1996. However, it was still part of the centre-right camp in a wider sense.

12 It is interesting to note that this combination of bipolarism and polarization corresponds to what Sartori wrote about the early French Fifth Republic (Sartori 1982: 310–15).

In the beginning of the Fifth Republic majoritarian logic had been imposed on a polarized pluralist party system through the absolute majority necessary for presidential elections. However, this majoritarian incentive to build party coalitions collided with two factors: first, persisting ideological polarization; and, second, the fact that parliamentary elections encouraged parties to focus also on their own benefit rather than the fate of their presidential coalition. Sartori called this formation 'polarized bipolarity' or 'bipolarization'.

13 I exclude those parties whose importance score for 'more services versus less taxes' is below their mean for all nine dimensions. A partial exception is made for PR because the highly related 'deregulation' dimension results as very important for this party.

14 See, for example, the concluding address to the Party Congress by party secretary Massimo D'Alema in 1997 (one year before PDS turned into PS).

15 However, it applies only to firms with more than 15 employees and, hence, less than half of the labour force.

16 The centrist UdC obtained 5.6 per cent of the vote and entered parliament but did not play a role in coalition formation and did not have a significant impact as opposition party either.

17 *La Repubblica*, 24 January 2011, '*E se il Cavaliere uscisse di scena*', by Ilvo Diamanti.

10 Party competition and benefit segmentation across advanced welfare states

1 A similar result can be obtained when taking the year of SA introduction as dependent variable. More dispersed party systems tended to introduce SA later. The correlation is not very strong, but mainly because of the exceptions: Austria (two-party system but late introduction) and Finland (polarized pluralism but early introduction). Both exceptions are ambiguous with regard to their type of party system.

2 Iversen and Soskice (2006) argue that the electoral system has an effect on the power relations between social classes that is then reflected in the partisan composition of government. As I show below, the composition of government does not have a lot of leverage to explain the segmentation of unemployment benefits.

3 The only difference is that for this section I calculated the average replacement rates of six model households (not four as in Chapter 3). The reason is that these six households (including two-earner couples) capture a broader range of policy features, while the four households show more directly the features of unemployment benefit systems (because there is no contemporaneous income of a second earner).

4 Australia, Czech Republic, Finland, Germany, Hungary, Iceland, Ireland, Italy, Japan, Netherlands, Norway, Poland, Slovak Republic, Sweden, and Switzerland. Therefore, I include also countries that were not included in the analysis for the phase of welfare expansion because at the time they did not have democratic party competition (Czech Republic, Hungary, Poland, and Slovak Republic). The point of this second analysis is not to trace the trajectory of the previous cases but to analyse the effect of party systems on benefit reforms in general.

5 The results are robust for different specifications of the dependent variable, such as percentage point changes instead of proportional changes and changes in the ratio of the replacement rates for outsiders/insiders.

11 Conclusions and future research

1 Note that the neglect of other social interests in centrist competition is assumed in a multi-party context. In a system with very few – say two – parties, the assumption would be that large parties take into account a wide range of interests, which mitigates the centrist focus.

Bibliography

Abelshauser, W. (2004) *Deutsche Wirtschaftsgeschichte seit 1945*, München: C.H. Beck.

Adams, J. and Merrill, S. (1999) 'Modeling Party Strategies and Policy Representation in Multiparty Elections: Why Are Strategies So Extreme?', *American Journal of Political Science*, 43: 765–91.

Adams, J. and Somer-Topcu, Z. (2009) 'Policy Adjustment by Parties in Response to Rival Parties' Policy Shifts: Spatial Theory and the Dynamics of Party Competition in Twenty-Five Post-War Democracies', *British Journal of Political Science*, 39: 825–46.

Alber, J. (1981) 'Government Responses to the Challenge of Unemployment: The Development of Unemployment Insurance in Western Europe', in P. Flora and A.J. Heidenheimer (eds) *The Development of Welfare States in Europe and America*, New Brunswick, NJ and London: Transaction Publishers.

Alber, J. (1987) 'Germany', in P. Flora (ed.) *Growth to Limits: The Western European Welfare States since World War II. Vol. 4. Appendix*, Berlin: Walter de Gruyter.

Alber, J. (1989) *Der Sozialstaat in der Bundesrepublik 1950–1983*, Frankfurt a.M. and New York: Campus Verlag.

Alemann, U.v. (2003) *Das Parteiensystem der Bundesrepublik Deutschland*, Bonn: Bundeszentrale für politische Bildung.

Allan, J.P. and Scruggs, L. (2004) 'Political Partisanship and Welfare State Reform in Advanced Industrial Societies', *American Journal of Political Science*, 48: 496–512.

Ansolabehere, S. and Snyder, J.M. (2000) 'Valence Politics and Equilibrium in Spatial Election Models', *Public Choice*, 103: 327–36.

Armingeon, K. and Bonoli, G. (eds) (2006) *The Politics of Post-Industrial Welfare States: Adapting Post-War Social Policies to New Social Risks*, London and New York: Routledge.

Armingeon, K., Engler, S., Potolidis, P., Gerber, M. and Leimgruber, P. (2010) *Comparative Political Data Set 1960–2008*, Berne: Institute of Political Science, University of Berne.

Arts, W. and Gelissen, J. (2002) 'Three Worlds of Welfare Capitalism or More? A State-of-the-Art Report', *Journal of European Social Policy*, 12: 137–58.

Arts, W. and Gelissen, J. (2010) 'Models of the Welfare State', in F.G. Castles, *et al.* (eds) *The Oxford Handbook of the Welfare State*, Oxford: Oxford University Press.

Baglioni, S., della Porta, D. and Graziano, P. (2008) 'The Contentious Politics of Unemployment: The Italian Case in Comparative Perspective', *European Journal of Political Research*, 47: 827–51.

Bardi, L. and Mair, P. (2008) 'The Parameters of Party Systems', *Party Politics*, 14: 147–66.

Bartolini, S. (1999) 'Collusion, Competition and Democracy: Part I', *Journal of Theoretical Politics*, 11: 435–70.

Bartolini, S. (2000) 'Collusion, Competition and Democracy: Part II', *Journal of Theoretical Politics*, 12: 33–65.

Bartolini, S., Chiaramonte, A. and D'Alimonte, R. (2004) 'The Italian Party System between Parties and Coalitions', *West European Politics*, 27: 1–19.

Becker, I. and Hauser, R. (2006) *Verteilungseffekte der Hartz-IV-Reform: Ergebnisse von Simulationsanalysen*, Berlin: Edition Sigma.

Benoit, K. and Laver, M. (2006) *Party Policy in Modern Democracies*, London and New York: Routledge.

Berton, F., Richiardi, M. and Sacchi, S. (2009) *Flex-insecurity: Perché in Italia la flessibilità diventa precarità*, Bologna: Il Mulino.

Birchfield, V. and Crepaz, M.M.L. (1998) 'The Impact of Constitutional Structures and Collective and Competitive Veto Points on Income Inequality in Industrialized Democracies', *European Journal of Political Research*, 34: 175–200.

Blancke, S. and Schmid, J. (2003) 'Bilanz der Bundesregierung Schröder in der Arbeitsmarktpolitik 1998–2002: Ansätze zu einer doppelten Wende', in C. Egle, *et al.* (eds) *Das Rot-grüne Projekt. Eine Bilanz der Regierung Schröder 1998–2002*, Wiesbaden: Westdeutscher Verlag.

Bleses, P. and Seeleib-Kaiser, M. (2004) *The Dual Transformation of the German Welfare State*, Basingstoke: Palgrave Macmillan.

Blome, A., Kech, W. and Alber, J. (2009) *Family and the Welfare State in Europe: Intergenerational Relations in Ageing Societies*, Cheltenham and Northampton, MA: Edward Elgar.

Blyth, M. (2002) *Great Transformations: Economic Ideas and Institutional Change in the Twentieth Century*, Cambridge: Cambridge University Press.

Blyth, M., Hopkin, J. and Pelizzo, R.X. 'Liberalization and Cartel Politics in Europe: Why Do Centre-Left Parties Adopt Market Liberal Reforms?' paper presented at the 17th International Conference of the Council for European Studies, Montréal, April 2010.

Bonoli, G. (2006) 'New Social Risks and the Politics of Post-Industrial Social Policies', in K. Armingeon and G. Bonoli (eds) *The Politics of Post-Industrial Welfare States: Adapting Post-War Social Policies to New Social Risks*, London and New York: Routledge.

Brady, H.E., Verba, S. and Schlozman, K.L. (1995) 'Beyond SES: A Resource Model of Political Participation', *American Political Science Review*, 89: 271–94.

Budge, I., Klingemann, H.-D., Volkens, A., Bara, J.L. and Tanenbaum, E. (eds) (2001) *Mapping Policy Preferences: Estimates for Parties, Electors, and Governments 1945–1998*, Oxford: Oxford University Press.

Bull, M.J. and Newell, J. (2005) *Italian Politics: Adjustment under Duress*, Bristol: Polity Press.

Bundesministerium für Arbeit und Soziales (2007) *Statistisches Taschenbuch*, Berlin: Bundesministerium für Arbeit und Soziales.

Castles, F.G. (ed.) (1982) *The Impact of Parties: Politics and Policies in Democratic Capitalist States*, London: Sage.

Cazzola, F. (1972) 'Consenso e Opposizione nel Parlamento Italiano: Il Ruolo del PCI dalla I alla IV Legislatura', *Rivista Italiana di Scienza Politica*, 2: 71–96.

Cherubini, A. (1977) *Storia della Previdenza Sociale in Italia (1860–1960)*, Rome: Editori Riuniti.

Cherubini, A. and Piva, I. (1998) *Dalla Libertà all' Obbligo. La Previdenza Sociale fra Giolitti e Mussolini*, Milano: FrancoAngeli.

Clasen, J. (1994) *Paying the Jobless: A Comparison of Unemployment Benefit Policies in Great Britain and Germany*, Aldershot: Avebury.

Clasen, J. (2005) *Reforming European Welfare States: Germany and the United Kingdom Compared*, Oxford: Oxford University Press.

Clasen, J. and Clegg, D. (2006) 'New Labour Market Risks and the Revision of Unemployment Protection Systems in Europe', in K. Armingeon and G. Bonoli (eds) *The Politics of Post-Industrial Welfare States: Adapting Post-War Social Policies to New Social Risks*, London and New York: Routledge.

Clegg, D. (2007) 'Continental Drift: On Unemployment Policy Change in Bismarckian Welfare States', *Social Policy & Administration*, 41: 597–617.

CNEL (2003). *Rapporto: La Situazione degli Ammortizzatori Sociali in Italia e in Europa*.

Corbetta, P. and Segatti, P. (2004) 'Un Bipolarismo Senza Radici?', in S. Ceccanti and S. Vassallo (eds) *Come Chiudere la Transizione: Cambiamento, Apprendimento e Adattamento nel Sistema Politica Italiano*, Bologna: Il Mulino.

Cotta, M. (1996) 'La Crisi del Governo di Partito all'Italiana', in M. Cotta and P. Isernia (eds) *Il Gigante dai Piedi di Argilla: La Crisi del Regime Partitocratico in Italia*, Bologna: Il Mulino.

Cotta, M. and Isernia, P. (1996) *Il Gigante dai Piedi di Argilla: La Crisi del Regime Partitocratico in Italia*, Bologna: Il Mulino.

Cotta, M. and Verzichelli, L. (2007) *Political Institutions in Italy*, Oxford: Oxford University Press.

Cox, G.W. (1990) 'Centripetal and Centrifugal Incentives in Electoral Systems', *American Journal of Political Science*, 34: 903–35.

Dalton, R.J. (2008) 'The Quantity and the Quality of Party Systems. Party System Polarization, Its Measurement, and Its Consequences', *Comparative Political Studies*, 41: 899–920.

Davidsson, J. and Naczyk, M. (2009) 'The Ins and Outs of Dualisation: A Literature Review', Edinburgh: RECWOWE Working Paper.

Downs, A. (1957) *An Economic Theory of Democracy*, Boston: Addison Wesley.

Duverger, M. (1959) *Political Parties: Their Organization and Activity in the Modern State*, 2nd edn, New York: Wiley.

Ebbinghaus, B. and Eichhorst, W. (2006). *Employment Regulation and Labor Market Policy in Germany, 1991–2005*. Bonn: Institute for the Study of Labor.

Eichhorst, W. and Marx, P. (2011) 'Reforming German Labour Market Institutions: A Dual Path to Flexibility', *Journal of European Social Policy*, 21(1): 73–87.

Emmenegger, P. (2009) 'Barriers to Entry: Insider/Outsider Politics and the Political Determinants of Job Security Regulations', *Journal of European Social Policy*, 19(2): 131–46.

Esping-Andersen, G. (1985) *Politics Against Markets: The Social Democratic Road to Power*, Princeton, NJ: Princeton University Press.

Esping-Andersen, G. (1990) *The Three Worlds of Welfare Capitalism*, Cambridge Polity Press.

Esping-Andersen, G. (1996) 'Welfare States without Work: The Impasse of Labour Shedding and Familialism in Continental European Social Policy', in G. Esping-Andersen (ed.) *Welfare States in Transition: National Adaptations in Global Economies*, London: Sage.

Esping-Andersen, G. (1999) *Social Foundations of Postindustrial Economies*, Oxford: Oxford University Press.

Estévez-Abe, M. (2008) *Welfare and Capitalism in Postwar Japan*, Cambridge: Cambridge University Press.

Estévez-Abe, M., Iversen, T. and Soskice, D. (2001) 'Social Protection and the Formation of Skills: A Reinterpretation of the Welfare State', in P.A. Hall and D. Soskice (eds) *Varieties of Capitalism: The Institutional Foundations of Comparative Advantage*, Oxford: Oxford University Press.

Ezrow, L., De Vries, C., Steenbergen, M. and Edwards, E. (2011) 'Mean Voter Representation and Partisan Constituency Representation: Do Parties Respond to the Mean Voter Position or to their Supporters?', *Party Politics*, 17(3): 275–301.

Fabbrini, S. (2000) *Tra Pressioni e Veti: Il Cambiamento Politico in Italia*, Bari, Italy: Laterza.

Fargion, V. (1996) 'Social Assistance and the North-South Cleavage in Italy', *Southern European Society & Politics*, 1: 135–54.

Fargion, V. (2001) 'Creeping Workfare Policies: The Case of Italy', in N. Gilbert and R.A. Van Voorhis (eds) *Activating the Unemployed: A Comparative Appraisal of Work-Oriented Policies*, New Brunswick, NJ and London: Transaction Publishers.

Faust, A. (1981) 'State and Unemployment in Germany 1890–1918 (Labour Exchanges, Job Creation and Unemployment Insurance)', in W.J. Mommsen (ed.) *The Emergence of the Welfare State in Britain and Germany, 1850–1950*, London: German Historical Institute.

Ferrera, M. (1984) *Il Welfare State in Italia: Sviluppo e Crisi in Prospettiva Comparata*, Bologna: Il Mulino.

Ferrera, M. (1987) 'Italy', in P. Flora (ed.) *Growth to Limits: The Western European Welfare States since World War II. Vol. 4. Appendix*, Berlin: Walter de Gruyter.

Ferrera, M. (1993) *Modelli di Solidarietà: Politica e Riforme Sociali nelle Democrazie*, Bologna: Il Mulino.

Ferrera, M. (1996) 'The Southern Model of Welfare in Social Europe', *Journal of European Social Policy*, 6: 17–37.

Ferrera, M. (2005a) *The Boundaries of Welfare: European Integration and the New Spatial Politics of Social Protection*, Oxford: Oxford University Press.

Ferrera, M. (ed.) (2005b) *Welfare State Reform in Southern Europe: Fighting Poverty and Social Exclusion in Italy, Spain, Portugal and Greece*, London and New York: Routledge.

Ferrera, M. (2008) 'The European Welfare State: Golden Achievements, Silver Prospects', *West European Politics*, 31: 82–107.

Ferrera, M. (2010) 'The South European Countries', in F.G. Castles, *et al.* (eds) *The Oxford Handbook of the Welfare State*, Oxford: Oxford University Press.

Ferrera, M. and Gualmini, E. (2004) *Rescued by Europe? Social and Labour Market Reforms in Italy from Maastricht to Berlusconi*, Amsterdam: Amsterdam University Press.

Ferrera, M., Maino, F., Jessoula, M., Madama, I. and Vesan, P. (2006) *Le Politiche Sociali: L'Italia in Prospettiva Comparata*, Bologna: Il Mulino.

Ferrera, M., Jessoula, M. and Fargion, V. (forthcoming) *Alle Origini del Welfare all'Italiana: le Politiche Sociali dalle Origini al 1970*, Bari, Italy: Laterza.

Flora, P. (1986a) 'Introduction', in P. Flora (ed.) *Growth to Limits: The Western European Welfare States since World War II. Vol. 1*, Berlin: de Gruyter.

Flora, P. (ed.) (1986b) *Growth to Limits: The Western European Welfare States since World War II*, Berlin: de Gruyter.

Flora, P. and Alber, J. (1981) 'Modernization, Democratization, and the Development of Welfare States in Western Europe', in P. Flora and A.J. Heidenheimer (eds) *The Development of Welfare States in Europe and America*, New Brunswick, NJ: Transaction Publishers.

Flora, P., Alber, J., Eichenberg, R., Kohl, J., Kraus, F., Pfenning, W., *et al.* (1983) *State, Economy, and Society in Western Europe: 1815–1975. A Data Handbook in Two Volumes*, Frankfurt a.M.: Campus Verlag.

Flora, P., Kraus, F. and Pfenning, W. (eds) (1987) *State, Economy, and Society in Western Europe: 1815–1975. A Data Handbook in Two Volumes*, Frankfurt a.M.: Campus Verlag.

Frerich, J. and Frey, M. (1996 (2nd edn)) *Handbuch der Geschichte der Sozialpolitik in Deutschland: Band 1: Von der vorindustriellen Zeit bis zum Ende des Dritten Reichs*, München: Oldenbourg.

Führer, K.C. (1990) *Arbeitslosigkeit und die Entstehung der Arbeitslosenversicherung in Deutschland 1902–1927*, Berlin: Colloquium Verlag.

Gallagher, M. and Mitchell, P. (eds) (2008), *The Politics of Electoral Systems*, Oxford and New York: Oxford University Press.

Gallego, A. (2007) 'Unequal Political Participation in Europe', *International Journal of Sociology*, 37: 10–25.

Gallie, D. and Paugam, S. (2000) 'The Experience of Unemployment in Europe: The Debate', in D. Gallie and S. Paugam (eds) *Welfare Regimes and the Experience of Unemployment in Europe*, Oxford: Oxford University Press.

Garrett, G. (1998) *Partisan Politics in the Global Economy*, Cambridge: Cambridge University Press.

Genschel, P. (2004) 'Globalization and the Welfare State: a Retrospective', *Journal of European Public Policy*, 11: 613–36.

George, A.L. and Bennett, A. (2004) *Case Studies and Theory Development in the Social Sciences*, Cambridge, MA: MIT Press.

Giger, N. (2011) *The Risk of Social Policy? The Electoral Consequences of Welfare State Retrenchment and Social Policy Performance in OECD Countries*, London and New York: Routledge.

Ginsborg, P. (1990) *A History of Contemporary Italy: Society and Politics. 1943–1988*, London: Penguin.

Ginsborg, P. (2001) *Italy and its Discontents: Family, Civil Society, State. 1980–2001*, London: Penguin.

Görtemaker, M. (1999) *Geschichte der Bundesrepublik Deutschland: von der Gründung bis zur Gegenwart*, München: C.H. Beck.

Green-Pedersen, C. (2001) 'Welfare State Retrenchment in Denmark and the Netherlands, 1982–1998: The Role of Party Competition and Party Consensus', *Comparative Political Studies*, 34: 963–85.

Green-Pedersen, C. (2002) *The Politics of Justification: Party Competition and Welfare-State Retrenchment in Denmark and the Netherlands from 1982 to 1998*. Amsterdam: Amsterdam University Press.

Grimshaw, D. and Rubery, J. (1997) 'Workforce Heterogeneity and Unemployment Benefits: The Need for Policy Reassessment in the European Union', *Journal of European Social Policy*, 7: 291–318.

Gualmini, E. (1997) *Le Rendite del Neo-Corporativismo: Politiche Pubbliche e Contrattazione Privata nella Regolazione del Mercato del Lavoro Italiano e Tedesco*, Soveria Mannelli, Italy: Rubbettino.

Gualmini, E. (1998) *La Politica del Lavoro*, Bologna: Il Mulino.

Guarnieri, C. (2006) *Il Sistema Politico Italiano*, Bologna: Il Mulino.

Haggard, S. and Kaufman, R.R. (1995) *The Political Economy of Democratic Transitions*, Princeton, NJ: Princeton University Press.

Hall, P.A. (1993) 'Policy Paradigms, Social Learning, and the State: The Case of Economic Policymaking in Britain', *Comparative Politics*, 25: 275–96.

Hall, P.A. (2003) 'Aligning Ontology and Methodology in Comparative Research', in J. Mahoney and D. Rueschemeyer (eds) *Comparative Historical Analysis in the Social Sciences*, Cambridge: Cambridge University Press.

Hall, P.A. and Soskice, D. (2001) 'An Introduction to Varieties of Capitalism', in P.A. Hall and D. Soskice (eds) *Varieties of Capitalism: The Institutional Foundations of Comparative Advantage*, Oxford: Oxford University Press.

Hall, P.A. and Taylor, R.C.R. (1996) 'Political Science and the Three New Institutionalisms', *Political Studies*, XLIV: 936–57.

Hall, P.A. and Thelen, K. (2009) 'Institutional change in Varieties of Capitalism', *Socio-Economic Review*, 7: 7–34.

Hassel, A. and Schiller, C. (2010) *Der Fall Hartz IV: Wie es zur Agenda 2010 Kam und wie es Weitergeht*, Frankfurt a.M.: Campus Verlag.

Häusermann, S. (2010) *The Politics of Welfare State Reform in Continental Europe: Modernization in Hard Times*, Cambridge: Cambridge University Press.

Häusermann, S. and Schwander, H. (2009) 'Identifying Outsiders across Countries: Similarities and Differences in the Patterns of Dualisation', Edinburgh: RECWOWE Working Paper.

Häusermann, S., Picot, G., Geering, D. (2010) 'Rethinking Party Politics and the Welfare State: Recent Advances in the Literature'. Paper presented at the 17th International Conference of the Council for European Studies, Montréal, April 2010.

Heclo, H. (1974) *Modern Social Politics in Britain and Sweden*, New Haven, CT: Yale University Press.

Hibbs, J., Douglas A. (1977) 'Political Parties and Macroeconomic Policy', *American Political Science Review*, 71: 1467–87.

Hine, D. (1993) *Governing Italy: The Politics of Bargained Pluralism*, Oxford: Oxford University Press.

Hinich, M.J. and Munger, M.C. (1997) *Analytical Politics*, Cambridge: Cambridge University Press.

Hobsbawm, E. (1994) *The Age of Extremes. The Short Twentieth Century 1914–1991*, London: Abacus.

Hockerts, H.G. (1980). *Sozialpolitische Entscheidungen im Nachkriegsdeutschland: Alliierte und Deutsche Sozialversicherungspolitik 1945–1957*. Stuttgart: Klett-Cotta.

Huber, E. and Stephens, J.D. (2001) *Development and Crisis of the Welfare State: Parties and Policies in Global Markets*, Chicago: University of Chicago Press.

Huber, E. and Stephens, J.D. (2005) 'State Economic and Social Policy in Global Capitalism', in T. Janoski, *et al.* (eds) *The Handbook of Political Sociology*, Cambridge: Cambridge University Press.

Immergut, E.M. (1992) 'The Rules of the Game: The Logic of Health Policy-Making in France, Switzerland, and Sweden', in S. Steinmo, *et al.* (eds) *Structuring Politics: Historical Institutionalism in Comparative Analysis*, Cambridge: Cambridge University Press.

Immervoll, H., Marianna, P. and Mira D'Ercole, M. (2004). *Benefit Coverage Rates and Household Typologies: Scope and Limitations of Tax-Benefit Indicators*. Paris: OECD.

Iversen, T. and Cusack, T.R. (2000) 'The Causes of Welfare State Expansion: Deindustrialization or Globalization?' *World Politics*, 52: 313–49.

Iversen, T. and Soskice, D. (2006) 'Electoral Institutions and the Politics of Coalitions: Why Some Democracies Redistribute More Than Others', *American Political Science Review*, 100: 165–81.

Iversen, T. and Wren, A. (1998) 'Equality, Employment, and Budgetary Restraint: The Trilemma of the Service Economy', *World Politics*, 50: 507–46.

Jessoula, M., Graziano, P.R. and Madama, I. (2010) ' "Selective Flexicurity" in Segmented Labour Markets: The Case of Italian "Mid-Siders" ', *Journal of Social Policy*, 39: 561–83.

Katz, R.S. and Kolodny, R. (1994) 'Party Organization as an Empty Vessel: Parties in American Politics', in Katz, R.S. and Kolodny, R. (eds) *How Parties Organize: Change and Adaptation in Party Organizations in Western Democracies*, London: Sage.

Katz, R.S. and Mair, P. (eds) (1994) *How Parties Organize: Change and Adaptation in Party Organizations in Western Democracies*, London: Sage.

Katzenstein, P.J. (1987) *Policy and Politics in West Germany: The Growth of a Semisovereign State*, Philadelphia: Temple University Press.

Katznelson, I. (2005) *When Affirmative Action Was White: An Untold History of Racial Inequality in Twentieth-Century America*, New York and London: W.W. Norton and Company.

Kemmerling, A. and Bruttel, O. (2006) ' "New Politics" in German Labour Market Policy? The Implications of the Recent Hartz Reforms for the German Welfare State', *West European Politics*, 29: 90–112.

Kinderman, D. (2005) 'Pressure from without, Subversion from within: The Two-Pronged German Employer Offensive', *Comparative European Politics*, 3: 432–63.

King, D. and Rueda, D. (2008) 'Cheap Labor: The New Politics of "Bread and Roses" in Industrial Democracies', *Perspectives on Politics*, 6: 279–97.

King, G., Keohane, R.O. and Verba, S. (1994) *Designing Social Inquiry: Scientific Inference in Qualitative Research*, Princeton, NJ: Princeton University Press.

Kirchheimer, O. (1966) 'The Transformation of West European Party Systems', in J. LaPalombara and M. Weiner (eds) *Political Parties and Political Development*, Princeton, NJ: Princeton University Press.

Kitschelt, H. (2001) 'Partisan Competition and Welfare State Retrenchment: When Do Politicians Choose Unpopular Policies?', in P. Pierson (ed.) *The New Politics of the Welfare State*, Oxford: Oxford University Press.

Kitschelt, H. (2003a) 'Political-Economic Context and Partisan Strategies in the German Federal Elections, 1990–2002', *West European Politics*, 26: 125–52.

Kitschelt, H. (2003b) 'Competitive Party Democracy and Political-Economic Reform in Germany and Japan: Do Party Systems Make a Difference?', in K. Yamamura and W. Streeck (eds) *The End of Diversity? Prospects for German and Japanese Capitalism*, Ithaca, NY: Cornell University Press.

Kitschelt, H. and Wilkinson, S.I. (eds) (2007) *Patrons, Clients, and Policies: Patterns of Democratic Accountability and Political Competition*, Cambridge: Cambridge University Press.

Klenk, T. (2009) 'Die Korporatistische Arbeitsverwaltung', *APuZ*, 27: 34–9.

Klingemann, H.-D., Volkens, A., Bara, J.L., Budge, I. and McDonald, M.D. (eds) (2006) *Mapping Policy Preferences II: Estimates for Parties, Electors, and Governments in Eastern Europe, European Union, and OECD 1990–2003*, Oxford: Oxford University Press.

Korpi, W. (1983) *The Democratic Class Struggle*, London: Routledge.

Korpi, W. and Palme, J. (2003) 'New Politics and Class Politics in the Context of Austerity and Globalization: Welfare State Regress in 18 Countries, 1975–95', *American
Political Science Review*, 97: 425–46.

Kreile, M. (1985) *Gewerkschaften und Arbeitsbeziehungen in Italien (1968–1982)*, Frankfurt a.M. and New York: Campus.

Laakso, M. and Taagepera, R. (1979) ' "Effective" Number of Parties. A Measure with
Application to West Europe', *Comparative Political Studies*, 12: 3–27.

Laver, M. and Hunt, B.W. (1992) *Policy and Party Competition*, New York: Routledge.

Lees, C. (2005) *Party Politics in Germany: A Comparative Politics Approach*, Basingstoke, UK: Palgrave Macmillan.

Lehmbruch, G. (2000) *Parteienwettbewerb im Bundesstaat: Regelsysteme und Span-
nungslagen im politischen System der Bundesrepublik Deutschland*, 3rd edn, Wiesbaden: Westdeutscher Verlag.

Leitner, S., Ilona, O. and Schmitt, C. (2008) 'Family Policies in Germany', in Leitner, S.,
Ilona, O. and Schmitt, C. (eds) *Family Policies in the Context of Family Change: The
Nordic Countries in Comparative Perspective*, Wiesbaden: VS Verlag für Sozialwis-
senschaften.

Lepre, A. (2004) *Storia della Prima Repubblica: l'Italia dal 1943 al 2003*, Bologna: Il
Mulino.

Leschke, J. (2008) *Unemployment Insurance and Non-Standart Employment. Four European Countries in Comparison*, Wiesbaden: VS Verlag für Sozialwissenschaften.

Lijphart, A. (1971) 'Comparative Politics and the Comparative Method', *American Political Science Review*, 3: 682–98.

Lijphart, A. (1999) *Patterns of Democracy: Government Forms and Performance in
Thirty-Six Countries*, New Haven, CT: Yale University Press.

Lindqvist, E. and Östling, R. (2010) 'Political Polarization and the Size of Government',
American Political Science Review, 104: 543–65.

Lipset, S.M., and Rokkan, S. (1990 [1967]) 'Cleavage Structures, Party Systems, and
Voter Alignments', in P. Mair (ed.) *The West European Party System*. Oxford: Oxford
University Press.

Lösche, P. (1994 (2nd edn)) *Kleine Geschichte der deutschen Parteien*, Stuttgart: Verlag
W. Kohlhammer.

Lynch, J. (2006) *Age in the Welfare State: The Origins of Social Spending on Pensioners,
Workers, and Children*, Cambridge: Cambridge University Press.

Mair, P. (2005) 'Introduction by Peter Mair', in G. Sartori (ed.) *Parties and Party
Systems. A Framwork for Analysis*, Colchester, UK: ECPR Press.

Manow, P. (2009) 'Electoral Rules, Class Coalitions and Welfare State Regimes, or How
to Explain Esping-Andersen with Stein Rokkan', *Socio-Economic Review*, 7: 101–21.

Manow, P. and Seils, E. (2000) 'Adjusting Badly: The German Welfare State, Structural
Change, and the Open Economy', in F.W. Scharpf and V.A. Schmidt (eds) *Welfare
and Work in the Open Economy. Vol. 2: Diverse Responses to Common Challenges*,
Oxford: Oxford University Press.

Mares, I. (2001) 'Strategic Bargaining and Social Policy Development: The Case of
Unemployment Insurance in France and Germany', in B. Ebbinghaus and P. Manow
(eds) *Comparing Welfare Capitalism: Social Policy and Political Economy in Europe,
Japan and the USA*, London and New York: Routledge.

Marshall, T.H. (1950) *Citizenship and Social Class*, Cambridge: Cambridge University
Press.

Marx, P. and Picot, G. 'Labour Market Integration and Political Integration in Germany', Paper presented at the Drei-Länder-Tagung 'Politische Integration', Basel, January 2011.

Mätzke, M. 'Political Competition in Redistributive Social Policy Legislation: Welfare Reforms in Germany since WWII', Paper presented at the 100th Annual Meeting of the American Political Science Association, Chicago, September 2004.

Ministero del Lavoro e della Previdenza Sociale (various years): Monitoraggio delle Politiche Occupazionali e del Lavoro. Rome: Ministero del Lavoro e della Previdenza Sociale. Online. Available: www.lavoro.gov.it/Lavoro/PrimoPiano/monitoraggio.htm (accessed: 15 June 2008).

Ministero Dell'Interno (2008) *Archivio storico delle elezioni*, Rome: Ministero Dell'Interno. Online. Available: http://elezionistorico.interno.it/ (accessed: 15 October 2008).

MISSOC (various years). *Mutual Information System on Social Protection, Bruxelles:* European Commission. Online. Available: http://ec.europa.eu/employment_social/spsi/ missoc_en.htm (accessed 15 June 2008).

Mitchell, B.R. (1975) *European Historical Statistics, 1750–1970*, London and Basingstoke, UK: Macmillan.

Möller, J. (2010) 'The German Labor Market Response in the World Recession – De-Mystifying a Miracle', *Zeitschrift für Arbeitsmarktforschung*, 42: 325–36.

Molina, O. and Rhodes, M. (2007) 'The Political Economy of Adjustment in Mixed Market Economies: A Study of Spain and Italy', in B. Hancké, *et al.* (eds) *Beyond Varieties of Capitalism: Conflict, Contradictions, and Complementarities in the European Economy*, Oxford: Oxford University Press.

Münnich, S. (2010) *Interessen und Ideen: Die Entstehung der Arbeitslosenversicherung in Deutschland und den USA*, Frankfurt a.M.: Campus.

Musso, S. (2002) *Storia del Lavoro in Italia: dall'Unità a Oggi*, Venezia: Marsilio.

Musso, S. (2004) *Le Regole e l'Elusione. Il Governo del Mercato del Lavoro nell'Industrializzazione Italiana: 1888–2003*, Torino, Italy: Rosenberg and Sellier.

Nachtwey, O. and Spier, T. (2007) 'Political Opportunity Structures and the Success of the German Left Party in 2005', *Debatte: Journal of Contemporary Central and Eastern Europe*, 15: 123–54.

Naldini, M. and Saraceno, C. (2008) 'Social and Family Policies in Italy: Not Totally Frozen but Far from Structural Reforms', *Social Policy & Administration*, 42: 733–48.

Neugebauer, G. and Stöss, R. (1996) *Die PDS: Geschichte, Organisation, Wähler, Konkurrenten*, Opladen, Germany: Leske + Budrich.

Niedermayer, O. (2006) 'Das Parteiensystem Deutschlands ', in O. Niedermayer, R. Stöss and M. Haas (eds) *Die Parteiensysteme Westeuropas*, Wiesbaden: Verlag für Sozialwissenschaften.

Nohlen, D. (2009) *Wahlrecht und Parteiensystem. Zur Theorie und Empirie der Wahlsysteme*, 6th edn, Opladen and Farmington Hills: Verlag Barbara Budrich.

O'Connor, J. (1973) *The Fiscal Crisis of the State*, New York: St Martin's Press.

OECD (2010a) *OECD Benefits and Wages.* Paris: OECD. Available: www.oecd.org/els/ social/workincentives (accessed 15 December 2010).

OECD (2010b) *OECD.Stat.* Paris: OECD. Online. Available: http://stats.oecd.org (accessed 1 December 2010).

Olson, M. (1971) *The Logic of Collective Action: Public Goods and the Theory of Groups* Cambridge, MA: Harvard University Press.

Orloff, A.S. and Skocpol, T. (1984) 'Why Not Equal Protection? Explaining the Politics of Public Social Spending in Britain, 1900–1911, and the United States, 1880s–1920', *American Sociological Review*, 49(6): 726–50.

Oschmiansky, F., Schmid, G. and Kull, S. (2003) 'Faule Arbeitslose? Politische Konjunkturen und Strukturprobleme der Missbrauchsdebatte', *Leviathan: Berliner Zeitschrift für Sozialwissenschaft*, 31(1): 3–31.

Padgett, S. (2004) 'Welfare Bias in the Party System: A Neo-Downsian Explanation for Gridlock in Economic Reform', *German Politics*, 13: 360–83.

Padgett, S. (2005) The Party Politics of Economic Reform: Public Opinion, Party Positions and Partisan Cleavages, *German Politics*, 14(2): 248–74.

Palier, B. (ed.) (2010) *A Long Goodbye to Bismarck? The Politics of Welfare Reforms in Continental Europe*, Amsterdam: Amsterdam University Press.

Palier, B. and Thelen, K. (2010) 'Institutionalizing Dualism: Complementarities and Change in France and Germany', *Politics & Society*, 38(1): 119–48.

Pappalardo, A. (2001) 'Il Sistema Partitico Italiano fra Bipolarismo e Destrutturazione', *Rivista Italiana di Scienza Politica*, 31: 561–600.

Parisi, A. and Pasquino, G. (1977) 'Relazioni Partiti-Elettori e Tipi di Voto', in A. Parisi and G. Pasquino (eds) *Continuità e Mutamento Elettorale in Italia: Le Elezioni del 20 Giugno 1976 e il Sistema Politico Italiano*, Bologna: Il Mulino.

Paster, T. (2010) 'Die Rolle der Arbeitgeber in der Sozialpolitik', in W. Schroeder and B. Wessels (eds) *Handbuch Arbeitgeber- und Wirtschaftsverbände in Deutschland*, Wiesbaden: VS Verlag für Sozialwissenschaften.

Pasquino, G. (2002) 'Italy: A Democratic Regime in Transition', in J.M. Colomer (ed.) *Political Institutions in Europe*, London and New York: Routledge.

Picot, G. (2009) 'Party Competition and Reforms of Unemployment Benefits in Germany: How a Small Change in Electoral Demand Can Make a Big Difference', *German Politics*, 18(2): 155–79.

Pierson, P. (1994) *Dismantling the Welfare State? Reagan, Thatcher, and the Politics of Retrenchment*, Cambridge: Cambridge University Press.

Pierson, P. (1996) 'The New Politics of the Welfare State', *World Politics*, 48: 143–79.

Pierson, P. (2001a) 'Post-industrial Pressures on the Mature Welfare States', in P. Pierson (ed.) *The New Politics of the Welfare State*, Oxford: Oxford University Press.

Pierson, P. (2001b) 'Coping with Permanent Austerity: Welfare State Restructuring in Affluent Democracies', in P. Pierson (ed.) *The New Politics of the Welfare State*, Oxford: Oxford University Press.

Pirrone, S. and Sestito, P. (2006) *Disoccupati in Italia: tra Stato, Regioni e Cacciatori di Teste*, Bologna: Il Mulino.

Porcari, S. (2004) 'Protezione Sociale e Disoccupazione in Italia', in Porcari, S. (ed.) *Sistemi di Welfare e Gestione del Rischio Economico di Disoccupazione*, Milano: Franco Angeli.

Przeworski, A. and Sprague, J. (1986) *Paper Stones. A History of Electoral Socialism*, Chicago and London: The University of Chicago Press.

Rabinowitz, G. and MacDonald, S.E. (1989) 'A Directional Theory of Issue Voting', *American Political Science Review*, 83: 93–121.

Regalia, I. (1984) 'Le Politiche del Lavoro', in Regalia, I. (ed.) *Welfare State all'Italiana*, Bari, Italy: Laterza.

Rehm, P. (2009) 'Risks and Redistribution: An Individual-Level Analysis', *Comparative Political Studies*, 42: 855–81.

Rehm, P. and Reilly, T. (2010) 'United We Stand: Constituency Homogeneity and Comparative Party Polarization', *Electoral Studies*, 29: 40–53.

Reyneri, E. (1987) 'Il Mercato del Lavoro Italiano tra Controllo Statale e Regolazione Sociale', in P. Lange and M. Regini (eds) *Stato e Regolazione Sociale: Nuove Prospettive sul Caso Italiano*, Bologna: Il Mulino.

Rodrik, D. (1997) *Has Globalization Gone too Far?*, Washington, DC: Institute for International Economics.

Roemer, J.E. (2001) *Political Competition: Theory and Applications*, Cambridge, MA: Harvard University Press.

Rohe, K. (2001) 'Entwicklung der Politischen Parteien und Parteiensysteme in Deutschland bis zum Jahre 1933', in O.W. Gabriel, *et al.* (eds) *Parteiendemokratie in Deutschland*, Bonn: Bundeszentrale für politische Bildung.

Rueda, D. (2005) 'Insider-Outsider Politics in Industrialized Democracies: The Challenge to Social Democratic Parties', *American Political Science Review*, 99: 61–74.

Rueda, D. (2007) *Social Democracy Inside Out: Partisanship and Labour Market Policy in Industrialized Democracies*, Oxford: Oxford University Press.

Sacchi, S. (2007) 'L'Esperienza del Reddito Minimo di Inserimento', in A. Brandolini and C. Saraceno (eds) *Povertà e benessere: Una Geografia delle Disuguaglianze in Italia*, Bologna: Il Mulino.

Sacchi, S., Pancaldi, F. and Arisi, C. (forthcoming) 'The Economic Crisis as a Trigger of Convergence? Short-time Work in Italy, Germany and Austria', *Social Policy & Administration*.

Salvati, M. (1982) *Stato e Industria nella Ricostruzione: Alle Origini del Potere Democristiano, 1944–1949*, Milano: Feltrinelli.

Sartori, G. (1982) *Teoria dei Partiti e Caso Italiano*, Milano: Sugarco Edizioni.

Sartori, G. (1990 [1968]) 'The Sociology of Parties: A Critical Review', in P. Mair (ed.) *The West European Party System*, Oxford: Oxford University Press.

Sartori, G. (2005 [1976]) *Parties and Party Systems: A Framework for Analysis*, Colchester, UK: ECPR Press.

Scharpf, F.W. (1985) 'Die Politikverflechtungs-Falle: Europäische Integration und deutscher Föderalismus im Vergleich', *Politische Vierteljahresschrift*, 26: 323–56.

Scharpf, F.W. (2000) 'Economic Changes, Vulnerabilities, and Institutional Capabilities', in F.W. Scharpf and V.A. Schmidt (eds) *Welfare and Work in the Open Economy. Vol. 1: From Vulnerability to Competitiveness*, Oxford: Oxford University Press.

Schmid, G. (2006) 'Der Mensch Denkt und die Institution Lenkt: Zur Reformfähigkeit von Staat und Gesellschaft am Beispiel der Deutschen Arbeitsmarktpolitik', *Politische Vierteljahresschrift*, 47: 367–79.

Schmid, G. and Oschmiansky, F. (2005) 'Arbeitsmarktpolitik und Arbeitslosenversicherung', in M.G. Schmidt (ed.) *Geschichte der Sozialpolitik in Deutschland seit 1945. Band 7: 1982–1989 Bundesrepublik Deutschland. Finanzielle Konsolidierung und Institutionelle Reform*, Baden-Baden: Nomos.

Schmid, G. and Oschmiansky, F. (2006) 'Arbeitsmarktpolitik und Arbeitslosenversicherung', in H.G. Hockerts (ed.) *Geschichte der Sozialpolitik in Deutschland seit 1945. Band 5: 1966–1974 Bundesrepublik Deutschland. Eine Zeit vielfältigen Aufbruchs*, Baden-Baden: Nomos.

Schmid, G. and Oschmiansky, F. (2007) 'Arbeitsmarktpolitik und Arbeitslosenversicherung', in G.A. Ritter (ed.) *Geschichte der Sozialpolitik in Deutschland seit 1945. Band 11: 1989–1994 Bundesrepublik Deutschland. Sozialpolitik im Zeichen der Vereinigung*, Baden-Baden: Nomos.

Schmid, G. and Oschmiansky, F. (2008a) 'Arbeitsmarktpolitik und Arbeitslosenversicherung', in M. Ruck and M. Boldorf (eds) *Geschichte der Sozialpolitik in*

Deutschland seit 1945. Band 4: 1957–1966 Bundesrepublik Deutschland. Sozialpolitik im Zeichen des Wohlstandes, Baden-Baden: Nomos.

Schmid, G. and Oschmiansky, F. (2008b) 'Arbeitsmarktpolitik und Arbeitslosenversicherung', in M.H. Geyer (ed.) *Geschichte der Sozialpolitik in Deutschland seit 1945. Band 6: 1974–1982 Bundesrepublik Deutschland. Neue Herausforderungen, wachsende Unsicherheiten*, Baden-Baden: Nomos.

Schmid, G. and Reissert, B. (1996) 'Unemployment Compensation and Labour Market Transitions', in G. Schmid *et al.* (eds) *International Handbook of Labour Market Policy and Evaluation*, Cheltenham and Brookfield, UK: Edwar Elgar.

Schmid, G., Wiebe, N. and Hoffmann, D. (2001) 'Arbeitsmarktpolitik und Arbeitslosenversicherung (Westzonen) und Arbeitskräftegewinnung und Arbeitslenkung (SBZ)', in U. Wengst (ed.) *Geschichte der Sozialpolitik in Deutschland seit 1945. Band 2/1: 1945–1949 Die Zeit der Besatzungszonen: Sozialpolitik zwischen Kriegsende und der Gründung zweier deutscher Staaten*, Baden-Baden: Nomos.

Schmid, G., Wiebe, N. and Oschmiansky, F. (2005) 'Arbeitsmarktpolitik und Arbeitslosenversicherung', in G. Schulz (ed.) *Geschichte der Sozialpolitik in Deutschland seit 1945. Band 3: 1949–1957 Bundesrepublik Deutschland. Bewältigung der Kriegsfolgen, Rückkehr zur sozialpolitischen Normalität*, Baden-Baden: Nomos.

Schmid, J. and Picot, G. (2001) ''Welfare to Work' bei Blair und Schröder – Eine Idee, Zwei Realitäten?', in G. Hirscher and R. Sturm (eds) *Die Strategie des 'Dritten Weges'. Legitimation und Praxis Sozialdemokratischer Regierungspolitik*, München: Olzog.

Schmidt, M.G. (1982) *Wohlfahrtsstaatliche Politik unter Bürgerlichen und Sozialdemokratischen Regierungen. Ein Internationaler Vergleich*, Frankfurt a.M.: Campus Verlag.

Schmidt, M.G. (2002) 'Germany: The Grand Coalition State', in J.M. Colomer (ed.), *Political Institutions in Europe*, London and New York: Routledge.

Schmidt, M.G. (2005) *Sozialpolitik in Deutschland: Historische Entwicklung und Internationaler Vergleich*, 3rd edn, Wiesbaden: VS Verl. für Sozialwissenschaften.

Schmidt, M.G. (2010) 'Parties', in F.G. Castles, *et al.* (eds) *The Oxford Handbook of the Welfare State*, Oxford: Oxford University Press.

Schmidt, V.A. (2002a) 'Does Discourse Matter in the Politics of Welfare State Adjustment?', *Comparative Political Studies*, 35: 168–93.

Schmidt, V.A. (2002b) *The Futures of European Capitalism*, Oxford: Oxford University Press.

Schofield, N. (2003) 'Valence Competition in the Spatial Stochastic Model', *Journal of Theoretical Politics*, 15: 371–83.

Schröder, G. and Blair, T. (1999) 'Der Weg nach vorne für Europas Sozialdemokraten. Ein Vorschlag', *Blätter für Deutsche und Internationale Politik*, 44: 887–96.

Schumacher, G. 'When does the Left do the Right Thing? A Study of Party Position Change on Welfare Policies', Paper presented at the Drei-Länder-Tagung 'Politische Integration', Basel, January 2011.

Schwarz, H.-P. (1981) *Die Ära Adenauer: Gründerjahre der Republik 1949–1957*, Wiesbaden: Brockhaus.

Scruggs, L. (2004) *Welfare State Entitlements Data Set: A Comparative Institutional Analysis of Eighteen Welfare States*, Version 1.1.

Shefter, M. (1977) 'Party and Patronage: Germany, England, and Italy', *Politics & Society*, 7: 403–51.

Sinn, H.-W. and Westermann, F. (2001). *Two Mezzogiornos*. Cambridge, MA: NBER.

SoVD (1997) *Dokumentation: Einschränkungen im Sozialen Bereich 1985–1995/7*, Berlin: Sozialverband Deutschland. Available: www.sovd.de/805.0.html (Accessed 15 November 2007).

Statistisches Bundesamt Deutschland (2006) *Datenreport 2006: Zahlen und Fakten über die Bundesrepublik Deutschland*, Bonn: Bundeszentrale für politische Bildung.

Streeck, W. and Thelen, K. (2005) 'Introduction: Institutional Change in Advanced Political Economies', in W. Streeck and K. Thelen (eds) *Beyond Continuity: Institutional Change in Advanced Political Economies*, Oxford: Oxford University Press.

Strøm, K. and Müller, W.C. (1999) 'Political Parties and Hard Choices', in W.C. Müller and K. Strøm (eds) *Policy, Office, or Votes? How Political Parties in Western Europe Make Hard Decisions*, Cambridge: Cambridge University Press.

Swank, D. (2002) *Global Capital, Political Institutions, and Policy Change in Developed Welfare States*, Cambridge: Cambridge University Press.

Swank, D. (2010) 'Globalization', in F.G. Castles, *et al.* (eds) *The Oxford Handbook of the Welfare State*, Oxford: Oxford University Press.

Swenson, P.A. (2002) *Capitalists against Markets: The Making of Labor Markets and Welfare States in the United States and Sweden*, Oxford: Oxford University Press.

Tamburrano, G. (1990) *Storia e Cronaca del Centro-Sinistra*, Milano: Rizzoli.

Tarrow, S. (2010) 'The Strategy of Paired Comparison: Toward a Theory of Practice', *Comparative Political Studies*, 43: 230–59.

Treves, C. (2007) 'La Riforma degli Ammortizzatori Sociali in Italia. La Posizione del Sindacato', *Rivista delle Politiche Sociali – Italian Journal of Social Policy*, 2: 199–211.

Tronti, L. (1991) 'Employment Protection and Labour Market Segmentation: the Fiftieth Anniversary of the "Cassa Integrazione Guadagni"', *LABOUR: Review of Labour Economics & Industrial Relations*, 5: 121–45.

Tsebelis, G. (2002) *Veto Players: How Political Institutions Work*, Princeton, NJ: Princeton University Press.

van Kersbergen, K. (1995) *Social Capitalism: A Study of Christian Democracy and the Welfare State*, London and New York: Routledge.

Vassallo, S. (2005) 'Italia', in Vassallo, S. (ed.) *Sistemi politici comparati*, Bologna: Il Mulino.

Verba, S., Schlozman, K.L., Brady, H. and Nie, N.H. (1993) 'Citizen Activity: Who Participates? What Do They Say?', *American Political Science Review*, 87: 303–18.

Vesan, P. (2008) 'Le politiche del Lavoro Italiane alla Luce del Dibattito Europeo sulla Flexicurity', Paper presented at the 22nd Annual Conference of the Italian Political Science Association (SISP), Pavia, September 2008.

von Beyme, K. (2000) *Parteien im Wandel: Von den Volksparteien zu den Professionalisierten Wählerparteien*, Wiesbaden: Westdeutscher Verlag.

Walter, F. (2002) *Die SPD: vom Proletariat zur Neuen Mitte*, Berlin: Fest.

Watson, S. (2008) 'The Left Divided: Parties, Unions and the Resolution of Southern Spain's Agrarian Question', *Politics & Society*, 36: 451–77.

Weimar, A.-M. (2004) *Die Arbeit und die Entscheidungsprozesse der Hartz-Kommission*, Wiesbaden: VS Verlag für Sozialwissenschaften.

Weisbrod, B. (1981) 'The Crisis of German Unemployment Insurance in 1928/1929 and its Political Repercussions', in W.J. Mommsen (ed.) *The Emergence of the Welfare State in Britain and Germany, 1850–1950*, London: German Historical Institute.

Weishaupt, J.T. 'Welfare States in Flux: Towards the End of the Continental Model?', Paper presented at the 66th Annual MPSA National Conference, Chicago, April 2008.

Weßels, B. (2000) 'Gruppenbindung und Wahlverhalten: 50 Jahre Wahlen in der Bundesrepublik', in M. Klein *et al.* (eds) *50 Jahre Empirische Wahlfaorschung in Deutschland: Entwicklung, Befunde, Perspektiven, Daten*, Wiesbaden: Westdeutscher Verlag.

Wilensky, H.L. (1975) *The Welfare State and Equality: Structural and Ideological Roots of Public Expenditures*, Berkeley: University of California Press.

Wilensky, H.L. and Lebeaux, C.N. (1965) *Industrial Society and Social Welfare*, 2nd edn, New York and London: The Free Press.

Wittman, D.A. (1973) 'Parties as Utility Maximizers', *American Political Science Review*, 67: 490–8.

Wolfrum, E. (2007) *Die geglückte Demokratie: Geschichte der Bundesrepublik Deutschland von ihren Anfängen bis zur Gegenwart*, 2nd edn, München: Pantheon.

Wolinetz, S.B. (2006) 'Party Systems and Party System Types', in R.S. Katz and W. Crotty (eds) *Handbook of Party Politics*, London: Sage.

Ziblatt, D. (2006) *Structuring the State: The Formation of Italy and Germany and the Puzzle of Federalism*, Princeton, NJ: Princeton University Press.

Zohlnhöfer, R. (2001) 'Parteien, Vetospieler und der Wettbewerb um Wählerstimmen: Die Arbeitsmarkt- und Beschäftigungspolitik der Ära Kohl', *Politische Vierteljahresschrift*, 42: 655–82.

Index

Page numbers in *italics* denote tables.

For Product Safety Concerns and Information please contact our EU
representative GPSR@taylorandfrancis.com
Taylor & Francis Verlag GmbH, Kaufingerstraße 24, 80331 München, Germany